party of five

The Unofficial Companion

Also by the Author

Hogan's Heroes: A Complete Reference
Rock Hudson: A Bio-Bibliography
Lauren Bacall: A Bio-Bibliography
Donna Reed: A Bio-Bibliography

party of five
The Unofficial Companion

Brenda Scott Royce

RENAISSANCE BOOKS
Los Angeles

This book is dedicated to Sharon,
who not only introduced me to *Party of Five*,
but fixed me up with a cute guy, named a
bunny rabbit after me, and forgave me for
humiliating her on her 55th birthday
(oops, I promised not to tell anyone her age).

Copyright ©1997 by Brenda Scott Royce
All rights reserved. This book may not be reproduced, in whole or in part, in any form, without written permission. Inquiries should be addressed to: Permissions Department, Renaissance Books, 5858 Wilshire Boulevard, Suite 200, Los Angeles, California 90036

97 98 99 00   10 9 8 7 6 5 4 3 2 1

Library of Congress Cataloging-in-Publication Data
Royce, Brenda Scott.
    Party of five: the unofficial companion/by Brenda Scott Royce.
        p. cm.
    Includes bibliographical references and index.
    ISBN 1-580673-000-6 (paperback: alk. paper)
    1. Party of five (Television program) I. Title
PN1992.77.P268R68   1997
791.45'72--dc21   97-34225
                                                                 CIP

Design by Deborah Daly
Manufactured in the United States of America
First Edition

Contents

Acknowledgments

I would like to express my sincerest gratitude to the following individuals and organizations for their assistance:

Heading the list is Jonathan Rosenthal of the Museum of Television & Radio in New York City, who kept a constant stream of information coming my way; Sharon Rhode, who tracked down facts that I had given up searching for; Jennifer Stoll, who was wise enough to tape the series from day one; and Lisa Hamameh, for helping to verify credits.

To the cast, creators, and crew of *Party of Five*, who all work so hard each week to produce an exceptional television show.

For miscellaneous assistance, my heartfelt thanks to: Archive Photos (Michael Shulman), Ian J. Ball, T. K. Baltimore, Kathy Bartels, Mary-Anne Batiato, Daniel Scott Burnford, Ernest Cunningham, Dave Dickerson, Nancy Dugan, the Everett Collection (Ron Harvey), George Fergus, GLAAD (Gay and Lesbian Alliance Against Defamation), Michael Graziano, Cindy Green, Steve Herbert, Lanette Hohl, Jani Klain, Jon Krieger, Janice Lange, John Lavalie, Josh Levine, Jonathan Levitt, Jason Liebman, Vicki, Ed & Bryan Linde, Pam Loveday, Phyllis Lycett, Madeline McGrail, Kathryn Mills, Photofest (Ronald Mandelbaum), Seth Poppel Yearbook Archives, Marcy Resnick, Barry Rivadue, Barney Rosenzweig, Jennifer Royce, Lauren Royce, Phyllis Royce-Repond, Bessie Lynn Sorge, Patrick Spreng, Catherine Sudeth, Allan Taylor, Viewers Voice, Arthur Wynne, Lynn Yanagihara, Amy Zachofsky.

The following libraries and research centers were particularly helpful: the Margaret Herrick Library of the Academy of Motion Picture Arts and Sciences; the Motion Picture, Broadcasting and Recorded Sound Division of the Library of Congress (Madeline F. Matz); the Museum of Television & Radio; and the Billy Rose Theater Collection of the New York Public Library at Lincoln Center.

As always, thanks to my family and friends for their support and encouragement.

Finally, thanks to my friend and editor, James Robert Parish, and my publisher, Bill Hartley, for believing in this project.

party of five

The Unofficial Companion

Party of Five billboard on the outside of the Sony Pictures lot.
PHOTO BY BRENDA SCOTT ROYCE.

Introduction

Welcome to *Party of Five: The Unofficial Companion*—the ultimate fan's guide to the hit FOX TV series, written by a fan who has been behind the scenes and talked to the people involved in the making of the show.

I have met every one of the regular and supporting cast members. (I've even seen one of them naked!) I've met Scott Wolf so many times he probably thinks I'm stalking him. He and Lacey Chabert are always the sweetest and most giving of their time. That's not to say anyone involved with the show has ever been rude. Everyone I have ever encountered on the set has been very friendly, from the cast and producers to the gaffers and grips.

I have been to the set at least a dozen times, and watched them film scenes from some of the series' most pivotal episodes, including "Thanksgiving" (the family confronts the drunk driver who killed their parents), "The Wedding" (or non-wedding), "Comings and Goings" (Grandpa moves in), "Spring Breaks" (Charlie almost loses the restaurant), and "A Little Faith" (Bailey falls off the wagon). I've met wardrobe and makeup people, editors, and other members of the technical staff.

I've also employed the resources of people even more fanatic about the show than myself—creators of Internet Web sites devoted to the series, fans who have amassed collections of clippings and videotapes, and the letter writers who helped keep the series afloat when it was in danger of cancellation.

It's all in here—facts about the cast, the history of the show, recaps of every episode of the first three seasons, behind-the-scenes photos, trivia, and more. Whether you watched the show from the beginning or joined the party late, you will find the answers to your questions in here.... Have fun!

chapter one

My Party of Five Encounters

I didn't want to like *Party of Five*. I heard raves about the show even before the pilot episode aired. Through my association with Viewers Voice, a nonprofit, international organization which campaigns to keep endangered television programs on the air, I knew that this show was going to be special. Sharon Rhode, the president of Viewers Voice, had screened a tape of the pilot episode and couldn't contain her enthusiasm. "The writing is terrific, the acting is dynamite, and it's a real tearjerker," she said. "Not to mention the guys are pretty cute!" she added with a wink.

Other than the cute guys, her description gave me all the more reason to avoid *Party of Five*. I just didn't want to get pulled into another heart-wrenching TV drama that would rip my heart out week after week, and then leave me devastated when it was canceled. I was still getting over the 1993 cancellation of *Life Goes On*. Was I going to watch a show about five orphans whose parents were killed in a car accident, which, I learned from Viewers Voice, was expected to face an uphill battle in the ratings from the beginning? No thanks.

So, I played hard to get. I let other people (obviously not enough of them) watch the first few episodes and get attached to those Salinger kids and their problems. Friends raved about how fantastic the show was while dabbing tear-filled eyes, and gushed about how "hot" Scott Wolf and Matthew Fox were while sighing dreamily. A few weeks after its debut, I checked the *Hollywood Reporter* and saw that *Party of Five* was landing in the bottom ten in the ratings. It would surely be canceled soon. "Ha ha, I'm the smart one," I told my gushing and sighing friends.

That all changed the first time I was invited to the set. Viewers Voice planned a visit to the sound stage during their annual convention in Los Angeles. *"Party of Five?"* I asked, "Is that the one with the cute guys?" It was. They didn't have to ask me twice. I figured that if I was going to the set, I should at least watch an episode first. It would be the polite thing to do.

I tuned in just in time to see Charlie cheating on his girlfriend, which was an apropos introduction to his character. Bailey was trying to win Kate away from her boyfriend, Tom. Tom seemed like a decent guy, but if Kate hadn't come to her senses and chosen Bailey by the end of the episode, I was ready to slap the silly girl. As Claudia would say, "Duh!" Julia was obviously going through a rebellious phase, lying about her age to get a job waitressing in a club. Claudia was also lying about her age so she could get the edge in a violin competition. I grew annoyed watching this child prodigy being so competitive, until she revealed that her mother had won second place in the same competition years before, and she was just trying to make Mom proud. Before you could say "pass the Kleenex," I was hooked.

It was mid-October 1994. The *Party of Five* gang were filming their tenth episode, "Thanksgiving," when our group from Viewers Voice descended upon the Sony Pictures lot in Culver City. The studio was once the home of MGM, and buildings on the lot are named after some of the glamorous stars who roamed the lot in a bygone era: Clark Gable, Myrna Loy, Judy Garland. Among the classic movies filmed at the studio were *Singin' in the Rain* and *The Wizard of Oz. Party of Five* sets occupy several soundstages in the middle of the lot. Stage 7 houses the Salingers Restaurant set; the family house and the coffee house are located on Stage 18; the school is on Stage 19; and the Salinger's attic and spillover sets are on Stage 20.

Before touring the soundstages, we were taken to the production offices, where then supervising producer (now co-executive producer) Ken Topolsky gave us a lesson in the art of television production. Next we subjected the show's creators, Chris Keyser and Amy Lippman, to numerous queries in a Q &A session on the Salingers Restaurant set. They talked about how the series was created, described a typical production schedule, and discussed the series' struggle for ratings. We were all impressed to learn that just as the Salingers get together once a week for a family dinner on the show, the cast had adopted the same practice, gathering on Friday nights for a group dinner. Chris and Amy also turned the tables on us, asking us to name our favorite episodes and describe what we liked most about the show. Sitting in the Salinger clan's usual booth on the restaurant set, I asked the question that was foremost in my mind: When are we going to meet the cute guys?

Matthew Fox had the day off, but we did meet Lacey Chabert, Neve Campbell and Scott Wolf, all of whom stopped to talk to us and answer our questions. Lacey talked about her work in *Les Miserables* on Broadway and *All My Children* on television before setting off on a bicycle ride around the studio lot. Scott interrupted his lunch to talk about his role as Bailey and pose for photos with our members. He thanked us all for supporting the show and said that he thought the program would benefit from a new time slot (which it got in January). Next, we caught a glimpse of Thurber, the family bulldog, as he was being loaded into a van by his trainer.

The episode they were filming—"Thanksgiving"—is one of the series' most powerful episodes, and the winner of a Humanitas Award for Outstanding Achievement in Writing. In the episode, each of the Salinger kids confronts the drunk driver who killed their parents. The episode features some heavy, emotional scenes between Scott Wolf, Neve Campbell, Matthew Fox, and guest star John Rubinstein. But the little scene I got to observe being filmed was nothing to break out the Kleenex for—Claudia, who has lost her sister's bracelet, walks down the hallway calling out nervously, "Julia?"

During our day on the set, we also sat in on an editing session, toured the makeup and wardrobe trailers, and talked to the associate producers responsible for selecting the background music used on the show.

Soon after that visit, I returned to the set of *Party of Five* to help them conduct a chat with fans on the online service America Online (AOL). At the time, there was a small but devoted group of fans on AOL who had been hooked from the very first episode. Producer Ken Topolsky, also an AOL user, had offered to gather the cast together to answer questions online. I had spotted a posted message from Ken in which he asked for someone in Los Angeles to help set up the chat. Since I lived nearby, had been to the set, and knew how to run an online chat, Ken invited me down.

The author with Matthew Fox and Scott Wolf. PHOTO BY MARCY RESNICK.

On December 6, 1994, the cast gathered in Ken's office for the first informal America Online *Party of Five* chat. For many of them, it was their first experience interacting with fans online. Matthew Fox, who had been conducting chats on CompuServe, another online service, was an old pro. But Matthew and Paula Devicq (Kirsten) were needed on the set and were only able to talk to fans for a few minutes. I sat at the computer, typing furiously as Scott, Neve, and Lacey fielded questions about their prior acting roles, future ambitions, and thoughts about the show. Sitting to my right, then 12-year-old Lacey watched my fingers tapping the keyboard with an expression of awe. "Wow, I wish I could type that fast," she said. I looked at this little girl, a talented actress, singer, and musician, who was living the dream that I had for myself at her age. And she was impressed by my 70-words-per-minute typing speed! I smiled and said, "Trust me, I'd much rather have your talents."

The cast enjoyed interacting with the fans online and were having fun joking around with each other as well. When an online fan asked

Scott how he felt about being compared to Tom Cruise, he paused only a moment before answering, "Tom who?" After Lacey revealed her desire to direct an episode, a fan asked what type of show she'd like to direct. She responded, "One about Bailey, guest-starring Tom Cruise!" Chris and Amy also got in on the fun, telling fans who asked if any of the cast wanted to try their hand at writing a script, "We won't act if they won't write!"

I went back to the set of *Party of Five* several times over the next few years, either with Viewers Voice, or a group of fans from America Online. Living in Los Angeles, I have also encountered some of the *Party* cast outside of the studio. At Wolfgang Puck's Cafe, I was seated at the table next to Michael Shulman (Claudia's first season friend, Artie) and his mother. At a dog adoption fair in Studio City, California, I petted pooches with Bryn Erin (Libby). I had an eye-opening experience while attending a play in Westwood in which Mitchell Anderson (Ross) appeared onstage completely naked. I also attended the *Party of Five* soundtrack release party at Universal Citywalk, and events honoring the show at the Museum of Television & Radio and the Academy of Television Arts and Sciences.

Neve Campbell, in a bathrobe, relaxes between takes.
Photo by
Brenda Scott Royce.

Having met the cast on several occasions over three years, I can honestly say that they have not changed. They were just as friendly and welcoming the last time I was at the set (while filming "A Little Faith," the next to the last episode of the third season) as the first. In between filming, they took the time to sign autographs and answer countless questions. Jeremy London (Griffin), who had been snoozing during his break, interrupted his nap when he heard that we wanted to meet him. Lacey spent so much time gabbing with us that she was late for her school session. The *Party of Five* cast has gone from being unknowns to having their pictures plastered on magazine covers, yet none of them appears to be suffering from star attitudes. They still seem genuinely happy to meet people who appreciate their work. And thankfully, those people are rapidly multiplying in number.

When it debuted in September 1994, *Party of Five* garnered immediate critical acclaim. Marvin Kitman of *Newsday* called it "a socially responsible, heartwarming, beautifully made, written and acted series." *New York Post* reviewer John Podhoretz found the series to be "terrifically intelligent and beautifully acted," and named it "the best new show of the season." Similar praise came from *USA Today*, *Variety*, and the *Los Angeles Times*, among others.

However, the public was slower to catch on to this extraordinary show. While there were thousands of fans who were hooked from the very first episode, the Nielsen ratings stayed dangerously low throughout the first two seasons. Finally, in the third season, the series exploded in popularity, attracting an additional one million viewers per week during Bailey's alcoholism story line. The hit theme song, "Closer to Free" by the BoDeans, saturated the airwaves; the cast graced the covers of *People*, *Entertainment Weekly*, *TV Guide*, and other magazines; and fans sported *Party of Five* T-shirts, while sipping from *Party* mugs and listening to the *Party* soundtrack. The show no one was watching became the show everyone was talking about.

Brilliant writing, exceptional acting, inventive cinematography, skillful direction, hip music, and cute guys. This show's got it all.

So, I got sucked in. Obviously, you did too.

chapter two

Planning the Party

We have found as we've gone along—although we never intended to do it—we've created a series that is in some ways the ultimate celebration of family. Because family is not taken for granted. It's something they create every day.

— Christopher Keyser, October 1996

The story behind the creation of *Party of Five* is atypical in that the show's creators, Christopher Keyser and Amy Lippman, did not conceive the series' basic premise. Most TV series originate with a concept dreamt up by a writer (or writing team), who then pitches the idea to the different networks and production companies. After a three-year stint as staff writers on the NBC series *Sisters*, Keyser and Lippman longed to create their own show. They developed a few ideas and brought them to FOX in November 1994. But the network was already nurturing an idea of its own: a TV series about kids living on their own, without parental guidance or interference. Lippman says, "Since their development season was almost over for the year, there were certain types of shows they were looking to put on. So while I think they were receptive to our ideas, they knew they were interested in putting on a show about 'kids on their own.'"

Realizing that their greatest hope of getting a show on the FOX schedule was to run with the network-supplied idea, Keyser and Lippman went off to think about the "kids on their own" concept. There was no question in their minds as to what kind of show the network had in mind. FOX, the home of *Melrose Place* and other guilty pleasures, was known for developing TV shows high in splash and low in substance, targeted for the 18- to 34-year-old demographic. In its effort to be the younger, hipper, edgier network, FOX often eschewed quality in favor

Co-creators Christopher Keyser and Amy Lippman. Photo by M. Victoria Batiato.

of sex appeal in its programming decisions. The gambit often worked.

The partying orphans concept was first presented to Keyser and Lippman by Sandy Grushow, then head of programming for FOX. The 34-year-old Grushow had joined FOX in 1983 as an intern in the feature films department, when he was fresh out of UCLA. He moved up through the ranks of the marketing and programming departments until 1992, when the network's chairman Jamie Kellner appointed him president of Fox Entertainment Group. Grushow's programming philosophy favored adhering to the strengths that made FOX famous.

Keyser and Lippman knew that the network was looking for a show similar in style to *Melrose Place* and *Beverly Hills 90210*, and they didn't want to deliver. Keyser says, "We sat down together and thought, 'this is a horrible idea for a show,' because we figured they wanted something along the lines of them driving across the Golden Gate bridge at three in the morning with the top down, screaming, and having parties, and it didn't feel real to us." Lippman agrees, "We weren't interested in telling a story about kids having a free-for-all, no parents present, it's a party every night. We were interested in telling a story about how the absence of parents affects children."

Had the network turned the partying orphans concept over to a producer like Aaron Spelling, progenitor of *Melrose Place* and *Beverly Hills 90210*, it probably would have gotten a series much more in keeping with its original vision. Instead, the fate of those fictional orphans was handed over to Chris Keyser and Amy Lippman, a duo who favored realism and small moments in their writing.

The pair brings a diversity of experience and background to their writing partnership. Christopher Keyser was born and raised on Long Island, New York. He was in his third year of law school at Harvard University when he decided that he didn't want to be an attorney. Uncertain of what he did want to do, he tried his skill at writing. He met Lippman, then an undergraduate at Harvard, in a playwriting class. Lippman had been reared in San Francisco and Los Angeles. After graduating in 1985, Keyser and Lippman each moved to New York separately. Lippman pursued a writing career, finding work almost immediately, including a stint on the soap opera *Loving*. Keyser worked part-time at a Manhattan law firm and held a number of other odd jobs. He gradually came to realize that writing was the one thing he enjoyed doing and, despite the incredible odds against making a living as a writer, decided to make it his career. Keyser and Lippman eventually discovered that they clicked as a writing team, and in 1988 they moved to Los Angeles to break into the television industry.

Following the course of most aspiring television writers, the duo wrote a spec script for a TV series they admired, *The Wonder Years*, and submitted it to the show's producers. Their script was rejected by *The Wonder Years*, but it was shopped around and eventually caught the attention of prolific TV producer Stephen Bochco (co-creator of *Hill Street Blues* and *L.A. Law*, among other series). Bochco hired them as staff writers for *L.A. Law*, where Keyser's legal background proved to be an asset. They also wrote for *Equal Justice*, but have since steered clear of legal dramas out of fear of being typecast. Later, they were hired as writers for *Sisters* in its first season, and eventually became co-executive producers of the hit series. They were with the program for three years, after which they left to develop *Party of Five*.

Around the FOX-supplied concept of kids without parents, Lippman and Keyser built a show about the Salinger family of San Francisco, five siblings ranging in age from one to twenty-four, who are struggling to stay together following the death of their parents in an automobile accident. They chose the characters' names, ages, and backgrounds without any input from FOX. They applied no magical formula in naming their characters; no trivia or hidden meanings lie behind the Salingers' names. They compare the process to choosing baby names or picking names from a phone book and point out that contrary to rumor, Bailey, the second oldest of the quintet, was not named after George Bailey of *It's a Wonderful Life*, although the characters do possess similar personality traits.

To allow themselves a wide range of storytelling possibilities, they placed their characters at different stages of maturation when life can be at its most turbulent. Teenagers Bailey and Julia would allow the writers to explore teen issues and emerging sexuality, while prepubescent Claudia's growing pains would provide plenty of story material. At 24, eldest sibling Charlie was at an age where he should have been free to explore his options and enjoy life, but he was saddled with the responsibility of caring for his younger siblings. In some ways, Owen, the littlest Salinger, is the most crucial member of the Salinger family, as Lippman explained to *Mediaweek:* "We decided to put a baby into the mix, and in a peculiar way it changed the stakes of the family. There was a new urgency in having this family stay together and preserve the memories of their parents."

In creating their fictional family, Keyser and Lippman defied TV stereotypes. Keyser says, "We tried to flip flop all those expectations we have about how a traditional family would work—the idea that the oldest would be the most responsible or that one of the women would take care of the family. We just threw those all up in the air and came up with new ideas about how a family might work." For that reason, when we first meet the Salingers of *Party of Five*, the eldest sibling is the least responsible member of the family, the eldest daughter is the least maternal, the smartest child is the youngest, and the middle son is the one who takes care of the baby and balances the checkbook.

Though their depiction of life in a large, parentless family is realistically rendered (sometimes heartbreakingly so), neither Lippman nor Keyser has a similar personal background. Each has only one sibling, and neither lost their parents young. However, as Lippman pointed out in a Viewers Voice interview, they each draw upon the experiences of loved ones. "Both of our spouses lost parents very early in life and I think both Chris and I have drawn off their experiences. Certainly there are story lines that I have taken directly from my husband's life and dramatized because they are very real and very moving. His response to being without a parent really forms, for example, Claudia's story, and to a certain extent, I used it in a story about Bailey. And Chris uses his wife's experience to form some of the work that he does on the show."

Keyser and Lippman set the series in San Francisco for a number of reasons, one of them very practical: they needed a city in which 13-year-old Claudia could get around on her own without being in danger. Keyser explains, "It's a city where you believe that these kids could exist and you're not afraid for them all the time because you know that they can take care of themselves in a city like that. Boston would have been another great choice." They also wanted to avoid the typical FOX show setting of Los Angeles, and liked the flexibility that San Francisco offered: a city that is both exciting and beautiful, with a character of its own that fit right in with the show.

When they returned to FOX with their retooled version of the "kids on their own" concept, Keyser and Lippman were apprehensive. Lippman recalls, "We said, 'This probably isn't what you want to hear, but this is the show we'd like to do.'" They explained that they didn't want to create a show which had a tragedy at its heart and then never deal with that tragedy. At a CompuServe online conference, Lippman said, "Even if the kids all said, 'Okay, it's behind us,' the loss of their parents would come up in different, subtle ways." Though the show they created was much darker in tone than FOX had originally envisioned, the network was receptive to their ideas and gave them the go-ahead with one basic caveat: that they infuse the drama with enough comedic elements to make the tragedy more palatable to audiences.

FOX development vice-president Bob Greenblatt, who oversaw the series' development, told *Entertainment Weekly*, "We were nervous that it wasn't quite as high-concept, quite as sexy, quite as cool as *90210*. We were thinking it should be more fun and light, while Chris and Amy really wanted to mine the dramatic side of it. But they were willing to do both, so we said, 'Go ahead.'"

chapter three

Building a Family

The exciting thing about casting unknown actors is watching the public discover them. It's been wonderful to see our actors, particularly Matthew and Scott, receive such recognition. And not just for being cute—but for being really fine actors.

— Amy Lippman, March 1995

Once FOX gave them the green light to proceed with the pilot, Keyser and Lippman set about casting the Salinger family, with the help of casting directors Mary V. Buck and Susan Edelman. Looking for unknown performers to inhabit the roles they created, they began auditioning actors for the four key roles in January 1994. Their task was made more difficult by the fact that they had to judge each actor not only on his or her own talents, but also on how they would interact with the other cast members. Instead of hiring four individual actors, they were assembling a family, and like an interlocking puzzle, every actor had to fit in place perfectly for the show to work. In a June 1995 *TV Guide* article, Chris Keyser explained, "The network was extremely concerned that every family member really fit. If any one of them wasn't right, it would undermine everything we were working for in dramatizing the struggles of this family."

The first piece of the puzzle to fall into place was Scott Wolf. Twenty-five-year-old Scott had been in Los Angeles for three years, pursuing an acting career. He had been working steadily—if forgettably—in commercials and episodic TV. He even had a leading role in a low-budget film, *Teenage Bonnie and Klepto Clyde* (1993). Scott had managed to avoid the typical struggling actor's fate of waiting tables for a living, but he still hadn't made a splash with his acting. Things began looking up for Scott after Burt Reynolds cast him in a few episodes of his sitcom, *Evening Shade*, in 1993. A featured role in an episode of *Blossom* followed, along with another feature film role in *Double Dragon* (1994). Poised on the precipice of stardom, Scott had yet to find the role which would allow him to make a name for himself in show business.

The moment Scott walked into the *Party of Five* audition, Keyser and Lippman knew they had found the right actor to play Bailey. Amy Lippman could immediately tell that Scott possessed the personality traits required to play big-hearted Bailey, the self-appointed caretaker of the family. "He's such a warm person that he seemed completely right for that character," she told *Entertainment Weekly*. Scott was among the first actors they saw, on the very first day of auditions, but they didn't hesitate in making their decision. In fact, they felt fortunate that Scott hadn't already been signed to another contract.

Chris Keyser recalls, "Our feeling when he walked in the room was, how can he still be available? We got really lucky. I imagine if we'd cast two weeks later, he might have been somewhere else."

Meanwhile, in New York, Matthew Fox and Lacey Chabert were among hundreds of performers taping audition scenes to be sent to the *Party* producers in L.A. When they saw Matthew's tape, Keyser and Lippman were impressed by his screen test but were concerned about his appearance. Lippman says, "He looked awful in this video—kind of green." However, screening a video of Matthew's 1993 afterschool special, *If I Die Before I Wake*, convinced the producers to fly Matthew out for additional testing.

Though he was 27 years old, Matthew looked much younger, and in each of his prior television roles he had played teenagers. He made his TV debut in a 1992 episode of the NBC sitcom *Wings* as a high school athlete. He also played high school athletes in his afterschool special and the feature film flop *My Boyfriend's Back* (1993). In the short-lived 1992 television series *Freshman Dorm*, he graduated to playing a college athlete. These roles hadn't been much of an acting challenge for Matthew, who had been a star athlete in high school and college. The role of Charlie in *Party of Five* would prove to be far more of a stretch for the actor. In order to appear old enough to play the 24-year-old irresponsible brother, Matthew grew a beard. With only a few days to go before the audition, he wasn't able to get a very full growth. Charlie's perpetual five-day stubble has since become the character's trademark.

Any reservations Keyser and Lippman had about Matthew disappeared when they met him in person in Los Angeles. "Once we saw him, that was sort of it," Lippman told *Us* magazine.

Lacey Chabert had been performing professionally since the age of nine, both on Broadway (*Les Miserables*) and in television (*All My Children*). Her audition tape was strong enough to merit a trip to Los Angeles to meet with the *Party of Five* producers. Lacey won the part, but it wasn't her performance that impressed Keyser and Lippman, it was her ability to follow complicated direction, and her engaging personality. "She just had this sparkle," Lippman told the *Los Angeles Times.*

Filling the role of Julia Salinger proved to be the most difficult task in casting *Party of Five.* "We had auditioned hundreds of actresses for Julia without finding one that FOX liked," Chris Keyser recalled in a 1995 interview. While they were searching, a Canadian actress with the unusual name of Neve Campbell was making the decision to move to the United States to further her acting career.

After injuries forced her to cut short her career as a professional dancer, Neve had been working steadily in film and television in her native Canada. She had a starring role in the syndicated Canadian TV series *Catwalk* (1992-93), which she quit after a year because she was unhappy with her character's metamorphosis into a sex symbol. Frustrated with the lack of opportunities in her homeland, 20-year-old Neve relocated to Los Angeles. She says, "You get to a certain point in Canada, unfortunately, where you can only get so far and then you have to move to the States to get big."

Within a week of arriving in Los Angeles, Neve found a manager, who set up auditions for her, including one for *Party of Five.* Her reading was over so quickly that Neve thought she hadn't made much of an impression. But like their experience with Scott Wolf, Keyser and Lippman knew instantaneously that Neve was the perfect choice for the role of the insecure 15-year-old Julia. Chris Keyser says, "Neve walked in the door on a Monday afternoon. We only had two days left to find our Julia and have her read with all of the family regulars for FOX before we flew to Vancouver to film the pilot. Neve read for two minutes and that was it. We called the casting director and told her to book Neve immediately."

The newly assembled Salinger clan still had one more obstacle to face before they were each signed to five-year contracts—approval from the network. The cast met for the first time at the FOX studios. After performing a scene for studio executives, the actors were ushered out of the room to await a decision. In a 1996 interview, Matthew Fox described the moment the cast became a true TV family, "They brought us all back in and they said 'Congratulations, you're the Salinger family.' From that second on we have always given of ourselves in those relationships, the brother and sister sibling relationships. Right from the get-go we were excited, we were fearless, we were taking a lot of chances with each other, getting emotional with each other. It's been really special."

chapter four

Creating the Salingers' World

In February 1994, the newly assembled cast flew to Canada to film the pilot episode of *Party of Five*. The pilot, like many pilots and television films, was filmed in Vancouver with a mostly local crew because production costs are lower than in Los Angeles. The production crew spent one day in San Francisco shooting exterior scenes to intersperse in the Canadian-shot footage.

The familial bond which exists between the actors and the crew developed during, and perhaps because of, the six-week location pilot shoot, according to Chris Keyser. He described that shoot during a seminar at the Museum of Television & Radio: "We all went off to Vancouver together and lived there together for about six weeks, away from everyone else, sort of locked in a hotel together. And got to know each other 'like a family.' Starting that way, all together, away from all the other distractions, I think it created some kind of atmosphere, particularly among the cast."

Matthew Fox agrees that the cast had an immediate rapport with one another. In a 1994 interview, he said, "It was shocking to me how wonderful it felt to meet these people. As an actor, when you get a chance to do something that is this relationship bound, you dive in. You commit to opening up to people so much more quickly, faster than you would on an everyday basis. People walk around in life with suspicions and they put up walls. As an actor, when you meet somebody who's going to be your sister, you open up so much quicker."

After filming on the pilot wrapped, the cast and producers returned to Los Angeles and awaited word from FOX on whether or not *Party of Five* would be picked up as a series for the 1994-95 season. When the network unveiled its fall schedule in May 1994, *Party of Five* was one of seven new series in the lineup. (Of the other six, only *New York Undercover* had staying power. The other five—*M*A*N*T*I*S*, *Wild Oats*, *Hardball*, *Fortune Hunter* and *Models, Inc.*—were canceled within one season.)

A few changes were made between the time the pilot was filmed and its September television premiere. Paula Devicq, who was hired for nothing more than a walk-on, was signed as a regular cast member. Amy Lippman recalls that Kirsten the nanny was never intended to become an ongoing presence in the Salingers' lives. In the pilot, Bailey has been searching fruitlessly for a nanny for baby Owen, when he opens the door to find a beautiful woman applying for the job. Paula, a former model, was hired strictly on the basis of her looks. The producers didn't have any idea if she could act. Nor did they care, since she was only intended, in Lippman's words, as a "sight gag."

Once FOX entertainment president Sandy Grushow saw footage from the pilot, he phoned Chris Keyser with the directive, "I want more Paula Devicq!" Chris and Amy agreed that throwing a beautiful nanny into a household with two young guys with raging hormones would provide great storytelling potential, so the role of Kirsten was expanded.

Another modification mandated by FOX involved the amount of money the Salinger kids receive from their parents' trust. In their script, Keyser and Lippman bucked a long-held TV taboo which held that no one on television discusses actual sums of money. A TV character might say, "We're really broke, what are we going to do?" However, actual sums, especially a character's salary or rent, are rarely mentioned. In an effort to make their story real, Keyser and Lippman came up with what they thought was a reasonable amount of money the children would have to live on each year. They researched the median income in the United States and the cost of living in San Francisco to come up with a figure which would be just enough for the kids to survive on, provided they didn't make any bad financial decisions (like Charlie losing $12,000 in a bad real estate investment or Julia squandering $800 on professional modeling photos).

However, the network didn't want the young characters to have any money worries whatsoever. Lippman says, "We had huge fights over

What's on the menu?

When *Party of Five* began, the family-owned restaurant, Salingers, was a family-style establishment where you could order a burger and fries, and most entrees cost under $10. In the second season, Salingers underwent a transformation when Charlie hired a distinguished chef at the suggestion of his wealthy girlfriend, Kathleen. Salingers now boasts a more upscale decor and a decidedly more elegant and pricey menu.

Here are some sample entrées from the Salingers menu:

Melrose Crabcakes
    with Grilled Plum Tomatoes & Lobster Aioli - $24.00
Charred Cajun Rack of Lamb
    with Minted Compote of Cucumber & Tomatoes - $30.00
Roast Carpenter Squash with Garlic Sausage, Fresh Bayleaves,
    Pancetta & Homemade Pappardale - $28.00
Grilled Free Range Chicken
    with Garlic Whipped Potatoes & Morel Sauce - $19.00

A meal for five, including appetizer (Pheasant & Foie Gras Ravioli with Oregano Soup), soup (Hearty Lobster Consommé with St. Peter's Bay Mussels), and entrée (Muscovy Duck Breast with Cepe Polenta & Spinach), would cost over $400. It's a good thing the Salinger kids can eat for free.

that issue, actually. Huge fights. FOX thought that they should live on $80,000 a year, and we thought that that was an extraordinary sum of money, and we thought we will completely alienate our viewership. I mean $80,000—a family of five can manage just fine on that. And yet, FOX was very concerned that an audience would think there's not enough money." But Keyser and Lippman wanted the family to have to struggle financially at times and to deal with the issue of financial responsibility.

Lippman says, "It's interesting to me, how paying the bills happens in a family where no one really knows how to balance a checkbook. Real issues of a family, I think are dramatic. I don't think you need to resort to melodrama to tell interesting stories."

In the end, the two sides reached a compromise. Instead of $80,000 a year, the family would receive $15,000 every four months from their parents' estate. Since the pilot had already been filmed, the actors had to loop (re-record dialogue) the new sums of money. If you watch the pilot closely, you can tell that when Julia talks about the check that has to last them four months, the dialogue does not match her lip movements.

Even though the figure was considerably less than $80,000, Lippman was still unhappy with the final outcome. She says, "It was the best compromise we could make, and I'm very uncomfortable with that. It makes me nuts."

With a 13-episode order from the network, *Party of Five* found a new home on the Sony Pictures studio lot and supervising producer Ken Topolsky set about assembling a crew. Topolsky started out in the music business in New York, producing albums for such artists as Paul Simon and Billy Joel. While in Los Angeles in 1982 assembling music for the film *Flashdance*, he decided that he wanted to be a filmmaker. He says, "What I loved about music was walking through a building and hearing something that you worked on, and seeing people respond to it. And realizing that the music doesn't belong to you, it belongs to the audience. And when I saw the response that people had to film and television, I said, 'Wow, this is good.'"

One of Topolsky's earliest producing credits was the acclaimed 1986 NBC miniseries *A Year in the Life* with Richard Kiley and Eva Marie Saint. Next, he was offered a position on ABC's *thirtysomething*, but in a career decision he has since regretted, opted instead to produce the

Co-executive producer Ken Topolsky. PHOTO BY BRENDA SCOTT ROYCE.

inferior 1987 television movie *The Bates Motel*. Since that professional blunder, he has only selected projects that live up to his personal standards of quality and integrity. After *The Bates Motel*, he produced the ABC drama *Men* (1989), and the feature film *The Wizard* (1989), about a mentally unstable boy who becomes a video game champion. He was a supervising producer on *The Wonder Years* (1989-93) and also directed 13 episodes of the series.

To complete his crew for *Party of Five*, Topolsky hired a number of people he had previously worked with. Costume designer Scilla Andreen-Hernandez had worked with Topolsky on *The Wizard*. Writer-producer Mark B. Perry had begun his writing career on *The Wonder Years* and went on to write for *Northern Exposure, Picket Fences*, and *Law & Order*. Bruce J. Nachbar also worked on *The Wonder Years*, starting as a post-production coordinator, then graduating to associate producer, co-producer, and finally producer. On *Party of Five*, he began as an associate producer and was promoted to co-producer in the second season. Bruce currently oversees the post-production of *Party of Five*, which includes choosing the background music.

The crew went about reconstructing the Salinger house set from the series' pilot, building other sets anew and filling them with the appropriate props and personal touches that would transform the soundstage into a home. According to Topolsky, the overriding concern of the producers was to create a world for the Salingers to inhabit that would seem tangible to viewers. He says, "We chose a very specific style for the show. We felt it was really important to make the home feel like a safe place, a very real place. Their whole world had to feel real." To achieve that goal, Topolsky and his crew defied convention in creating the sets for *Party of Five*. For one thing, the rooms were built life-size, whereas most sets are much smaller in actuality than they appear on TV. The *Party of Five* sets are also equipped with ceilings, another rarity in television. Most sets have open ceilings to allow stage lights to be hung overhead.

Topolsky further explains, "We purposely put the ceiling pieces on, so that when you have to light the set—where does light come from? Well, when you're in a house, a good place for light to come from is the window. So if you look at our show, you'll see light always comes in from the window. If you're sitting next to a lamp, that seems like another good place. Light comes in from another room. Seems like a pretty good place. And you have shadows, and people walk in and out of shadows. And some people claim, often times, that our characters are in the shadows. But that felt real. On other shows, they put lights shining down from overhead, and they tend to look very flat, and the shadows tend to dissipate all over the place, so you don't really have any shadows. And you don't have any character, or any kind of distinguishing lighting source."

Roy H. Wagner, director of photography for the series' first two seasons, says that the unusual construction of the sets made them more difficult to work in than conventional sets. However, the end result, according to him, was worth the extra effort. Wagner, who previously worked on the CBS drama *Beauty and the Beast* (1987-90) and in feature films, says that in his career he has often been criticized for caring "too much" about the look of the shows he works on. He adds, "Many years ago a network executive confided in me on the set [of *Beauty and the Beast*] that all we were doing was creating filler that was just good enough to keep the audience watching until the next commercial." Wagner refused to adopt the network exec's cavalier attitude toward his art and continues to go to great lengths to achieve inventive and moving effects with his camera.

His work did not go unnoticed by critics or by fans. *The Hollywood Reporter*'s review of the second season premiere commended Wagner for creating an intimate atmosphere with his images. Visitors to the America Online *Party of Five* bulletin board have frequently commented on the unique cinematography. Among the scenes to receive the most mention by fans: a kitchen scene from "Ready or Not" (9/27/95) with Bailey and Will shot mainly through an open refrigerator door, and a scene from "Valentine's Day" (2/14/96) in which Julia looks out of the kitchen window at Griffin in the backyard, and her reflection in the window merges with his.

The same type of meticulous care that Topolsky and his crew took in staging *Party of Five* was applied to every aspect of the show, from choosing the wardrobe to dressing the set. As the series opens six months after the kids have lost their parents, when money is tight and household chores are being neglected, it would be unlikely for any of the main cast to wear new or freshly-pressed clothes. Their wardrobe had to reflect the Salingers' situation—kids on a limited budget living in the San Francisco climate.

Costume designer Scilla Andreen-Hernandez buys much of the actors' wardrobe at second-hand stores. She also picks through her grandmother's closet. "She's saved everything from the 1940s," she explains. When she does buy new clothing, Andreen-Hernandez will send the actors home with the clothes to break them in. The wardrobe department will take a new shirt and age it by using a sander, pulling out seams with a needle, or dirtying it up with Fuller's Earth (a non-odorous type of dirt frequently used in the movies).

Even seemingly minute details, like the pizza boxes on the counter tops in the early stages of the show, were painstakingly planned by the producers. Topolsky recalls, "We talked a lot about the archaeology of the family. How six months before the pilot, the parents were there, and the house was probably well-kept, clean, neat, and things weren't lying around. A month after they died, there were more and more newspapers left lying around. Three months after they died, there were clothes lying around. Six months after they died, there were pizza boxes lying around. And then, of course, as the children adjusted to their situation, we started making them a bit neater, a bit cleaner, and it seems to go away. And I think all of these little things that we've done, all the care that we've tried to take, trying to create the world, I think it does get appreciated. And it does touch the audience emotionally."

Production coordinator Carol Kravetz is responsible for overseeing the production schedules, which can get difficult since, while one episode is being filmed, another is being prepped and still another is in post-production. She explains the standard procedure, "Each episode is prepped in seven days and shot in seven days. Prepping is finding locations, props, wardrobe, building and dressing sets, and casting, and so on. Then about a month to do editing and other post-production stuff."

Though the show is set in San Francisco, nearly all of the filming is done in Los Angeles, either on the Sony lot or at various locations around town. The company travels to San Francisco once or twice per season, for a few days of filming exteriors. A typical shooting day on *Party of Five* begins at 7 a.m. and ends at 8 p.m. The cast actually arrives an hour early, at 6 a.m., for hair and makeup. The actors work five days a week on the show, and they often have to do publicity or make personal appearances on the weekends. The show is filmed nine months out of the year, and most of the cast spend their hiatuses working on feature films or other projects.

The exhausting schedule is made tolerable for the actors by the fact that they all get along very well. As clichéd as it sounds, they insist that they feel as though they have formed a real family. When the series began, most of the cast members were new to Los Angeles and had few friends in the area. They began getting together on Saturday evenings for "family" dinners, just like their TV counterparts. They would alternate hosting and cooking duties. Eventually, as soaring careers and other relationships placed more demands on their free time, they abandoned the weekly ritual. They agree that the time they spent together off camera in the early days helped them to form a familial bond that time hasn't diminished.

Lacey says that her older cast members act protectively toward her. She told *Teen Beat*, "I feel so much that they're like my real brothers and sister. We all make each other laugh so much. Neve is the nicest person in the world. I call her Nevey Neve. Scott makes me laugh. It's kind of bad sometimes! At table readings, it's supposed to be dramatic, and you just look at him and start laughing."

Neve concurs, "We all hit it off really, really well. Matthew has a great deadpan when he's joking around. You can never tell if he's joking or not. Scott is very outgoing and charismatic. He loves to work his dimples. Lacey is a doll. We like to sing and dance together. She really reminds me of me when I was her age."

Like any family, the cast members have their own in-jokes and running gags, such as the nose-tweaking contest, or the bad joke contest.

Scott Wolf fielding calls on the set. PHOTO BY M. VICTORIA BATIATO.

Jennifer Love Hewitt (Sarah) says that Scott's puns are the worst, "Like, 'Why is a sea gull by the sea? 'Cause if it were by the bay, it would be a bagel.'"

Lacey says that, occasionally, the jocularity of the cast gets them in trouble on the set. She told *People* magazine, "We're always being told, 'Okay guys, settle down.' We have too much fun. When someone laughs, that's it. We're all gone." The actors concur that Scott Wolf is the resident prankster on the set, but Love Hewitt says that sometimes the normally reserved Matthew Fox is the one scoring the laughs. She says, "He can be as funny as Jim Carrey. He does this dance that's a combination of Elvis and a serious twitching disease. Even when he's being serious, I can't take him seriously anymore because I've seen him dance."

chapter five

An Uphill Climb

The buzz about *Party of Five* began even before it premiered. Before the public had a chance to meet the Salinger clan, the pilot episode was being circulated to the press. One of the show's earliest supporters was John Podhoretz of the *New York Post*, who wrote in his July 15, 1994 column: "FOX's *Party of Five* is hands-down the best pilot of the upcoming fall season. It's a terrifically intelligent, emotionally restrained drama... and it is beautifully acted by a cast of unknowns."

Another ardent early supporter was reviewer Matt Roush of *USA Today*, who wrote, "If you're at all inclined to fall for a new TV family of considerable charm and four-handkerchief heart, by all means crash FOX's *Party of Five*." But while some reviewers became early boosters of the show's quality, other members of the media focused on the series' unsettling premise and its similarity to another new series.

Debuting in the same season as *Party of Five* was *On Our Own*, an ABC sitcom with a remarkably similar premise: seven siblings struggle to stay together after their parents are killed in a car crash. There were more similarities: the eldest brother takes charge, working in a restaurant to help pay the bills. The *On Our Own* family even had a bulldog. Plots involved outmaneuvering social workers who wanted to separate the kids. But the similarities ended there. *On Our Own's* Jerrico family was black, they lived in St. Louis, and the eldest son was prone to cross-dressing. The biggest difference of all was that *On Our Own* was played strictly for laughs, which were supplied by a loud laugh track.

On Our Own, which debuted the same month as *Party of Five,* had a remarkably similar premise. EVERETT COLLECTION

The media wondered if the two shows represented the beginnings of a trend and tended to lump the two together in its coverage of the fall season even though the series were strikingly dissimilar in style and content. As the season got underway, *Party of Five* was in danger of being dismissed as one of the "orphan shows," rather than gaining a reputation on its own merits.

The similarity between the two shows was strictly coincidental. The creators of *On Our Own* did not initially set out to do a show about orphans. Instead, they envisioned a family with two working parents and "latchkey" kids who have to fend for themselves while the parents are away. It was only after they cast the Smolletts, a real-life family of six siblings, that they dropped the parents. Robert L. Boyett, the executive producer of *On Our Own*, told the *Los Angeles Times* that with seven kids (comedian Ralph Louis Harris played the oldest child) in the cast, they didn't have room for more characters. Thus, the "orphan" concept was born. The comparisons ended as the season got underway, and viewers could see for themselves how disparate the two shows were. ABC bounced the low-rated *On Our Own* all over its schedule, until canceling it at the end of the season.

Party of Five was also struggling in the ratings (routinely landing in the bottom ten of all prime-time network shows), but it had the distinct advantage of being on FOX, a network whose shows seldom rank in the top ten. Because their ratings expectations aren't as high as their big three competition, the network has the ability to nurture lower-rated shows they believe in. Amy Lippman told the *Hollywood Reporter*, "Only FOX could look at the ratings and see value in keeping the show on the network." ABC Entertainment chairman Ted Harbert agrees. He said in a *People* magazine interview, "FOX has the great benefit of being able to live with smaller numbers. If *Party of Five* were on ABC, it probably wouldn't last."

At a June 1997 panel discussion at the Academy of Television Arts & Sciences, Chris Keyser recalled that during the series' first season, industry insiders jokingly referred to the show as "*Party of Five* Share." ("Share" represents the percentage of television sets in use which are tuned in to a particular show. Top ten hits such as *ER* and *Seinfeld* generally garner at least a 30 share.)

One reason FOX is willing to take time to develop their shows is that, historically, the network's dramas have not garnered strong ratings right from the start. Keyser explains, "*Melrose* was only a hit in its second season. *90210* similarly became a hit later on. I don't know whether it's because FOX has a slightly smaller viewing audience, therefore its on-air advertising doesn't reach quite as many people, or whatever it is about FOX, it really takes time for them to nurture their programs. We don't expect to come out of the box as an overnight hit because it's just not traditionally true with FOX dramas."

The series lost its champion at FOX when Sandy Grushow left the network on September 27, 1994, only three weeks into the series' run. At a 1995 panel on creating television, Amy Lippman remembered her fear that Grushow's departure would spell the end of *Party of Five*. "Sandy Grushow called us in very bleak times, and said, 'I know your ratings are miserable. I love the show, I'm going to stand by it for as long as I'm president.' And then he left the next day. Not a high point in the history of the show."

Grushow's displacement was blamed on the network's overall poor ratings, especially in the wake of a $395 million acquisition of the NFL broadcasting rights that failed to make an impact on ratings. Grushow also clashed with FOX chairman Rupert Murdoch's vision of the network. While Grushow wanted to maintain FOX's image as the maverick youth-oriented network, Murdoch wanted to move into the mainstream and gain equal respectability alongside the other major TV networks.

Murdoch appointed John Matoian as Grushow's replacement. Matoian began his career as an elementary school teacher in Fresno, California, before moving to New York. There he worked for Scholastic Productions, and later, CBS, where he became senior vice president for the network's television movies and miniseries division. He was responsible for developing such acclaimed telefilms as *The Betty Broderick Story*, *David's Mother*, *To Dance with the White Dog*, and *Sarah, Plain and Tall*. He left CBS to join FOX as president of the network's family films division. He was in the position only a few months before succeeding Grushow.

Matoian announced that his programming agenda at FOX would revolve around a commitment to quality. While he didn't abandon the network's sexy centerpieces, *Melrose Place* and *Beverly Hills 90210*, he immediately pulled the plug on some of FOX's new, lower-rated fare: *Wild Oats*, *Fortune Hunter*, and *Encounters: The Hidden Truth*. Matoian also entered into a multi-picture agreement with Hallmark Entertainment to produce original, family-oriented movies for FOX, while backing away from the network's development of celebrity TV biographies. (FOX had previously produced biopics on Roseanne, Madonna, and O. J. Simpson.)

Keyser and Lippman's fears were allayed when they learned that Matoian liked *Party of Five* and intended to give it a chance to build an audience. In fact, in mid-October, as proof of his faith, Matoian ordered an additional three episodes to be shot, and scripts written for the entire season. He also increased the show's promotional budget and sent the cast around the country on promotional appearances. He further agreed to test the show in a different time slot.

Airing on Monday nights at 9 p.m. after *Melrose Place, Party of Five* lost a significant share of that show's audience each week. Initially, Keyser and Lippman thought that the network was giving the show a leg up by scheduling it after their most successful property. Two weeks before the series premiered, Keyser told Viewers Voice, "I think that we have a fantastic time slot, coming after *Melrose* and opposite football, which is obviously one of the strongest programs of the week. On the other hand, it probably doesn't necessarily appeal to quite the same type of audience that our show does."

However, he and Lippman soon realized that the *Melrose–Party* pairing was, in Lippman's words, "not a marriage made in heaven." The bedhopping, backstabbing adventures of *Melrose's* inhabitants provided a jarring contrast to *Party's* realism and sentimentality. The producers now felt that their show would perform better if it aired on Wednesday nights at 9 p.m., after the less outrageous *Beverly Hills 90210*.

FOX tested the theory by scheduling an episode on Wednesday, November 2, 1994, in the slot usually occupied by *Models Inc.* The *Party of Five* cast appeared in a promotional spot just prior to the episode, urging *Beverly Hills 90210* fans to stay tuned and give the show a try. Scott Wolf talked to *USA Today* about his apprehension over the ratings for the special Wednesday episode. "I'm going to have to drive to the studio, park my car there and wait for the producers to get there (in the morning) with the ratings," he said. The episode gained a ratings point over the series' average, but still ranked in the week's bottom ten of all network TV series.

In a 1997 *People* magazine interview, Scott looked back on the early days when his show was constantly hovering on the brink of cancellation. "It was so frustrating," he said. "You start to think, 'Am I pouring my heart into something that will be gone next week?'"

John Matoian admits that his decision to continue to support the series when ratings sagged was a risky one. He told the *New York Times*,

Matthew Fox signing auto-
graphs. PHOTO BY BRENDA
SCOTT ROYCE

"My competitors at the other networks thought I was out of my mind.
They were thanking me for letting *Party of Five* sit there as a soft spot
on our schedule."

In November 1994, the network picked up the series for the remainder of the season. FOX executive Dan McDermott explained to *USA
Today*, "Without a doubt, this is one of the best shows on any network,
and it has our 100% unconditional support."

Despite such assertions, prognosticators remained doubtful that *Party
of Five* would be renewed for a second season unless its ratings picked up
substantially. Fans of the show began campaigning for its renewal in
December 1994. Through united efforts or under their own individual
steam, viewers began bombarding FOX with letters and e-mails in support of the show. Members of the television advocacy group Viewers
Voice launched a letter-writing campaign urging members to recruit
friends, family, and strangers to watch the show and write to the network
and the show's sponsors. In a December column, *Newsday* critic Marvin
Kitman called *Party of Five* "the best family drama in the history of FOX"
and asked Santa Claus to save the series as his Christmas present.

In January 1995, *USA Weekend* ran an article on two endangered
series, *Party of Five* and *My So-Called Life.* Viewers were asked to write
in if they wanted to save either show. Over 15,000 readers wrote to the

magazine in support of *Party of Five*. In response to the letters, FOX's John Matoian told *USA Weekend*, "The letters to your magazine are fabulous. That's an astounding number of people taking the time to write a letter. It absolutely makes an impact in terms of our decisions later."

On January 2, 1995, *Party of Five* made the permanent move to Wednesday nights, following *Beverly Hills 90210*. Amy Lippman was optimistic about the change, saying, "I think the two shows are not totally similar, but not so wildly dissimilar that audiences have trouble making the leap from one show to the other."

The new time slot paid off, though not dramatically. The ratings began a slow, incremental climb, inching their way out of the bottom ten. Though its overall rating was still relatively low, the series experienced a noticeable increase in viewers in the 18-to-34-year-old demographic. At a January 1995 press conference, John Matoian said, "*Party of Five* has definitely turned the corner. It is winning its time period in adults 18 to 34, beating *Grace Under Fire* and *The Naked Truth*. And I think the best is yet to come."

Nevertheless, as the first season of *Party of Five* came to an end, its future was uncertain. Critics predicted the finale would be the series' swan song. *USA Today* critic Matt Roush wrote, "The ratings. So poor for something so rich." John Martin of the *New York Times* used his column to make a public plea to the network: "Think hard FOX. *Party of Five* may not be a ratings hit. Don't forget it's opposite *Roseanne*. But it's a show you can be proud of."

Meanwhile, devoted fans continued to rally for the show's renewal. In April 1995, approximately 28,000 viewers cast their vote to save *Party of Five* in *TV Guide's* annual "Save Our Shows" poll. The Gay & Lesbian Alliance Against Defamation, which had commended the series for its depiction of Ross as a gay male role model, distributed "Don't Stop the Party" postcards pre-addressed with the FOX network address to their members. Internet denizens used their Web sites to put forth *Party's* plea. On America Online, fans, led by Lisa Hamameh and Daniel Scott Burnford, banded together to distribute FOX's address to online fans and motivate them to write to the network. Other groups, including Viewers for Quality Television, also organized letter-writing crusades.

The efforts paid off. On May 22, 1995, FOX announced that *Party of Five* would return in the fall of 1995. It was the lowest-rated prime-time series on a major network to ever be renewed.

Though *Party of Five* still struggled in the ratings in its second and third years, times were never as tough as in its perilous first season. In its campaign to redefine itself as a network that cared about quality, FOX couldn't do better than to use *Party of Five* as its poster child. However, tense moments were in store for the *Party* gang when the network's champion of quality, entertainment president John Matoian, resigned from his post in September 1996. He was replaced by Peter Roth, who had been running Twentieth Century-Fox's TV production division for the previous four years. Once again, the producers of *Party of Five* felt fortunate that the FOX network could look beyond the ratings and find value in keeping the show on the air. Shortly after Roth's appointment, Amy Lippman said, "We've been very lucky. We've been through three presidents at FOX since we've been on the air. And we have the support of the new president, Peter Roth." Stressing that Roth shared his predecessors' belief that *Party of Five* would eventually experience an increase in viewers, Lippman stated, "We would not be on the air if we were not on FOX."

Party of Five averaged a 7.1 rating in the second season, up one ratings point from its first season average of 6.1 (In the 1994-95 season, one ratings point represented 954,000 households, which meant that an average of 6.7 million households tuned into *Party* in its second season.) The third season peaked with a 9.6 rating for "Hitting Bottom" (2/26/97) and averaged a 7.4 rating overall.

On December 15, 1995, *Party of Five* graced the cover of *TV Guide*, which hailed the series as "The Best Show You're Not Watching." In the same month, *Time*, *People*, and *USA Today* all listed *Party of Five* in their wrap-ups of the year's best television. In January 1996, the series won the Golden Globe award for best television drama. As *Party of Five* accumulated honors and accolades, media coverage of the show and its stars increased. The stars were featured on the covers of *People*, *Entertainment Weekly*, and other magazines, and were mobbed by fans at publicity events.

Scott Wolf described the change in his recognizability factor over the course of the series in a November 1996 interview. "First they'd look and they'd go 'no', and then they'd look and think they knew me, and then they'd look and say, 'oh he's on TV,' and then they'd look and go, 'oh the guy from *Party of Five*.' And now, actually, people say my name, which is probably the strangest thing. To have strangers come up and say, 'You're Scott Wolf,' that's weird."

On March 7, 1997, *Party of Five* was picked up for a fourth season. FOX entertainment president Peter Roth said, "It's gratifying that *Party of Five* continues to attract tremendous reaction from the media, and most importantly, the American TV viewing public." Americans aren't the only ones enjoying the *Party*—as of June 1997, the series is also airing in a number of other countries, including Argentina, Australia, Belgium, Canada, England, France, Italy, Israel, and Sweden.

chapter six

The Salingers

Scott Wolf
(Bailey Salinger)

One of the things that I love about Bailey as a character is that no matter how far he gets into his own world and no matter how far he goes from the house to find his own stuff, he'll always be driven by this sense of how important his family is to him.

— Scott Wolf, October 1995

Had it not been for the advice of a family friend, Scott Wolf probably would have ended up being an accountant rather than an actor. As a business major at George Washington University, he thought he had his life mapped out. "I was all ready to get a sensible degree, get a sensible job and live a sensible life, sensibly," he told *Us* magazine. Luckily for Scott and his countless fans, he followed his heart and chose an unsensible career path.

Scott Richard Wolf was born on June 4, 1968, in Boston, Massachusetts. His parents divorced in 1973 when Scott was five years old. Scott and his siblings—Michael, Gary, and Jessica—were raised by their mother, Susan, a substance abuse counselor, in West Orange, New Jersey. His father Steven Wolf, a health care executive, now lives in St. Louis.

At West Orange High School, Scott was a B-student. He participated in sports and theater productions. Though he thought he had a knack

Scott Wolf as Bailey in the first season of *Party of Five*. PHOTOFEST.

for acting, he didn't consider it a realistic career possibility. He says, "Growing up in the town I grew up in, you just didn't go to Hollywood and be an actor."

Things changed when Scott attended a party his father threw in honor of his best friend's fiftieth birthday. In attendance was the best friend's brother, an actor-turned-accountant, who noticed Scott's natural charm and exuberance, and thought he could make a living as an actor. Scott recalled in a *TV Guide* interview, "He told my dad that if I had any interest in acting, he should push me toward it. He said he'd never met anybody who struck him so strongly as having the potential to do well."

Suddenly the notion of acting was no longer just a dream, it was a possibility. Because someone with show business experience had expressed a belief in his ability to succeed, Scott felt that he had to give it a shot. While finishing up his course work towards his degree in finance, Scott was already making prepara-

Scott Wolf's senior yearbook photo. West Orange High School, West Orange, New Jersey, 1986. SETH POPPEL YEARBOOK ARCHIVES.

tions for his new career: he wrote his thesis paper on show business.

After graduation, Scott enrolled in acting classes at H. B. Studios in New York City. He got a role in an NYU student film entitled *Grease Monkey*. After a few months he decided to try his luck in Los Angeles. He loaded up his car and made the cross-country trip in three days. Such a move must have been daunting for a formerly business-minded young man on a sensible career track, but he was bolstered by the support of his mother, whom he credits with giving him the best advice he ever received. He says, "While I was packing the car, my mom came over and said, 'I just want you to know that you're already a star.'"

In Los Angeles, Scott enrolled in acting classes at Playhouse West, where he studied under Robert Carnegie and Jeff Goldblum. Shortly after his arrival, he signed with an agent who found him work in television commercials. Among his first gigs were commercials for Yoshinoya Beef Bowl, a Japanese restaurant chain, and an ad for Aqua Fresh toothpaste. He recalls, "I sit in a dentist's chair and say, 'Tartar-control Aqua Fresh fights cavities!' Then there's a lightning effect, and suddenly, magically, I'm on a waterslide, and I say, 'It makes you feel this fresh!'" Perhaps his most memorable commercial was a spot for Frosted Flakes, in which Scott played tennis with Tony the Tiger. He told *People* magazine, "Tony and I beat the crap out of two other guys."

Not every job came easily for Scott. In fact, one of his early failures endures as one of his most embarrassing experiences—he was rejected for a one-line role on the syndicated series *Baywatch!* He described the audition on *Late Night With Conan O'Brien*: "I get there and there's a room full of guys, like fifty guys. And there's a sheet with the dialogue on it. The dialogue is 'Please help me!' That's it. And one at a time, the door opens, the door closes, and you hear this muffled, 'Please help me!' The door opens, the guy is out, and they're shuffling us through. So I go in there, and I walk in the room and I introduce myself, and they say, 'Go ahead and get on the ground.' So I get down on the ground. This character has a rock pinning his leg, so I said, 'PLEASE HELP ME,' and they said, 'Thank you very much.' And that was it. I didn't get the part."

Scott made his television series debut on a November 1990 episode of the sitcom *Saved by the Bell*, in a bit role as a waiter. He told fans on America Online, "I actually had such a small part, if you blinked you missed me." He appeared on a subsequent episode of the series in a non-speaking role as a choir member.

In a 1991 episode of the Disney Channel series *Kids Incorporated*, Scott played a dual role as twins Billy and Bobby. In the thinly-plotted segment, "Double Trouble," Eric (Eric Balfour) wonders why his new friend acts differently each time he meets him. Twenty-three-year-old Scott, whose baby face and small build (he is 5'8") enabled him to play characters much younger than his actual age, played opposite kids a decade younger than him, including 12-year-old Jennifer Love Hewitt, his future *Party of Five* costar.

Scott had a supporting role in an NBC pilot *Yesterday Today*, which aired in July 1992. The proposed series starred Nick Gregory as a man who awakens from a coma twenty years after suffering a football injury. Among the changes that have occurred since 1972 was the marriage of his girlfriend to his best friend! Also in the cast were Daniel Baldwin, Eve Plumb (of *The Brady Bunch* fame) and Kevin Tighe. Despite receiving positive reviews, the pilot was not picked up as a series.

Scott continued to work in episodic television, with guest appearances on *Down Home*, *The Commish*, and *Parker Lewis Can't Lose*. In the final episode of *The Trials of Rosie O'Neill*, he played Eric, a high school student who sexually harasses Rosie's stepdaughter. Rosie (played by Sharon Gless) sees to it that Eric gets his comeuppance by episode's end. Scott played a similarly slimy character in an episode of *Blossom*, in which he makes a play for Blossom while her boyfriend is in the next room.

One evening after a play, a mutual friend introduced Scott to Burt Reynolds and his then-wife, Loni Anderson. Scott recounted the meeting on *Live With Regis and Kathie Lee*. "We were introduced, and he grabbed my face, and he said, 'Look at this face.' And he pointed it at Loni, 'Look at that face.' And Loni said, 'What a face!'"

Reynolds was so impressed by Scott's face that he gave him a guest shot on his series *Evening Shade*. Scott appeared in the series' 1992-93 season finale as David Kilmer, a high school quarterback with a great throwing arm and a bright smile. When the series returned in the fall, Scott's character returned for another guest appearance.

Scott made his feature film debut in the low-budget Trimark film, *Teenage Bonnie and Klepto Clyde*, an updating of the 1967 Faye Dunaway–Warren Beatty classic about the 1920s gangster duo. Scott was cast as Clyde, opposite Maureen Flannigan (star of the syndicated television series *Out of This World*) as Bonnie. Filmed in Salt Lake City, Utah, the film was released in 1993 and received a tepid review from *Variety* which concluded, "The young actors are adequate."

In June 1993, Scott began work on his second movie role, *Double Dragon*. Based on the video game of the same name, *Double Dragon* was a futuristic karate film set in earthquake-ravaged Los Angeles. Scott and Mark Dacascos played brothers Billy and Jimmy Lee, possessors of one-half of a dragon amulet that bestows special powers upon its holder. The plot concerns their quest to retrieve the other half from a power-mad mogul as they are befriended by a gang of vigilante teens. Scott learned some basic martial arts moves in preparation for the film, but he says when it came time to film the fight scenes, "I just wung it. Billy Lee was a scrappy fighter, so I got away with it." The more elaborate karate scenes were filmed using stunt doubles.

Double Dragon's November 1994 release went largely unnoticed by filmgoers, and the movie quickly disappeared from theaters. *Variety* observed, "The best things *Dragon* has going for it are the appealing leads, although Dacascos and Wolf are rendered so dopey by the script that teen heartthrob status will have to wait for better vehicles."

While making *Double Dragon*, Scott became romantically involved with his costar, former *Who's the Boss?* star Alyssa Milano. Determined that their offcamera relationship would not become another doomed on-set romance, they moved in together shortly after returning to Los Angeles. They got engaged just before Halloween 1993. In a March 1994 *People* magazine interview, Scott said, "I could have asked her to marry me two weeks after we met. I'm convinced we're like two halves of the same soul." However, by April 1994 they had separated, and the *People* article—in which the couple posed together in their bathtub—may have been a contributing factor.

Scott told *TV Guide*, "There was nothing wrong with the relationship. She's great and I still love her. The only thing I would change is putting my private life out there in public. But I learned: one bubble

Before starring in *Party of Five,* Scott battled evil thugs in *Double Dragon.*
EVERETT COLLECTION.

bath in *People* and I'm done." On *Regis & Kathie Lee*, he said that the experience with Alyssa taught him to keep the details of his love life private. "It's so hard to have a relationship period, and to make that work, it's a complicated thing. And then you sort of invite 50 million people to watch."

When Scott read the pilot script for *Party of Five* in January 1994, he knew immediately that he could portray Bailey. He recalled, "I put it down and said, 'I have to do this. It's the most honest thing I've ever read.'" He had no trouble convincing the series' producers of his suitability for the role. The minute Scott auditioned, they knew that he was the right actor for the part. He was the first of the regular cast members to be selected.

Soon after *Party of Five* premiered in September 1994, Scott was being singled out by teen magazines as TV's hottest new hunk. Equally hunky Matthew Fox didn't mind being eclipsed by Scott in the press. He said, "I'm very happy for him. Maybe it's the dimples." Scott was flattered by the attention but feared that he would be dismissed as a "teen idol" instead of being taken seriously as an actor. "I think if you look on the actor's career lifeline chart, 'teen idol' doesn't go quite as far as I think I'd like to go," he told Conan O'Brien on his late night talk show. Scott was also a little embarrassed by his coverage in teen magazines, because he was 26 years old when the series debuted.

The fact that Scott was a full ten years older than his character came as a surprise to most fans, not to mention the producers. Amy Lippman told *Us* magazine, "When we were shooting the pilot, I actually made Scott show me his license just to get the facts!" Scott's approach to his role has less to do with the character's age than his situation, Scott explained in *Us*, "My job when I was cast wasn't to play 16. My job was to find Bailey, to determine how he relates to people and how his mind works."

Comparisons to superstar Tom Cruise came early in Scott's career. Scott was characteristically good-humored about the comparisons. He joked to *Movieline* magazine, "At least no one says I'm a short Marty Feldman." He told TV talk show host Regis Philbin, "You expect to some extent when you're starting out, everyone sort of stamps a label on you, a young this or a new that. I could have done a lot worse." Eventually, Scott grew tired of the Tom talk, noting that it was mentioned in every article written about him. In a June 1996 interview with the British magazine *Empire*, Wolf said, "You know, I've talked so much about it for

Scott Wolf in 1994. Photo by M. Victoria Batiato.

the past year and a half. First of all, it's flattering. If there's anyone I'd want to be compared with it's him—he's a great actor and has a great career and so forth—but ultimately no one wants to be compared with anyone, you want to be seen for what you're doing." Then he quipped, "I just wonder if Tom Cruise is getting tired of being told by people that he reminds them of Scott Wolf."

Wolf spent his first hiatus from *Party of Five* filming the Ridley Scott high-seas adventure film *White Squall*. The film was based on the true story of the 1961 wreck of the Ocean Academy brigantine, the *Albatross*, in which four students and two crew members were killed. The production took the mostly-male cast to exotic locales, including Malta, South Africa, and Bermuda. During the grueling shoot, Scott overcame his fear of the sea and endured a bout with seasickness. When it was released in February 1996, *White Squall* received mixed reviews, but most of the critics had high praise for Scott. The *Los Angeles Times* wrote, "Scott Wolf, the hot young star of TV's *Party of Five*, is by far the main attraction... his is a compelling presence in the company, and the young audience for whom the film seems intended will appreciate the strength he brings."

Next Scott took a supporting role in *Evening Star*, the long-awaited sequel to the 1983 tearjerker *Terms of Endearment*. The movie was filmed in Houston in the fall of 1995. Though he knew that accepting the role would mean a back-breaking schedule, flying back and forth between Los Angeles and Houston each week, Scott couldn't pass up the opportunity to work with the film's stars, Shirley MacLaine (reprising her role as Aurora Greenway) and Juliette Lewis. In the film, he played Bruce, the boyfriend of Aurora's granddaughter, Melanie (played by Lewis).

The film's producer David Kirkpatrick said, "It's a great role for Scott. He plays a handsome, self-effacing nitwit." The role was quite a departure for Scott, who was beginning to be pegged for playing only good guy roles. In a *Cosmopolitan* interview, he said, "It was a relief to play the selfish guy, who really hurt people even though he didn't mean to." Scott got a kick out of filming a scene in which his character, an aspiring underwear model, demonstrates his talents for his girlfriend. He said, "It's like goofy beefcake."

While he was working on *Evening Star*, rumors began to circulate that Scott was involved with his leading lady, Juliette Lewis. But by February 1996, he was spotted around New York and Los Angeles with another actress, Paula Devicq, who plays Kirsten on *Party of Five*. Having learned from his experience with Alyssa, Scott remained tight-lipped about his relationship with Paula. He told inquisitive reporters only that he was involved with a "secret person." Eventually, after they were seen together at the World Series and other public events, Scott became a bit more revealing. In a *Sassy* cover story, he talked about their relationship: "We met on the show and were friends first for a couple of years. All that first-date stuff was already known, so it made things much easier when we actually began dating."

Scott Wolf in the third season of *Party of Five*. EVERETT COLLECTION.

During a November 1996 appearance on the *Tonight Show*, Scott confirmed that he and Paula were living together in his new house. But by Valentine's Day 1997, the couple had broken up. Neither has commented on the reason for their breakup. A tabloid reported in April 1997 that Scott has been dating his ex-fiancée Alyssa Milano, once again.

Though he has a promising feature film career, Scott says he won't let the movies lure him away from his television show. He told columnist Marilyn Beck, "People are wondering, 'Are you going to stay with the series?' Well, there's no question of that. I'm very proud of this television show, and I think that it would be a huge mistake to break away. I'm happy where I am, working with people I love, playing a character I love."

When the series ends, Scott would like to do more films and theater, but for now, he's not looking ahead but is savoring the success he is currently enjoying. He says, "I think 20 years from now, I'll be grateful that I tried—and did—appreciate it as much as I possibly could. Because I know that this is as good an opportunity as any actor could have in their career."

Selected Credits

Feature films

Teenage Bonnie and Klepto Clyde (1993) 'Clyde'
Double Dragon (1994) 'Billy Lee'
White Squall (1995) 'Chuck Gieg'
Evening Star (1996) 'Bruce'

Television

Saved by the Bell ep. "The Prom" (NBC, 11/8/90) 'Waiter'
Saved by the Bell ep. "The Glee Club" (NBC, 12/23/90) 'Choir Member'
Kids, Incorporated ep. "Double Trouble" (The Disney Channel, 1991) 'Billy/Bobby'
Down Home (NBC, 1991)
The Trials of Rosie O'Neill ep. "Role Reversal" (CBS, 5/30/92) 'Eric'
Yesterday Today (NBC pilot, 7/3/92)
The Commish (ABC, 2/13/93) 'Todd Clements'
Parker Lewis Can't Lose ep. "The Rocky Kohler Picture Show" (FOX, 6/6/93) 'Brian Sommerville'
Evening Shade (CBS, 5/17/93, 10/4/93) 'David Kilmer'
Blossom (NBC, 1/94) 'Gordy'
Nickelodeon's 10th Annual Kids' Choice Awards (Nickelodeon, 4/20/97) 'Presenter'

Stage

Dead End, Williamstown Theatre Festival (Williamstown, MA), July 9-20, 1997

Commercials

Aqua Fresh, Yoshinoya, Frosted Flakes, others

Matthew Fox as Charlie Salinger in the first season of
Party of Five. PHOTOFEST.

Matthew Fox
(Charlie Salinger)

*Charlie has a good heart. His intentions are good, he just doesn't
always do the right thing. I think that's very human.*
— Matthew Fox, Spring 1995

Perhaps the least likely success story in the *Party of Five* cast belongs
to Matthew Fox. Not only did he harbor no fantasies of stardom while
growing up on his family's 120-acre ranch in Wyoming, but he admits

he had little ambition to do much of anything. He assumed he would probably fall into the life of a farmer like his father, Francis. But it was his father who pushed him to make something of himself and gave him the motto, "Life is what you make of it."

The second of three sons, Matthew was born on July 14, 1966, in Crowheart, Wyoming, which he describes as "nothing but a post office along a highway in between two towns that are 90 miles apart." The town also has a combination gas station/general store and a one-room schoolhouse where Matthew's mother Loretta teaches primary school.

A self-described country boy, Matthew learned to ride horseback at the age of six, and throughout his youth he helped out on the ranch, feeding the cows and pigs, and working with his father in his outfitting business. The Fox family didn't have a television while Matthew was a child. TV addict Rosie O'Donnell teased him when he appeared on her TV talk show: "Matthew, what the hell kind of life is that? It's like child abuse!"

Matthew Fox was a star athlete at Wind River High School in Kinnear, Wyoming. SETH POPPEL YEARBOOK ARCHIVES.

Matthew, who calls his youth "the greatest childhood you could possibly imagine," disagrees. He explained, "My father was just one of those people who was not a big fan of television, and always wanted us to read books, which I really appreciate." He added that the family did eventually buy a set. "When I was around fifteen or sixteen, my dad finally broke down," he told Rosie.

At Wind River High School, Matthew excelled at sports (he was on the basketball and football teams, and was the state long jump champion), but was an unmotivated student. He told *Soap Opera Digest*, "In high school, I had no vision for my future. I wasn't looking toward college." Even if Matthew had few goals for himself beyond farm life, his father did. A University of Pennsylvania alumnus, Francis Fox wanted his son to see more of the world before deciding to settle down on the farm. At his urging, Matthew went East for a postgraduate year of high school after graduating from Wind River in 1984. At Deerfield Academy, an all-boys preparatory school in Massachussets, he felt completely out of his element. He told *People* magazine, "I was a total hick. I chewed tobacco." His classmates voted him "Most Likely to Appear on *Hee Haw*."

Matthew's senior yearbook photo from 1984. SETH POPPEL YEARBOOK ARCHIVES.

However, the strict atmosphere and emphasis on scholastic achievement worked wonders for Matthew, who became an excellent student. While at Deerfield, Matthew's best friend was Nelson Rockefeller's son, Mark.

After graduating from Deerfield Academy, Matthew attended Columbia University in New York City, on a football scholarship. The 6'4" student was a wide receiver for four years, and he majored in economics. During his sophomore year at Columbia, Matthew saw the 1987 film *Wall Street*, and thought he'd found his calling. He wanted to be like Charlie Sheen's character, Bud Fox, a high-rolling stockbroker. "I really wanted to go down on Wall Street and make a million dollars," he said on PBS's *In the Mix.* "Sad to say, that was really a motivating factor for me at the time. My parents are ranchers and farmers so I guess going to the big city and getting into that big-time money excitement stuff was really appealing to me then."

First he had to finish his education, which was an expensive proposition in spite of his scholarship. A girlfriend whose father was in the modeling business suggested he try modeling. He signed with the Ford Agency and landed several modeling assignments, mostly catalog work, working strictly for the money. He told *TV Guide*, "I hated it. It's just completely contingent on selling your looks and your smile. *Selling yourself.* I hated that." When his agent suggested he quit school and go work in Europe, he refused.

Modeling led to commercials, including ads for Clearasil, Dr. Pepper, and milk. His motives were still purely financial. Then an agent suggested that he take some acting classes and give some thought to pursuing it as a career. He told Viewers Voice, "That was still in my senior year of college and I was way too busy with other things that I was doing to seriously consider taking acting classes on the side, too."

Matthew graduated in 1989 with a Bachelor of Arts degree in Economics. Following his *Wall Street*-inspired plan, he started interviewing at brokerage firms. Then he began to question his career choice. "I was literally going on interviews to Merrill Lynch and other Wall Street financial firms when all of a sudden I said to myself, 'I'm not going to rush into this. I have the rest of my life to put on a suit,'" he told *Television Today*.

He signed up for acting classes, but at first he was too terrified to perform in front of his classmates. He says, "At first it was really frightening. I was horrible, and I was scared and nervous. To get up in front of people and actually perform was just gut-wrenching. But gradually it became easier and I was really fascinated by it, so even though I wasn't really enjoying it in the beginning, something inside of me said that if I kept with it, I would at some point."

Matthew says that he never had an epiphany in which he realized he would be an actor. As he overcame his fears and perfected his craft, he gradually developed a love of acting. He recalled in a 1995 *Los Angeles Times* interview, "It was never like a bolt of lightning. The more I uncovered, the more passionate I got about it."

His first television job was a 1992 guest spot on the NBC sitcom *Wings*. He played Ty Warner, the star player on Joe's old high school baseball team. The plot concerned Joe's jealousy when Ty breaks his old strikeout record. Clean-shaven and baby-faced, Matthew easily passed for 17, although he was 25 at the time.

Next, Matthew landed a regular role in the CBS hour-long drama *Freshman Dorm*. Again, he played a student and an athlete. Filmed at Pepperdine University in Malibu, *Freshman Dorm* was set at the fictional Western Pacific University and centered on six freshmen students from diverse backgrounds. Matthew Fox played campus jock

Matthew (top right) was miserable while working on the short-lived CBS series *Freshman Dorm*. EVERETT COLLECTION.

Danny Foley, and Robyn Lively played his girlfriend, theater major Molly Flynn. The series debuted in August 1992 and was roundly and justifiably lambasted by critics. The *Hollywood Reporter* called it a "hopeless mishmash that's juvenile at best." *Variety* gave the series an F in originality, describing it as "a pretty shallow look at campus life, all wrapped up and packaged for the *Melrose* crowd."

Freshman Dorm was pulled from CBS's schedule after only five episodes had aired. The cancellation was somewhat of a relief for Matthew, who was unhappy with the quality of the series. In an interview with *Television Today* he described *Freshman Dorm* as "one of the worst written shows ever. They wouldn't even let us mess around with the stuff so we were stuck with this material that was almost impossible to do. It was also one of my first jobs and I was very, very nervous. I was so terrified and unhappy with my work; it was a very frustrating time."

His next project was hardly an improvement. Touchstone Pictures' 1993 release *My Boyfriend's Back* starred Andrew Lowery as a lovesick teen who returns from the dead to claim a date with the most popular girl in school. Matthew played Buck Van Patten, the handsome but obnoxious campus jock. When Johnny returns to town as a zombie to win pretty Missy away from Buck, the townsfolk are more perturbed

Matthew Fox as Charlie Salinger in the second season of
Party of Five. PHOTOFEST.

with him than horrified. The film's attempts at humor arise from Johnny's decaying body parts and penchant for cannibalism. The *Hollywood Reporter* called *My Boyfriend's Back*, "a slim-witted glop of gross-out humor mixed with teen-dream goop." *Variety* praised the film's talented ensemble cast, but called the movie itself, "so moonbeam-silly and so embarrassingly offensive—to the ear and to the eye—that it's hardly worth talking about."

Following those two disasters, Matthew was more careful choosing scripts. He starred in the CBS afterschool special *If I Die Before I Wake*, playing (yet again) a high school athlete. The one-hour telefilm concerned a track star whose teammates are killed in a plane crash, which would have killed him, too, had he not been sidelined by an injury. He turns to friends, family, and finally, religion in his search for comfort and answers. The Emmy-nominated special aired in October 1993. The *Hollywood Reporter* had mixed praise for the special and little for Matthew's performance: "The matinee-idol-handsome Fox confuses spirituality with being blandly serene or rolling his eyes upward."

In February 1994, Matthew was one of thousands of actors in New York and Los Angeles competing for roles on upcoming television pilots. Among the 25 pilot scripts he read, Matthew felt most drawn to *Party of Five*. "I loved it, and I really saw myself as Charlie immediately," he says. "I felt like I had it in me to tell the story." He made an audition tape in New York that impressed creators Amy Lippman and Chris Keyser enough to have him flown to Los Angeles to test in person.

Charlie's perpetual five-day stubble was Matthew's idea. He told *Soap Opera Digest*, "Up until that point, the oldest character I had played was 18 or 19. Charlie was supposed to be 24. I had a few days before the audition, so I decided to grow a goatee." He also felt that the scruffy look fit Charlie's slacker persona. Apparently, it was a good call. Amy Lippman told *Us* magazine, "Once we saw him, that was sort of it."

Of all the actors on the show, Matthew is the least like his TV character. While Charlie was a womanizer at the series' outset, in real life Matthew is a devoted husband. He met his wife, former model Margherita Ronchi, in 1987, while at Columbia University. Born and raised in Venice, Italy, Margherita was visiting New York City when a friend introduced her to Matthew and love bloomed. They dated for five years and were married in August 1992. Matthew also cannot relate to Charlie's initial reluctance to accept responsibility for his brothers and sisters. He says, "I would like to think that in his situation I would do a better job of taking care of my siblings."

Despite their differences, Matthew has compassion for his character, as well as an appreciation of Charlie's three-dimensionality, which makes this acting job more fulfilling than his prior roles. He told *Soap Opera Digest*, "I never wanted Charlie to be this cliché, irresponsible brother who's always screwing up and fooling around. I think I've made him human. Sure, he makes mistakes. But he pays. He truly is the tragic character on the show. Look at the hand he's been dealt. He's 24, and he'll never be able to live a life for himself. And while he really loves these kids, he hates them too. That's what makes this so worthwhile."

Matthew and costar Scott Wolf were singled out early in *Party of*

Matthew appeared in an ad touting the benefits of drinking milk.
COURTESY OF THE NATIONAL FLUID MILK PROCESSOR PROMOTION BOARD.

Five's run as the stars to watch out for. While he appreciates the plaudits he has received for his work on *Party*, Matthew is unnerved by the attention he receives from fans in public. At an October 1994 promotional appearance in New York City, he and Scott were mobbed by 2,000 female fans. He calls the experience flattering but scary and admits that he shuns such crowds. Matthew was named by *People* magazine as one of the 50 Most Beautiful People in the World in 1996, but he told Viewers Voice that he is not comfortable with his status as a sex symbol. "Getting recognized...has been hard for me. The work I love. Being on the set I love. The bit of fame that comes from being on a television series has probably been the most surprising thing to me. I kind of prepared myself for that, but in hindsight, I didn't know what it would be like, and I didn't prepare myself as well as I thought I did."

The reticent Matthew prefers less public ways of interacting with his fans. He has conducted several online chats on CompuServe throughout the series' run. In the show's first two years, he personally answered all of his fan mail, with the help of his wife. Eventually, the fan mail reached unmanageable proportions and he had to hire someone to handle it for him.

Unlike his costars, Matthew hasn't striven to fill his hiatuses with feature film roles, preferring instead to spend time with his wife, relaxing and traveling. Their visits to Margherita's family in Italy are complicated by communication barriers, as Matthew told Rosie O'Donnell on her talk show: "I can't really communicate with her family very well. They don't speak English. So I just pretty much sit at the table and eat everything that's put in front of me, and smile a lot and just say how good it is and go "mm mm" a lot, and they love me."

They also go back to Matthew's home state of Wyoming at least a couple of times a year. He says, "It's like recharging my batteries. When I feel like I'm kind of getting stressed out and burnt out, I go home and spend two weeks there and I come back completely invigorated and excited. It's very beautiful country and there's something very spiritual about it and something that makes you feel very connected to yourself."

In the fall of 1996, Matthew returned to Wyoming to host a TBS special, *Survival of the Yellowstone Wolves*. The documentary charted the activities of the Wolf Restoration Project, in which wolves were reintroduced into Yellowstone Park, bringing the park back to a full state of ecological balance. Growing up in the area, Matthew was aware that wolves had been eliminated from Wyoming sixty years before. Matthew enjoyed filming the special, although he admits to being nervous when meeting the wolves eye-to-eye. He told *TV Guide*, "They were pacing all around me, completely wild, and then they started running frantically. It was pretty intense."

Matthew's commute to his next guest appearance was much shorter. The TV game show *Jeopardy!* is filmed on the Sony lot, one soundstage over from *Party of Five*. So when Matthew was asked to appear on *Celebrity Jeopardy!*, the trek to Alex Trebek's set was a literal hop, skip, and a jump from his trailer. Competing against comic actor Jon Lovitz and Olympic athlete Carl Lewis, Matthew was trailing throughout both rounds of questions. All three stars missed the final

Jeopardy question, on which they each bet their entire winnings. The game ended with a three-way tie of 0! His loss was for a good cause, however. The charity he played for, the Make-a-Wish Foundation, received a $10,000 donation in his name.

In the spring of 1997, Matthew and Margherita had their first child, a daughter named Kyle Allison Fox. In a *People* magazine interview, his costar Jennifer Love Hewitt recalled that Matthew had tears in his eyes when he told his castmates about his impending fatherhood. "He said, 'Hey guys, I'm going to be a daddy!' It was one of the sweetest things Matthew has ever done," she recalled. Matthew turned down all offers for work during his third season hiatus so he could spend time with his child. He told *People*, "I want to be there and be present every second that I possibly can." While he hopes his series will continue for years to come, it would come as a surprise to few if, when *Party* ends, Matthew retreats with his wife and daughter to a cabin in the wilds of Wyoming, where he will pass on the values he learned from his own father to his child. "Life is what you make of it," he says. "My dad gave me that. He meant that happiness depends on that set of eyes you use to view the world."

Selected Credits

Feature films
My Boyfriend's Back (1993) 'Buck Van Patten'

Television
Wings ep. "Say It Ain't So, Joe" (NBC, 4/30/92) 'Ty Warner'
Freshman Dorm (CBS, 8/11/92 - 9/9/92) 'Danny Foley'
If I Die Before I Wake (CBS Schoolbreak Special, 10/26/93) 'Charlie Deevers'
Survival of the Yellowstone Wolves (TBS, 11/3/96) 'Host'

Commercials
Clearasil, Milk, Dr. Pepper

Neve Campbell
(Julia Salinger)

No one conveys the fractured emotions of a TV teen better than Neve Campbell on Party of Five. *In any given episode, viewers can expect to witness ecstasy, angst, and all the fleeting feelings that occur in between.* —TV Guide, *May 1997*

Neve Campbell as Julia Salinger in the first season of *Party of Five.* ARCHIVE PHOTOS.

Aside from fans who approach her in inappropriate places—like bathroom stalls—Neve Campbell's biggest pet peeve is the mispronunciation of her first name. Neve, derived from the Spanish word for snow, is pronounced "Nev". The actress complains, "I get Neevay, Nevay, Navy, Neeve. No one says Neve." The worst case of mangling her moniker occurred when she auditioned for *Phantom of the Opera* in Canada. She recalls, "I was at a cattle call audition, and when they called my name to go in they said, 'Nevay Camembera.' Now how they got that, I have no idea. All of a sudden I was a cheese. That was probably the most interesting one."

The answer to one of the questions she is asked most frequently is yes, Neve is her real name; it was taken from her mother's maiden name. Neve Adrianne Campbell was born on October 3, 1973, in Guelph, Ontario, Canada, about an hour's drive outside of Toronto. Neve likes to say that performing is in her blood—not only were both her parents actors, but so were both sets of grandparents! She says, "Both my Scottish grandparents used to perform for the soldiers during World War II, and my Dutch grandparents owned a theater in Holland." Neve's father, Gerry Campbell, a Scottish immigrant, is a drama teacher. Her mother, Dutch-born Marnie Neve, is a yoga instructor and former theatre owner.

Neve's parents met while doing a play together at the University of Windsorin Ontario. Both had aspirations of being actors but they didn't pursue it after they married and their first child, Christian, was born. (Christian has starred in several television movies, as well as the short-lived 1996 series *Malibu Shores*.) The Campbells divorced while their second child, Neve, was still an infant. Each of her parents subsequently remarried and divorced, and her father wed a third time. Neve has two half-brothers, Damien and Alex.

Growing up, Neve was close to both her parents, and she alternated living with each for periods of time. No matter where she lived, she was exposed to the theater, and from an early age she knew that she wanted to perform. Her father, a high school drama teacher, often directed school and community theater productions. Her mother owned a dinner theater, and Neve would sit in the back and watch the performances over and over again, studying people's reactions. In a July 1995 interview, she said, "My parents were frequently involved in theater productions during my childhood, so I would spend hours hanging about during rehearsals, watching, listening, fantasizing." Neve and Christian often had small parts in their father's productions.

When she was six years old, Neve attended a performance of *The Nutcracker* and decided that she wanted to be a ballerina. She was enrolled in dance classes at age six, and at eight, she auditioned for the National Ballet School in Toronto. Approximately two thousand youngsters try out each year to attend the prestigious school, and less than a dozen are accepted.

Neve entered the National Ballet School as a full-time resident student at nine years of age. She endured a rigorous training schedule, which included up to five hours of dance instruction daily, as well as a full academic program. In her first year at the school, she performed in the National Ballet of Canada's production of *The Nutcracker.* She later appeared in *Sleeping Beauty.*

At 14, Neve suffered an emotional breakdown as a result of the highly stressful conditions at the school. She explained to the *Toronto Sun,* "The school was very tough. It was very intense, had a lot of favoritism, lots of competition, and lots of backstabbing." Additionally, Neve had sustained hip injuries, which were exacerbated by the harsh training schedule. In a *TV Guide* interview, Neve said, "I got to a place at that school where I hated dance, and that was really tragic for me. I had no friends, I didn't fit in, and I was living in residence. When you live with the people you don't fit in with, you're in trouble." She quit the school and enrolled in a public high school for her tenth grade year.

Neve found that she fit in no better at her "regular" school than she had at the ballet company. In fact, she says that throughout her schooling, she was unpopular and was often picked on by her classmates. "They even had a song about me, and how ugly I was," she told the *New York Daily News.* "I was the kid who had to sit with the chaperones, or the matrons, at lunch, because no one would sit with me."

A year later, Neve switched schools again. She attended an alternative school where students chose their own hours and courses. She longed to get back into performing, and when she heard that the first Canadian production of Andrew Lloyd Webber's musical *The Phantom of the Opera* was to be mounted in Toronto, she decided to audition. She says she never really expected to be cast, but went to the audition for the experience. When she arrived at the theater and saw that there were hundreds of other dancers trying out, she felt so intimidated that she almost didn't go through with the audition. She remembers, "When they called me in, I ran off to the dressing room, bawling my eyes out. Some dancers convinced me to go ahead with it anyway, so I did—and then they kept calling me in, again and again, all day long. Everyone got cut but eight of us."

Neve made the cut and was chosen to be one of the ballet chorus members, as well as the understudy for the singing role of Meg. After she was cast, the show's American director, Hal Prince, was shocked to discover that Neve was only 15 years old. The next youngest dancer in the production was 24. Neve said that being the youngest member of the troupe had its advantages. "I was at least ten years younger than everyone else in the cast, so I was treated like the little sister. Everyone was very protective of me."

The Phantom of the Opera opened at Toronto's Pantages Theatre on September 20, 1990. Neve stayed with the production for two years, performing in over 800 shows. She looks back on *Phantom* as the best experience of her career to date, not only because she was fulfilling her dream to dance professionally, but also for the acting and voice training that she received. The production marked the end of her scholastic career (she had dropped out of high school when she landed the role). As she reasoned, "It didn't make a lot of sense to say, 'Oh, I'm not going to take *The Phantom of the Opera* because I need to learn more about history.'"

An agent spotted Neve during a performance of *Phantom* and suggested she try modeling. She did, with disastrous results. Neve not only hated modeling and found it boring, but she also felt she had been exploited. She told *Detour* magazine, "I did a photo shoot for Sony, and I was in a bathing suit or something like that. It was only supposed to be in a catalogue, and all of a sudden there was this huge, huge, huge poster in Toronto. I had been taken for a ride."

After a few months of modeling, Neve graduated to TV commercials. Her first job was a spot for the Eaton Centre, a mall in Toronto. She filmed ten commercials in five months, including one for Tampax, which she calls a career low point.

Neve stopped doing commercial assignments when she began winning roles in film and television. In the 1994 sci-fi/horror feature *The Dark*, she played a police deputy who investigates strange goings-on at a cemetery where a prehistoric creature has been devouring people. She also appeared in the 1994 film *Paint Cans*, about the bureaucracies of filmmaking in Canada. Neve had a starring role in the short film *Love Child*, about the budding sexuality of a pre-teen boy named Murray. She played Deidre, the 16-year-old object of Murray's desire.

Neve (lying on the sofa) played the resident sex symbol on the Canadian series *Catwalk*. EVERETT COLLECTION.

Her largest role, and most adventure-filled movie experience to date, came in *Baree*, where she plays Nepeese, a half-Indian, half-French Canadian young woman. Baree is her half-dog, half-wolf companion. Jeff Fahey plays Paul, a rugged environmentalist who befriends Nepeese and her father. When a depraved trader becomes obsessed with Nepeese and kills her father so that he can claim her, Paul and Baree come to her rescue. The film was released to home video in 1995, under the title *Northwest Passage*.

Neve had a life-threatening experience while making *Baree*, in a scene that called for Nepeese to be chased through the woods by a bear. To achieve this, the director had put honey on Neve's hand and had her run through the woods as the bear pursued her.

Even though the bear used in the film had no claws or teeth, its strength alone made the stunt a dangerous one. Prior to shooting the scene, Neve overheard the stunt coordinator warn the director, "If he takes her by the arm, he's going to rip it off. If he takes her by the leg, he's going to break it, and if he takes her by the neck, he's going to kill her." Despite the admonition, she filmed the stunt, allowing the bear to chase her through the forest. Then the bear caught her and began dragging her by the leg and gumming her. Neve escaped the bear's clutches and suffered no injuries, but as she later described the experience on *Late Night with Conan O'Brien*, "It really sucked."

Neve landed her first regular television role in 1992, on the syndicated Canadian series *Catwalk*. The show followed the struggles of six people in their early twenties who form a band (named Catwalk). Neve, who was 17 when she was cast, played Daisy, a singer and dance teacher. Behind-the-scenes problems and politics early in the series' run led to a personality redo of Neve's character. She recalled in a Canadian *TV Guide* interview, "The creator was fired two weeks into the run, so my character was changed from kind of a spiritual chick with a lot to say to this sex symbol instead... wearing less clothes than I thought she should, and a lot of plot lines were based around her and guys rather than dealing with life, which is what I signed on for." Frustrated with her character's loose morals and tight clothing, Neve quit the show after one season.

She continued to work in Canadian-produced film and television, including guest-starring roles on *My Secret Identity*, *The Kids in the Hall*, and *Are You Afraid of the Dark?*

She had a brief but memorable role in the 1994 American television movie, *Janek: The Forget-Me-Not Murders*. As Jess, the goddaughter of NYPD detective Frank Janek (Richard Crenna), she is the eighth victim of a serial killer. Due to his personal involvement with the case, Janek relentlessly pursues the killer, who is somehow linked to Jess's therapist, played by Tyne Daly. Neve's character is killed in the film's first minutes, and her only dialogue is a message left on Janek's answering machine, played after her death. *The Hollywood Reporter* praised the telefilm as one of the best in a string of *Janek* mysteries CBS had produced.

In the NBC TV movie *I Know My Son is Alive*, Neve played a young nanny who conspires with her boss and lover, Mark (played by Corbin Bernsen), to drive his wife (Amanda Pays) crazy and steal her baby. The producers of *I Know My Son is Alive* arranged for her to fly to Los Angeles to meet the network executives. Neve had been contemplating moving to L.A., where the opportunities for stardom are far greater than in Canada. She says, "I knew I needed to come [to L.A.] because you get to a certain point in Canada, unfortunately, where you can only get so far and then you have to move to the States to get big. Canadians really don't acknowledge their stars until they get big in the States, which I really think needs to change."

On January 17, 1994, a magnitude 6.7 earthquake wreaked havoc on Los Angeles and its surrounding communities. Neve arrived in town a week after the quake, eager to make the rounds of the agents and cast-

Neve Campbell as Julia Salinger in the second season of *Party of Five*, PHOTOFEST.

ing directors, but she found that everyone was busy picking up the pieces and putting their homes back together. Neve, however, did meet a manager, Arlene Forester, who offered to help set up some auditions for her until she found an agent. One of the auditions she arranged was for *Party of Five.*

Neve loved the pilot script when she read it, but she was also attracted to the project because the production was being supervised by Ken Topolsky, who had been a producer on the well-regarded *The Wonder Years.* She says, "*The Wonder Years* was an incredibly written and produced show. When my manager told me *Party of Five* was with the same producer, that's what made me so enthusiastic about the show."

Close to 300 actresses had auditioned for the role of Julia Salinger before Neve impressed the producers with her audition. She only read for two minutes before they offered her the plum role. Had Neve harbored any doubts about relocating to the States, they were quelled when she was offered the role of Julia—two weeks after arriving in L.A.!

Like Neve, her character Julia Salinger grew up fast and was an outsider at school. Neve could relate to Julia's insecurities and lack of social standing at school. She has said, "I'm very similar to Julia in the sense that I had difficulty relating to people my age because of my family circumstances or because of my work circumstances and Julia has difficulty relating to people her own age too."

One of Neve's favorite *Party of Five* story lines was Julia's pregnancy and her decision to have an abortion. Whereas usually the actors don't know about future episodes until they read the script, the producers consulted Neve ahead of time about the pregnancy story line. She says, "Because it's such a sensitive issue, the producers and writers approached me about two weeks before we started the episode and asked me my opinions, and what I was comfortable with." Neve was excited about the plot line, which would have made her character the first regular on a prime-time drama series to have an abortion. She was disappointed when the network, succumbing to pressure from advertisers, ordered the producers to change the script. Though she decides to have an abortion, Julia suffers a miscarriage. She calls the decision a "cop out," but thinks that as long as the story prompted discussion about the subject among viewers, it was worthwhile.

Neve has made the most of her breaks from *Party of Five,* taking on feature film and television projects. She hopes that if she builds a movie career during the series, she won't have trouble being pigeonholed as

"Julia" after the series ends. During her first hiatus from the series, she made a feature film, *The Craft*, and a made-for-television movie, *The Canterville Ghost*. One of the lures of *The Canterville Ghost* was the opportunity to work with Patrick Stewart, of *Star Trek: The Next Generation* fame. She says, "I love Patrick, not only because I'm a Trekkie, but because he's just an incredible actor." The story, an adaptation of Oscar Wilde's novella, starts when an American family moves into stately Canterville Hall in Great Britain. The daughter, Ginny Otis, meets and befriends the 400-year-old ghost (Stewart) of the hall's original owner, and tries to save him from his horrible, haunted fate.

The Canterville Ghost aired on ABC on January 27, 1996. *The Hollywood Reporter* enthused, "Those looking for an engrossing, absorbing spot of entertainment are more than urged to tune into *The Canterville Ghost*... this kicky yet affecting update of Oscar Wilde's treatment of undying love is a blast that is, in the parlance of the reviewer's lexicon, fun for the whole family." The telefilm received a Family Film Award for Outstanding Television Movie from the World Film Institute. Neve Campbell received the Family Film Award for Outstanding Actress in a Television Movie.

While filming *The Canterville Ghost* in London, Neve married her longtime boyfriend Jeff Colt in a spur-of-the-moment ceremony at the Registry Office of Westminster. The couple had met in 1990 when she was in *The Phantom of the Opera* and he was a bartender at the theater. They moved in together when Neve was 17 and Jeff was 25. When Neve relocated to Los Angeles for *Party of Five*, Jeff stayed behind in Canada (where he hosted a TV talk/game show, *It's Alive!*) and they maintained a long-distance relationship.

Due to her parents' divorce (and subsequent remarriages and divorces), Neve had little faith in the institution of marriage when she was growing up. She told *Us* magazine, "I swore up and down that I would never, ever get married. Then I swore up and down that if I married, I'd never marry young." However, meeting Jeff changed her mind. She said, "Jeff is extremely supportive and has been wonderful for me."

The couple married on April 4, 1995. Neve invited 13 people to the ceremony—all were friends she made on location during the movie. None of her family members were invited. She explained the difficult decision to exclude her family from her wedding in a *TV Guide* interview: "My immediate family, they're all incredible—but not in the same room, you know?"

After honeymooning in Paris, Venice, and Zurich, Neve returned to Los Angeles to work on her next project, *The Craft*. In this horror film, four teenage girls, all outcasts in school, join forces to tap into malevolent supernatural powers. They use witchcraft to settle some scores, then things get out of hand when they begin turning on each other. Neve was Bonnie, a girl who had been badly burned in a fire as a child. Bonnie employs witchcraft to rid her body of her disfiguring scars. (Bonnie's doctor was played by Brenda Strong, who later turned up on *Party of Five* as Charlie's vindictive girlfriend Kathleen.) Bonnie's transformation—both physical and emotional—is what drew Neve to the role. She told *Venice* magazine, "She goes from being a real insecure 'freak type' who can't relate to anybody to becoming a very strong, empowered young woman. To play transitions like that is a wonderful thing because it's almost like you get to play two characters."

The Craft opened without much advance media attention in May 1996. Surprisingly, it earned $7 million in its first weekend and ranked number one at the box office for the week. The picture itself received mixed reviews, but critics universally praised the four leads. *Variety* judged, "Four gifted and attractive actresses struggle hard to lend a semblance of dramatic coherence to *The Craft*, a neatly crafted film that begins most promisingly as a black comedy à la *Heathers*, but gradually succumbs to its tricky machinery of special effects."

Neve spent her second *Party of Five* hiatus, the summer of 1996, filming the lead role in the Dimension Films release, *Scream*. She played the horror movie's central character, high school student Sidney Prescott. Still traumatized by her mother's murder a year earlier, Sidney is the prime target of a serial killer stalking the town of Woodsboro, California. Again, what attracted Neve to the role was her character's transition from victim to heroine. In a Prodigy online chat session, she said, "When I read the script it was one of those scripts where I literally couldn't put it down. [It was] extremely intriguing and witty. And I liked the fact that my character goes from being somewhat of a victim in the beginning of the film, to becoming much stronger and empowered by the end."

As a dancer, Neve enjoyed the physical demands of the role. Though professional stunt people performed the more dangerous action sequences, Neve did as many of her own stunts as the director would allow. These included hanging from a two-story window and falling

Though she starred in *Scream,* the highest-grossing horror film to date, Neve admits that she's not a fan of scary movies herself. "I have to sit with a pillow in front of my face." EVERETT COLLECTION.

from trucks and cars. In one of her favorite scenes of the film, she punched one of her costars, *Friends* star Courteney Cox. She explained to *TV Guide* Online, "I was really psyched about being able to fight and punch and do stunt work. I think a lot of that comes from being physically active, because I'm a dancer, so anything physical on a set that's challenging is a lot of fun for me and that's what I enjoyed."

Originally titled *Wes Craven's Scary Movie, Scream* is not a traditional horror movie. Filled with in-jokes and broad clichés, *Scream* satirizes the horror genre while at the same time providing a chilling suspense story. *Entertainment Weekly* assessed, "Poised on the knife edge between parody and homage, *Scream* is a deft, funny, shrewdly unsettling tribute to such slasher-exploitation thrillers as Craven's own *A Nightmare on Elm Street.*"

The film's director, horror master Wes Craven, attributes the film's success to Neve's performance: "The whole film depended on her. We

Neve Campbell sports a milk mustache in this 1996 advertisement. Photo courtesy of the National Fluid Milk Processor Promotion Board.

agonized over who to cast because her role was instrumental. But ultimately, she was the linchpin without whom the movie wouldn't work. She's very wry and witty." Ironically, the *Scream* queen can't stand to watch horror flicks. Neve admitted, "I hate horror films. I'm one of those people that are terrified watching them. I have to sit with a pillow in front of my face, and I scream a lot. But I love playing in them."

Scream opened on December 20, 1996, and was the surprise hit of the holiday movie season, scaring up $40 million in box office receipts in its first three weeks. (The film only cost $15 million to make.) After its successful first run, it was re-released on April 11, 1997. As of June 1997, the film had racked up $100 million in domestic box office receipts alone. It is the highest-grossing horror movie of all time, far eclipsing such genre classics as *Nightmare on Elm Street, Friday the 13th,* and *Halloween.* It's no surprise that screenwriter Kevin Williamson quickly penned a sequel, and Neve Campbell signed on as star. *Scream Again* is targeted for a Christmas 1997 release. Also in the works for Neve is a thriller, *Wild Things,* with Kevin Bacon and Matt Dillon, in which she plays an ex-convict drug addict whose affair with a high school guidance counselor sets off a string of murders.

In the wake of *Scream,* Neve found her margin of fame widening. She was now in high demand for talk shows and magazine covers. In February 1997, she posed for the cover of *TV Guide* and hosted *Saturday Night Live.* (She had previously hosted the FOX network's Saturday night variety show, *Mad TV,* which featured a hilarious send-up of *Party of Five.* In "Republican *Party of Five,*" Julia was being wooed by presidential candidate Bob Dole, who tried to win her heart with his poetry: "I love you, Julia. Let's face it, you rule-ia.")

On July 29,1997 *Entertainment Tonight* reported that Neve and her husband Jeff have separated.

Though she struggled for many years to achieve the level of success she is currently enjoying, Neve still has difficulty adjusting to fame. She says, "It just seems absurd to me. I'm still the little girl that was really insecure and didn't fit in at school and who was really unpopular and considered to be the ugliest in the class. And then I'll stand in a room with thousands of people screaming and whatever—it's overwhelming."

Selected Credits

Feature films
Baree (aka *Northern Passage*) (1994; Canadian) 'Nepeese'
The Dark (1994; Canadian) 'Deputy Jesse'
Paint Cans (1994; Canadian)
Love Child (1995; short) 'Deidre'
The Craft (1996) 'Bonnie'
Scream (1996) 'Sidney Prescott'

Scream Again (1997) 'Sidney Prescott'
Wild Things (1998) 'Susie Toller'

Television
Catwalk (Canadian syndicated, 10/92 - 1993) 'Daisy McKenzie'
I Know My Son is Alive (NBC, 2/20/94) 'Beth'
Janek: The Forget-Me-Not Murders (CBS, 3/29/94) 'Jess Foy'
Are You Afraid of the Dark? ep. "'The Tale of the Dangerous Soup" (Nickelodeon, 4/16/94) 'Nonnie'
Kung Fu: The Legend Continues ep. "Kundela" (Syndicated, 10/94) 'Trish Collins'
The Canterville Ghost (ABC, 1/27/96) 'Virginia Otis'
Mad TV (FOX, 11/2/96) 'Host'
Politically Incorrect (Comedy Central, 1996)
Saturday Night Live (NBC, 2/8/97) 'Host'
MTV Movie Awards (MTV, 6/12/97) 'Presenter/Nominee'
Also, episodes of *My Secret Identity* and *The Kids in the Hall*

Stage
Sleeping Beauty, National Ballet of Canada
The Nutcracker, National Ballet of Canada
The Phantom of the Opera, Pantages Theatre, Toronto, 1990-92

Video
The Lion King II (Disney Home Video; animated) 'voice of Kiara'

Commercials
Coke, Tampax, others

Awards
1996 Family Film Award for Outstanding Actress in a Television Movie, for *The Canterville Ghost*
1997 MTV Movie Award nomination for Best Female Performance, for *Scream* (lost to Claire Danes of *Romeo and Juliet*)
1997 Saturn Award from the Academy of Science Fiction, Fantasy and Horror Films, for Best Actress in a Horror Film, for *Scream*

I'm not a Salinger, but I play one on TV

Are the stars of *Party of Five* anything like the characters they play? Ask anyone on the set and they'll say that Matthew Fox is the least like his character, while Jennifer Love Hewitt is the most like hers. In an October 1996 interview, Amy Lippman said that Matthew, who is happily married and ultra-responsible, really had to struggle to love and understand his character during the show's first two seasons. Luckily for Matt, his character evolved and matured into a more likable guy by season three. Perhaps the biggest difference between the cast and their characters is that the actors are all extremely lucky individuals, living out every actor's dream by starring on a popular TV series, while the Salingers are the most preternaturally unlucky family to hit the tube in years. As Love Hewitt told E! Online in April 1997, "The biggest difference is that in real life, none of us have quite as depressing a life as our character does!"

Here's what the actors have to say:

Scott Wolf: "I'm just as stupid as Bailey, but a little taller."

Lacey Chabert: "I hope when it comes to Claudia's bratty side that I am NOT. I think I'm a little more grounded than Claudia."

Neve Campbell: "Julia's pretty close to how I was when I was in high school. I didn't fit in and I didn't have many friends. I couldn't relate to people my age because of family circumstances and stuff like that so I can really relate to Julia on that level."

Matthew Fox: "I like to think I'd behave differently from Charlie, that I'd be a little bit more responsible for my brothers and sisters in that situation."

Jennifer Love Hewitt: "I'm completely like Sarah in every way possible. Like in the first couple of episodes when she was chasing after Bailey, those are totally the things that I would do and say. And all the embarrassing things she did as far as like being the klutz and everything, that is completely me."

Bullseye could not be reached for comment, but I'm told that he's not nearly as moody as his character, Thurber.

Lacey Chabert as Claudia Salinger in the first season of *Party of Five*. ARCHIVE PHOTOS.

Lacey Chabert
(Claudia Salinger)

> *Claudia figures that she has an answer for every little thing that happens and if everyone would just listen to her, everything would be okay.* — Lacey Chabert, May 1996

The youngest member of the regular cast, Lacey Chabert had more show business experience going into the series than most of her adult costars. Born in Purvis, Mississippi, on September 30, 1982, Lacey knew by the time she reached kindergarten that she wanted to be a star. She liked to sing in the bathroom using a hairbrush as a mock microphone, in imitation of her older sister, Wendy, a singer. Her mother Julie, a pianist, nurtured Lacey's musical talent, enrolling her in singing lessons at age five. Lacey's father, Tony, worked in the oil industry.

Thoughts of stardom may have seemed farfetched while growing up in rural Purvis, but Lacey's dream came within reach when the family went on vacation to New York City in the summer of 1991. She spotted a notice in the newspaper for an open call for the Broadway production of *Les Miserables*. Even though she had never taken an acting lesson, Lacey decided to audition. Lacey says she never expected to land a part, she just wanted to see what the audition process was like. To her surprise, she was cast in the role of Young Cosette. (Actually, Lacey played three roles in the stage production. She was one of three young actresses who shared the roles of Young Cosette and Young Eponine, and she also understudied the role of Gavroche.) In a 1997 interview with *React* magazine she recalled, "I couldn't believe I actually got it. It was the first time I ever tried anything like that." Lacey's luck meant prolonging the family vacation—the Chaberts took an apartment in New York. What they thought would be a short-term stay lasted three years.

Lacey relished performing live for an audience of 1,600 every night. She described her experience in a 1994 *Los Angeles Times* interview: "I loved it! I got to wear makeup and get a huge black eye every night and that was so fun. I got to get beaten up. I also had a solo song." As much as she enjoyed Cosette's black eye and "Castle on a Cloud" solo, one of Lacey's most memorable performances occurred when she stepped into the male role of Gavroche. She told fans during an America Online chat, "I was understudy for a boy's part, Gavroche, and on my birthday, I got to do it. I got shot three times and had a great time! And at the end when I bowed I took my hat off and some people were like, 'Oh my God . . . it's a girl!' It was one of the most exciting things I ever had to do!"

Lacey stayed with *"Les Miz"* for two years. She was with the company when pop singer Debbie Gibson made headlines by stepping into the role of Eponine. Also in the cast during Lacey's run was Michael Shulman, who was later cast as Claudia's pal, Artie, on *Party of Five*.

Between performances of *Les Miserables*, Lacey went on hundreds of auditions, and worked steadily in TV commercials. (You may have heard her voicing the Zest jingle, "You're not fully clean unless you're

Lacey Chabert on the set of *Party of Five* in 1994. PHOTO BY M. VICTORIA BATIATO.

Zest-fully clean.") She appeared on *Star Search '91* as a junior vocalist, making it to the finals. She played the role of an abused girl in the NBC television movie *A Little Piece of Heaven*, with Kirk Cameron and Chelsea Noble. In the story, Cameron's character kidnaps Lacey from her abusive parents, claiming to be her guardian angel. *A Little Piece of Heaven* aired on December 2, 1991, and received mixed praise from *Variety:* "Despite a far-fetched plot, this Christmas telepic manages to be a heartwarming tale thanks to some terrific acting." *TV Guide* called it "a big hunk of nonsense bordering on the grossly distasteful."

In 1993, Lacey was cast in the ABC daytime drama *All My Children.* She played Erica Kane's daughter Bianca for six months. Next, Lacey was cast as Baby June in the TV version of the musical *Gypsy,* opposite Bette Midler as Mama Rose. In a May 1996 interview, Lacey shared this memory of working with Midler, "Bette was crazy and fun! She would bring her dog, Puddles, on the set. She was called Puddles because if you spoke to her in a high voice she peed." *Gypsy* aired on CBS on December 12, 1993. The three-hour special garnered a great deal of media attention, as it marked Midler's television movie debut and the network's first musical production in 25 years. Lacey appeared (as a blonde) in two musical numbers early in the special.

In early 1994, the producers of the upcoming *Party of Five* were scouring the country for new faces to play the Salinger siblings. On the basis of an audition tape she had made in New York, Lacey was flown to Los Angeles to meet the producers. The role of Claudia, a smart, sassy 13-year-old violin prodigy, seemed tailor-made for Lacey's talents. Not only did she possess a wiser-than-her-years demeanor, but Lacey had been taking violin lessons for two years. She says, "My Mom is a trained musician, and my family is very musically-oriented. In my family you have to play an instrument." Her musical ability may have been a plus, but it was not what landed her the part. Chris Keyser told the *Los Angeles Times*, "We would have cast her anyway if she didn't play an instrument. Her personality won us over.

Lacey Chabert on the set of *Party of Five* in 1996. PHOTO BY BRENDA SCOTT ROYCE.

She was given very complicated direction and just impressed us with how bright she is." Co-creator Amy Lippman added, "She just had this sparkle. It's a strong sense of irony that she also plays violin."

Lacey says she "went through the roof" when she learned she won the part. Lacey's good fortune meant uprooting the family once again. The family still called Mississippi home. In between Lacey's New York gigs, they retreated to her uncle's 20-acre farm in Purvis. With only a 13-episode initial commitment from the network, the Chaberts decided not to rush into purchasing a Los Angeles home. Lacey, her mother Julie, and sister Wendy moved into a rented beachfront apartment in Los Angeles, while her sister Chrissy and younger brother T. J. stayed in Purvis with their father. Julie Chabert brought her daughters home to Purvis for weekend visits whenever Lacey's shooting schedule allowed, which was usually every three or four weeks. The trip entailed flying into New Orleans and driving two-and-a-half hours to Purvis. When the series was picked up for a second season, the Chaberts bought a home in Ventura County, California, and officially made the move. Lacey loves Los Angeles, which she calls "a mix between Mississippi and New York."

As a minor, Lacey's working hours are restricted by child labor laws. She can work no more than nine-and-a-half hours per day, and three of those hours must be set aside for school. A trailer parked outside one of the *Party of Five* soundstages serves as her schoolhouse, and she is its only pupil. She spends one hour per day on homework, and at least an hour each day on music lessons. One of the questions she is most frequently asked is whether she really plays Claudia's violin numbers. It's also the question she finds most difficult to answer. While Lacey does actually play the violin, when filming she plays a muted violin and the sound (recorded by another musician) is dubbed in later in post-production. She has to learn the bowing and fingering in order to make her performances look believable. She explained in a 1994 *Teen Beat* interview, "If you have any musical knowledge, you'd know if my finger was bent half an inch off—you'd notice. So, I really have to work hard on it."

Lacey's mother makes sure that in between her work, schooling, and music lessons, she has time for some leisure activities. On weekends, she likes to play golf with her father and brother. When she has downtime on the set, she likes to ride her bike around the Sony lot, or play with her pogo stick or hula hoop. In the early days she would spend time in her trailer playing agent or businesswoman (complete with working cash register), but lately her interests have turned more to fashion and makeup than dolls and make-believe.

Claudia Salinger has done a lot of growing up on screen, causing the actress who plays her to experience some of her most embarrassing moments on television. An episode that dealt with Claudia getting her period had Lacey so mortified that she didn't show up for the table reading of the script. She was eventually coaxed into doing the episode, which includes one of the series' funniest scenes—big brother Bailey helps Lacey shop for feminine hygiene products and is clearly out of his element. "Wings? What's that about, huh?" he asks, before Claudia sends him away so she can figure it out for herself.

Another episode had Claudia stuffing her bra in an attempt to fit in at junior high school. But Lacey's most nerve-wracking moments have involved Claudia's romantic encounters. In episode 32 ("Grand Delusions," 12/20/95), Claudia meets a boy on vacation in Mexico and has her first kiss. The kiss was also a first for Lacey, who isn't allowed to

Lacey Chabert as Claudia Salinger in the third season of
Party of Five. ARCHIVE PHOTOS.

date in real life until she is sixteen. She described the experience as
"excruciating" in *React* magazine: "I had no idea what to do. I tried prac-
ticing on my pillow, but I still didn't know what to expect because, you
know, the pillow didn't kiss me back. I had to wait until the actual
moment to discover what it was all about. I was so nervous my palms
were sweating!"

She was still nervous when her next screen kiss came along in the
third season opener ("Summer Fun, Summer Not"). This time, she had
to smooch *Boy Meets World* star Rider Strong. She recalls, "My palms
were sweating, my heart was beating. I was really nervous. My Mom
said I didn't have to do it, but then I'm like, 'What? Not kiss Rider Strong?

He's very cute.'" That onscreen romance only lasted two episodes, as Rider's character Byron developed a crush on Claudia's older sister, Julia.

Lacey has clearly overcome her nervousness about kissing, as she has been begging producers to give Claudia a steady boyfriend, even offering helpful casting tips (that they hire someone cute). One romantic fantasy Lacey has left behind is her childhood crush on costar Scott Wolf, who is 14 years her senior. In the early days of *Party of Five*, 12-year-old Lacey freely admitted that she had the hots for Scott. She told fans on AOL, "Who wouldn't like working with the two hottest guys?" She has since outgrown the crush, as she told *TV Guide*. "I was in love with him at first. I used to think, maybe he'll wait for me. But as we got to know each other, suddenly we became best buddies. So I gave up on that."

Lacey considers her costars a second family and says that she has a different relationship with each one. "Scott and I are like the jokesters and partners. Matthew treats me like my big brother; he helps me out on the set. And Neve is like my big sister on the set. I love them all!"

One benefit of stardom for Lacey is that she has an opportunity to help other people. Her charitable instincts are at least partially motivated by an illness in her family. Her sister Chrissy was diagnosed with a rare form of muscular dystrophy in 1993. Lacey told *TV Guide*, "I think it made me want to help people. When you have somebody in your family who is really sick, you understand other people." When her schedule permits, Lacey likes to take part in charity events. In October 1996, she was one of several celebrities who waited tables in the third annual Celebrity Server Dinner benefiting the Homeless Health Care Los Angeles.

Lacey also finds that just doing her job portraying Claudia Salinger helps people. She says, "One of the great things is I get fan mail from kids who have lost their parents [saying that] I have helped them through it. One of the great things about acting is that I am able to touch some of these people." Though she is glad that people can relate to her character's struggles, Lacey sometimes feels that being a role model to millions of young people can be a bit of a burden. She told FOX news reporter Linda Mour, "It's kind of scary. It's a big responsibility for lots of people to be looking at you and following your actions, so I think it's very important that, even when I do these bad things on the show, the writers always send a message, why I did that." Her father hopes that by enacting Claudia's mistakes, Lacey will learn a few lessons herself. She says, "He called me up after the smoking episode and said, 'I hope you learned something!'"

While working on *Party of Five*, Lacey fit in several other acting assignments. First was the 1995 ABC AfterSchool Special *Educating Mom*, about a mother of two (Jane Kaczmarek) who returns to high school to get her diploma, sixteen years after she dropped out. Unfortunately, her teenage son (Will Friedle) attends the same school and is none too pleased to have Mom as a classmate. Lacey played younger daughter Carly, a computer whiz and soccer player. Jane Kaczmarek later appeared on *Party of Five* as Justin's mother, while Will Friedle got to know another *Party* star, Jennifer Love Hewitt. They met and began dating while costarring in the feature film *Rescue Me*.

In the summer of 1996, while on hiatus from *Party of Five*, Lacey went to Toronto to film the ABC television movie *Mother's Day*, with Gregory Harrison and *Chicago Hope*'s Roxanne Hart. Lacey played an adopted girl whose biological mother comes back into her life on Mother's Day, setting off a mysterious chain of events. The film was renamed *When Secrets Kill* by the time it aired on April 6, 1997. *Variety* called the plot "muddled," but awarded Lacey high praise: "Chabert's lively performance, a tight script and snappy directing will keep audiences tuned for the hollow denouement." Indeed, 14.9 million viewers tuned in, and the telefilm scored a higher rating than any episode of *Party of Five* to date.

Lacey spent her third season hiatus from *Party of Five* in London, filming the big screen version of the TV series *Lost in Space*, with Mimi Rogers, William Hurt, and *Friends* star Matt LeBlanc. Prior to landing the role of Penny Robinson (played in the original 1960s series by Angela Cartwright), Lacey had only seen one episode of the original show. The role was exciting to Lacey in that it involved her first trip to England, the chance to work with robots and space creatures, and her first live-action feature film appearance. Her prior film work had been strictly in animated features. She enjoys doing animation because she can play a wide range of characters. She has lent her voice to various cartoons, as well as the animated films *Anastasia* with Meg Ryan and Angela Lansbury, *Babes in Toyland* with Christopher Plummer, *The Prince of Egypt* with Michelle Pfeiffer and Val Kilmer, and the direct-to-video releases *Lion King II*, *An American Tale III*, and Mikhail Baryshnikov's *Stories From My Childhood*. She also voices the role of Eliza Thornberry in the Saturday morning Nickelodeon series, *The Wild Thornberries*.

Among Lacey's future career ambitions is directing. She has asked producers to let her direct an episode of *Party of Five*, but they advised her to come back when she turns eighteen. She fears they don't take her seriously and plans to keep asking until they give her a chance. Her bosses at *Party of Five* may be reluctant to let her helm an episode, but they acknowledge that she is far advanced in maturity for her age. Amy Lippman told *TV Guide*, "Sometimes I think Lacey is older than I am."

Lacey doesn't like getting the star treatment and describes herself as a normal person who does something that is not normal. She told the PBS series *In the Mix*, "My parents keep me focused on just being normal and having friends, and family is really, really important, so I hope I'm not affected by it in the way I act. This is just something that I love to do and I feel very lucky that my parents let me do it."

Selected Credits

Feature Films

Anastasia (animated) (1997)
Lost in Space (1998) 'Penny Robinson'
The Prince of Egypt (animated) (1998) 'Young Miriam'
Babes in Toyland (animated) - upcoming

Television

Star Search '91 (Syndicated, 1991) 'Contestant'
A Little Piece of Heaven (NBC, 12/2/91) 'Princess'
All My Children (ABC, 1993) 'Bianca Montgomery'
Gypsy (CBS, 12/12/93) 'Baby June'
Educating Mom (ABC, 3/14/96) 'Carly'
Nickelodeon's 9th Annual Kids' Choice Awards (Nickelodeon, 5/11/96) 'Presenter'
When Secrets Kill (ABC, 4/6/97) 'Jenny Newhall'
The Wild Thornberries (animated) (Nickelodeon, Fall 1997) voice of 'Eliza Thornberry'

Stage

Les Miserables, Imperial Theatre, New York, 1991-93 'Young Cosette/Young Eponine/Gavroche'

Recordings

The Broadway Kids Sing Broadway
Gypsy Soundtrack album (Atlantic Records, 1993)

Video

Kidz 'N Commercials (1996)
The Lion King II (animated; Disney Home Video) - upcoming
An American Tale III (animated; Universal Home Video) - upcoming
Little Redux Riding Hood (animated; Disney Home Video) - upcoming
Stories from My Childhood (animated; Family Home Entertainment) -
    upcoming

Commercials

Zest, others

Awards

1997 *Hollywood Reporter* YoungStar Award for Best Performance
    by a Young Actress in a Drama TV Series, for *Party of Five*

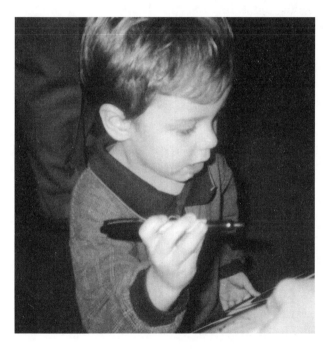

Andrew Cavarno, one of the twins who plays Owen, the littlest Salinger, signs autographs at the *Party of Five* soundtrack release party. PHOTO BY BRENDA SCOTT ROYCE.

Andrew and Steven Cavarno
(Owen Salinger)

The third set of twins to share the role of Owen, Andrew Scott and
Steven Anthony Cavarno were born on July 1, 1992, in San Bernardino,

California. They spent a season on the ABC series *Homefront* (1992-93) and also appeared in the 1994 made-for-cable movie *The Cool and the Crazy*. They live in Redlands, California, with their parents and older sister. Twins Alexander and Zachary Ahnert appeared as Owen in the *Party of Five* pilot, which was filmed in Canada. When the series was picked up, the role of Owen was filled by Brandon and Taylor Porter. Prior to *Party of Five*, the Porter twins had played baby Superman on *Lois and Clark: The New Adventures of Superman* and appeared on the NBC sitcom *The Mommies*. The Cavarnos took over the role of Owen in December 1995.

Bullseye
(Thurber, the family dog)

Bullseye plays Thurber, the Salingers' moody but lovable English bulldog. Bullseye was picked from a kennel in Riverside, California, by his trainer, David McMillan of Worldwide Movie Animals. The four-year-old, brown-eyed pooch weighs 50 pounds.

chapter seven

Friends, Lovers, and Others

Paula Devicq
(Kirsten Bennett)

Co-creator Amy Lippman calls Paula Devicq "the total surprise of the first season." The character of Kirsten was not envisioned as being part of the regular cast. In fact, she was only intended as a sight gag! After a long, unfruitful search for a nanny, Bailey opens the door to find a beautiful woman applying for the job—the answer to his prayers.

Lippman explains, "Paula was cast literally to open a door in the pilot. There's a beautiful nanny there and Bailey is very happy about it. And the truth is... we only auditioned Paula with 'hello, I'm the nanny.' So, we didn't know if she could act."

But after filming of the pilot commenced, the producers decided to expand Paula's role. Chris Keyser says that the one note he received from FOX network executives about the pilot was that they wanted to see "more Paula Devicq." Paula was given a little more screen time in the pilot beyond the door opening scene, and the possibility was left open for her character's integration into the series. When FOX picked up *Party of Five* as a series, Paula was signed to a contract as a regular member of the cast. Her character's romance with Charlie has provided one of the series' most enduring and pivotal story lines.

Paula Michelle Devicq was born on July 7, 1965, in Edmonton, Alberta, Canada. While working at McDonald's during high school, she

Paula Devicq as Kirsten
Bennett. Photofest.

was approached by someone who suggested she try modeling. She
didn't hesitate in choosing modeling over serving french fries. After she
graduated from high school, her mother enrolled her in modeling
classes. On the advice of a talent scout, she moved to New York to pursue a modeling career full-time. Among her modeling assignments was a
job for L'Oreal. She appears on the cover of their packaging for L'Oreal
Excellence Ash Blond hair color.

On the basis of her popularity in *Party of Five*, Paula was cast in the
1995 USA Network TV movie, *Wounded Heart*, opposite *As the World
Turns* star Jon Hensley. Paula played Tracy Lance, a tough-as-nails cor-
porate financier who returns to her Texas roots when she learns that
her estranged father is dying. Her plans to sell the ranch are impeded
by her half-brother, Sean (played by Hensley), who wants to preserve
their father's legacy. Eventually, Tracy and Sean fall in love and join
forces to save the ranch from foreclosure. *People* magazine graded the
film a "C +" and judged, "This movie starts smartly but gets a little soft-
headed and predictable—although Devicq and Hensley look great
together."

On *Party of Five*, Paula was paired with Matthew Fox's character, Charlie. In real life, the actress fell in love with Scott Wolf, who is three years her junior. In early episodes, Scott's character harbored a crush on Kirsten, who was oblivious to his attentions and laughed off his suggestion of dating a younger man: "I take care of babies, Bailey, I don't date them." After working together for nearly two years, Scott and Paula began dating and eventually moved in together. But they broke up in February 1997, and neither has spoken publicly about the reasons for the split.

In the third season of *Party of Five*, Paula's character developed a debilitating case of depression, triggered by the events which occurred in "The Wedding" episode. To prepare for the story line, Paula read William Styron's *Darkness Visible: A Memoir of Madness*, an 84-page book in which the author describes his devastating descent into depression. The actress says that the story line, while difficult, has been rewarding. She said, "Though it was very draining, it was the best experience I've had. And I've learned a lot from it. And I've learned to be much more compassionate towards people that go through it."

Throughout three seasons on *Party of Five*, Charlie and Kirsten have split up and reconciled several times. Telling the story of their rocky romance has necessitated long stretches in which Paula does not appear on the series and fans are left wondering, "Will she return?" In October 1996, Amy Lippman said, "What you see us doing is trying to put her in wherever we can because we don't want to lose her. I think our instincts—it feels like this couple belongs together and we keep fighting for ways to both keep them together and split them apart because that's where the drama is."

In May 1997, Paula began filming the independent film *Dinner and Driving*, opposite *The Single Guy's* Joey Slotnick.

Selected Credits

Feature films
Dinner and Driving (upcoming)

Television
Wounded Heart (USA, 8/16/95) 'Tracy Lance'

Stage
The Wild Geese, Ensemble Studio Theatre, New York

Michael Goorjian as
Justin Thompson.
Archive Photos.

Michael Goorjian
(Justin Thompson)

It's frustrating sometimes to play a character where you're like, 'Oh God, why's he doing this?'

—Michael Goorjian, February 1996

When he was first starting out in show business, Michael Goorjian received plenty of advice, including the suggestion that he adopt a more marquee-friendly moniker. But Michael says his family, which is of Armenian descent, "wouldn't have taken too well" to the idea of him changing his name.

Michael was born in Oakland, California, on February 4, 1973. His father is a NASA scientist and his mother is a nurse. He has one sister, a landscape architect. Michael became involved in theater while attending Bishop O'Dowd High School in Oakland. After high school, he studied at San Francisco's American Conservatory Theater before moving to Los Angeles and enrolling in UCLA's Theater Arts program.

He found UCLA's curriculum unsuited to his needs. He felt he was spending too much time learning about the technical aspects of the theater rather than exploring acting techniques. He told *Back Stage West,* "Many theater programs teach you everything about the theater—how to drop a curtain, how to build a block and all that, which is fine and fun, but I don't find it the best way. I had one acting class and the rest [of my time was spent] sewing costumes for the graduate school. I dropped out."

Michael, who had also trained as a dancer, performed as a singer/dancer in seven episodes of the 1990 ABC series, *Hull High,* an hour-long musical drama series set in a high school. The misguided series, which interlaced teen drama with song and dance numbers, was yanked after four months on the air. More chorus work was to come: he was cast in a small role in the Disney musical *Newsies.* The 1992 film was based on the 1899 newsboys' strike against newspaper magnates Joseph Pulitzer and William Randolph Hearst. As Skittery, Michael performed in the chorus of several musical numbers.

In a 1991 episode of *Life Goes On,* Michael played Ray Nelson, a bully who cheats series regular Corky (played by Chris Burke) out of his money. The character underwent a bit of a metamorphosis when he was brought back for several episodes in the series' fourth and final season. Here, Ray was depicted as a wiseacre, but not a hoodlum, as he befriended the series' central characters, Becca and Jesse (Kellie Martin and Chad Lowe) during Jesse's battle with AIDS. Ray's unrequited love for Becca provided some poignant moments in the series' final episodes.

After small roles in such films as *Forever Young* and *Chaplin,* and the telefilms *Never Forget* and *The Flood: Who Will Save Our Children?,* Michael got the chance to sink his teeth into a challenging role: an autistic teen in the 1994 television movie *David's Mother.* In the critically acclaimed film, Michael commands almost equal screen time with his costar, Kirstie Alley. In preparing for his part, Michael drew upon memories of an autistic teenager he knew in his youth. He also spent months with a group of autistic children in Toronto (where the movie was filmed), observing their behavior and mannerisms. The film's director, Robert Allan Ackerman, told the *Los Angeles Times* that Michael was so convincing in his performance that many members of the crew believed he was actually autistic, causing confusion when Michael would step out of character at the end of the day.

In a highly laudatory review, the *Hollywood Reporter* commended the stars: "These two deliver a profoundly believable portrait of human beings joined by tragedy." The *Daily Variety* reviewer noted, "Goorjian deserves special credit for his realistic portrayal of the autistic teen."

Despite such glowing reviews, Michael was astounded when he learned he had been nominated for an Emmy for his performance. Especially shocking was that he was nominated in the company of four much more established actors: Matthew Broderick, Richard Gere, Alan Alda, and Sir Ian McKellan. "I thought it was unusual that I was put in with them," he told the *Los Angeles Times*. "It's not just that I was surprised to be nominated, I was even more surprised about who else was on the list."

At the Emmy Awards ceremony in September 1994, Michael Goorjian was named Outstanding Supporting Actor in a Miniseries or Drama. He told *Soap Opera Digest*, "I became numb. I don't remember much of the evening. No one knew who I was. I do recall walking off the stage and the gal from *Picket Fences* [Kathy Baker, who presented the award] looking at me like, 'I hope this kid is going to be okay."

The Emmy brought a deluge of offers, but Michael was wisely choosy about his roles. He told *Drama-Logue*, "Part of the reason I won an award is not just because of my performance, but because the piece itself was good. It is pretty hard to do good work in something that is not so good."

He did accept a guest-starring role in a 1994 episode of the NBC drama series *Sweet Justice*, with Melissa Gilbert and Cicely Tyson. In the story line, he played opposite future *Party of Five* actress Megan Ward. Megan played Deidra, a female cadet suing for the right to attend Stonewall Jackson Military Academy. Michael was Jimmy, a cadet who becomes romantically involved with Deidra, but is coerced by his fellow cadets into lying on the stand to keep her out of the academy.

The role of Justin on *Party of Five* was created specifically with Michael in mind, signaling a change of status for the actor, who had often been rejected for roles due not to a lack of talent, but a lack of 'star power.' "It's the story of my life," he told *Soap Opera Digest*. "The director will write, 'I really wanted you, but they made me hire a name.' And I'm not a name." Intended as a six-episode stint, the character of Justin proved so popular with fans that Michael was added to the regular cast for the second season.

Michael has had a love-hate relationship with his character over the duration of the series. He likes the fact that Justin is one of few intelligent teens on television to avoid the stereotype of being a nerd. He says, "Very often, when they want to show an intelligent teenager on TV, they have to be a nerd. Justin is about something. He's honest and respectable."

On the other hand, Michael was unhappy with the way his character dealt with his relationship with Julia. He feels that Justin shouldn't

Neve Campbell and Michael Goorjian take a coffee break during the filming of "The Wedding" episode. PHOTO BY BRENDA SCOTT ROYCE.

have taken Julia back after she cheated on him with Griffin and that relationship ended. "I said to the producers, 'And I'm taking her back? Excuse me, why?' In real life, I would never stand for that."

In fact, Michael is one of the few cast members who challenges the *Party of Five* writers about his character's actions and motivations. While the other actors have stated that they feel no need to tinker with the writing because the scripts are always so well written, Michael feels that questioning the writing is part of his job as an actor. In an interview on the PBS series *In the Mix*, he said, "For me it's about the argument. If everybody sits there and goes, 'O.K., well I write this and you say it,' and everybody fits into their places, it gets stagnant and boring. Hopefully people understand that to me it's part of it. Nothing personal, I want to argue. I want to fight for what I think is the right decision. So, I try to have a say [in the writing], as best I can."

The writers seem to relish pulling Julia between her two onscreen loves, Justin and Griffin. At an October 1996 panel discussion, Amy Lippman responded to questions about Justin's future on the show in light of the fact that Griffin was once again returning. She said, "It's such a hard question to answer, because you fall in love with these characters and you fall in love with the actors who play them, and you have to look and see what the actual life of the story is. We would like to keep Michael a part of the show."

His character's transitory nature on the show has allowed Michael the time to work on other projects. He appeared against type in the 1996 feature film *Leaving Las Vegas* as a college boy who participates in a gang rape. He has also written screenplays, including *Walking the Magician*, which was optioned by Metafilmics in December 1996. Michael plans to star in and direct the film if he can get a studio's backing.

When he isn't working in film or television, Michael spends much of his time working with the Buffalo Nights Theatre Company in Los Angeles. He co-founded the group in 1992 with some of his UCLA classmates. He feels that the group allows him the freedom of artistic expression that is difficult to achieve when working in more commercial venues. He says, "With television and film work it's easy to fall into tricks and patterns, especially if you're under contract to a show for five years. It's difficult to grow or to get better as an artist in that medium." Michael has performed in several productions with Buffalo Nights, including a 1996 revival of *Modigliani*, for which he received rave reviews for his portrayal of the famed Italian painter. The *Los Angeles Times* reviewer wrote,

"Goorjian is charmingly dissolute—an impassioned, reckless child in tattered rags ruled by a twitchy addiction to whiskey."

While film and television are more lucrative, Michael generally finds working in the theater to be more rewarding, and has therefore turned down many well-paying offers that he felt lacked artistic merit. He told *Back Stage West*, "You have to have the guts to say, 'I'm not going to get this paycheck. I'm not playing the nerd again. I'm going to go for what I really want to do.'"

Making it clear that he's not in acting for the money, Michael says, "My personal approach is that I would rather be unemployed than do things that I don't find creatively interesting. It is difficult, but financially I don't really care. As long as I have enough money to eat some soup, I am happy."

Selected Credits

Feature films
Newsies (1992) 'Skittery'
Forever Young (1992) 'Steven'
Chaplin (1992) 'Adult Charles Chaplin, Jr.'
Leaving Las Vegas (1995) 'College Boy #1'

Television
Hull High (NBC, 8/90 - 12/90) 'Dancer'
Never Forget (TNT, 4/8/91) 'Chuck'
Life Goes On ep. "Sweet 16" (ABC, 10/20/91) 'Ray Nelson'
Life Goes On ep. "Exposed" (9/27/92)
Life Goes On ep. "Babes in the Woods" (11/29/92)
Life Goes On ep. "Udder Madness" (12/13/92)
Life Goes On ep. "Visions" (2/13/93)
Life Goes On ep. "Five Minutes to Midnight" (2/21/93)
Life Goes On ep. "Last Wish" (3/7/93)
Life Goes On ep. "Life Goes On (and On ...)" (5/22/93)
The Flood: Who Will Save Our Children? (NBC, 10/10/93) 'Scott Chapman'
Blind Justice (HBO, 1994) 'Soldier #1'
David's Mother (CBS, 4/10/94) 'David Goodson'
Sweet Justice ep. "One Good Woman" (NBC, 9/24/94) 'Jimmy Childers'
Under Suspicion (CBS, 11/11/94) 'Johnny'

Stage

All with Buffalo Nights Theatre Company

AS ACTOR

Hope on the Range, UCLA's Little Theatre, 1992
Hope on the Range, The Complex, Hollywood, 1993
Sophistry, The Lost Studio Theatre, Los Angeles, 1995
Modigliani, The Lost Studio Theatre, Los Angeles, 1996
The Firebugs, The Powerhouse Theatre, Santa Monica, 1997

AS CHOREOGRAPHER

Salome, Second Stage Theatre, Hollywood, 1995

AS DIRECTOR/CO-WRITER

The Beautiful Love, Coast Playhouse, Santa Monica, 1996

Commercials

Mazda

Awards

1994 Emmy Award as Outstanding Supporting Actor in a Miniseries or Special for *David's Mother*

Scott Grimes
(Will McCorkle)

Scott Grimes (who is called "Scotty" on the set of *Party of Five* to distinguish him from Scott Wolf) was born on July 9, 1971, in Lowell, Massachusetts. He got started acting as a child, playing precocious preteens in the made-for-television movies *A Doctor's Story*, *It Came Upon a Midnight Clear*, and *The Night They Saved Christmas*.

Many viewers recognize Scott from his recurring role as Chad McCann (Alyssa Milano's love interest) on the ABC sitcom, *Who's the Boss?* (1985-86). Next, he was a regular on the sitcom *Together We Stand*, with Dee Wallace Stone and Elliott Gould. After two months on CBS's schedule, the show was taken off the air and reworked. It returned in February 1987 as *Nothing Is Easy*, with the same cast minus Gould, whose character had been killed in a car accident.

Scott played Brian Dennehy's son in the 1994 medical series *Birdland* and has guest-starred on several series, including *Star Trek: The Next Gen-*

Bailey and Will (Scott Wolf and Scott Grimes) say farewell in "Summer Fun, Summer Not." ARCHIVE PHOTOS.

eration, *21 Jump Street*, and *Wings*. His feature film credits include the first two *Critters* movies (1986, 1988) and *Crimson Tide* (1995).

Scott had no trouble fitting in with the *Party of Five* cast—he and Scott Wolf were already buddies. Wolf told MTV viewers, "I really love my scenes with Scotty. Scotty and I were actually friends. We met playing ice hockey before *Party of Five* ever started. So we were already friends and then he was cast as my friend on the show, and so we spend a lot of time laughing when we're doing the scenes. We have a good time."

After two seasons on *Party of Five*, Scott left the series to work on the UPN sitcom *Goode Behavior*, starring Sherman Hemsley. In the series, which debuted in the fall of 1996 and was canceled after one season, Hemsley played Willie Goode, a recently paroled con artist who moved in with his estranged son Franklin, the Dean of Humanities at a North Carolina college. Scott played Garth, Franklin's kowtowing teaching assistant.

Scott has a band, "Scott Grimes and the Misdemeanors," and one of their songs was used in the episode "Strange Bedfellows."

Selected Credits

Feature films

Critters (1986) 'Brad'
Critters 2: The Main Course (1988) 'Brad'

Night Life (1989) 'Archie Melville'
Crimson Tide (1995) 'Petty Officer Hilaire'

Television

A Doctor's Story (NBC, 4/23/84) 'Charles Wickes'
The Night They Saved Christmas (ABC, 12/13/84) 'David Baldwin'
It Came Upon a Midnight Clear (NBC, 12/15/84) 'Robbie Westin'
The Twilight Zone ep. "Little Boy Lost" (CBS, 10/18/85)
Who's the Boss? (ABC, 1985-86) 'Chad McCann'
Together We Stand/Nothing is Easy (CBS, 9/22/86 - 4/24/87)
    'Jack Randall'
Bring Me the Head of Dobie Gillis (CBS, 2/21/88) 'George Gillis'
Star Trek: The Next Generation ep. "Evolution" (Syndicated, 9/23/89) 'Eric'
21 Jump Street ep. "Buddy System" (FOX, 10/27/90)
Wings ep. "Noses Off" (NBC, 10/8/92) 'Marty'
Birdland (ABC, 1/5/94 - 2/9/94) 'Scott McKenzie'
Goode Behavior (UPN, 8/26/96-1997) 'Garth Shoup'

Stage

Nine, Broadway production, 'Pepe'
Traveler in the Dark, Mark Taper Forum, Los Angeles
Chaplin, Dorothy Chandler Pavilion, Los Angeles

Jennifer Love Hewitt
(Sarah Reeves)

> *I used to make goals for things I wanted to do. The amazing thing
> is, the last seven years, my goals have gone 100 percent more than
> I had wanted them to!*
>
>   — Jennifer Love Hewitt, October 1996

Anyone who knows anything about Jennifer Love Hewitt knows
that she prefers to be called Love. Love is her middle name, but it's the
only one she has ever gone by, and the name her mother intended to
give her all along. Pat Hewitt wanted to name her daughter after her
best friend in college, a beautiful blonde named Love. It was Love's
well-meaning brother Todd, aged eight at the time, who suggested that
they give the baby a "normal" name so that she wouldn't get picked on

Jennifer Love Hewitt as Sarah Reeves. Archive Photos.

growing up. Pat let Todd choose another name, and he picked Jennifer, after a little girl down the street whom he had a crush on. Pat thought that Jennifer Love Hewitt sounded better than Love Jennifer Hewitt, but the baby who was born Jennifer Love Hewitt on February 21, 1979, in Waco, Texas, has always been known as Love.

Love finds it ironic how different she is from the woman she was named after. In an E! Online Q&A session, she said, "[She] was like five-eleven, long blonde hair past her butt, big blue eyes, freckles, and an hourglass figure. She was the most beautiful woman my mom had ever seen. My mom said if she ever had a little girl, she would name her

Love, so when I was born she of course named me Love—even though I came out, like 5'3", brown hair, half an hourglass figure and completely different looking."

Love's parents, Pat and Tom Hewitt, divorced in September 1979, when Love was just six months old. Love was raised by her mother, a speech pathologist, in Killeen, Texas, a small town north of Austin.

From the time she was a toddler, Love craved the spotlight. Always dancing and singing, she would perform at dinners, parties—anytime there was a group of people assembled. Her mother recalls that the family was dining at a supper club one night when they noticed that three-year-old Love had disappeared from the table. They panicked, then heard the little girl's voice coming from an adjoining room. They rushed in to find her perched on top of a baby grand piano, entertaining a roomful of guests. For Love, whose grandmother's third cousin was Patsy Cline, show business was in her blood.

Pat Hewitt encouraged her daughter's interest in performing, enrolling her in dance lessons before she even started kindergarten. Love studied tap, jazz, and ballet, quickly taking center stage in all of her classes because of her extroverted nature. Before long, Love was performing at livestock shows around Texas. Her love of show biz set her apart from her friends. She told *People* magazine, "I never really fit in where I lived in Texas. I would host and direct and star in these little plays, and my friends never really wanted to do it. I thought there was something wrong with them."

As a youngster, Love was inspired by the TV series *Punky Brewster* (NBC, 1984-87). She watched Soleil Moon Frye perform as Punky every week and thought that she could do it, too. By this time, she wasn't just performing in living rooms and supper clubs. When she was nine, Love was chosen to tour Russia with the Texas Show Team. Shortly after she returned from the tour, a local talent scout referred Love's mother to a manager in Los Angeles. Pat and Love traveled to L.A., arriving on February 21, 1989, Love's tenth birthday.

Within days of their arrival, Love signed with an agent and began going on auditions. What was originally intended as a one-month stay turned into a permanent move, as Love landed a role in the Disney Channel series *Kids Incorporated*. The series was already in its sixth season when Love joined the cast. She was one of 1,100 girls who auditioned for the role of Robin. The series combined singing, dancing, and

Love Hewitt (top right, on ladder) starred in the Disney Channel's *Kids Incorporated* from 1989 to 1991. EVERETT COLLECTION.

skits. Love revealed to fans during an America Online chat that while the kids all sang their own songs, they were fake-playing their instruments. Love stayed with the show for three years. In a 1991 episode, she worked with her future *Party of Five* costar, Scott Wolf, who guest-starred as twins. Love looks back fondly on her *Kids Inc.* days, saying, "It was my first job and it was kind of like a dream come true because I loved to sing, loved to dance, and loved hanging out with people my own age, so it was a lot of fun."

During this time, Love also appeared in dozens of commercials, including over twenty "Barbie" spots for Mattel Toys. She was hired by footwear manufacturer L.A. Gear as part of an international touring group, traveling throughout the U.S., Europe, and Asia, singing and dancing in four 30-minute performances each day. She and the other kids in the group were tutored in between performances, and Love also wrote about her travels for her school back home.

When she wasn't working, Love attended a regular school. She went through a difficult period when her schoolmates picked on her for being different and her teachers discouraged her from following her dreams. In an interview for *Real* magazine, she recalled, "My teachers said that I was ruining my life because I was acting, and that I was going to end up stupid because I wasn't going to have a good education. Yet, I had traveled the world, I had social skills, and I was a straight-A student."

Luckily for Love, her mother's support and encouragement was unflagging. Not the stereotypical stage mother, Pat never pushed her daughter to perform. Love told *Seventeen* magazine, "On my first day of work on my first job, my mom and I did our secret handshake and said that the minute it stopped being fun, I wouldn't do it anymore."

Love was one of nine young girls chosen to perform aerobics with an animated Barbie doll in the 1991 video, *Dance! Workout With Barbie.* In addition to dancing alongside Barbie, Love performed all of the songs used in the bouncy 30-minute exercise tape. The following year, twelve-year-old Love became an international singing sensation, when her first album, *Love Songs*, was released in Japan. She recalls, "It did really, really well. I had the number one dance song on the charts for four weeks. It was called 'Dance With Me.'" Singles from the album were released in England, Germany, Austria, and Switzerland.

Love's first feature film role was 1992's *Munchie*, Roger Corman's spoof of *Gremlins.* The campy kids' film starred Jaime McEnnan as Gage Dobson, a lonely boy who discovers a centuries-old creature named Munchie (voiced by Dom DeLuise). Munchie's mystical powers help Gage best the school's bullies and win the attentions of a pretty classmate, but they also land him in hot water with his mother and school authorities. Love played Andrea, the young hero's love interest. That same year, Love filmed an NBC pilot *Running Wilde*, with Pierce Brosnan as a reporter for *Auto World* magazine who lives the stories he covers. The proposed series was not picked up, and the pilot never aired.

She landed the title role in Concorde Pictures' holiday film, *Little*

Miss Millions (1993). Love played Heather Lofton, a wealthy nine-year-old who runs away from her money-grubbing stepmother in search of her real mom. *WKRP in Cincinnati* star Howard Hesseman played Nick Frost, a private eye who tracks Heather down. Nick and Heather form an uneasy alliance as they try to elude the Feds and re-unite Heather with the mother who loves her, instead of the stepmother who only loves her money. *Little Miss Millions* was released in 1993. It often pops up on television during the holidays, under the alternate title *Home for Christmas.*

Jennifer Love Hewitt at a 1997 promotional appearance. PHOTO BY LAUREN ROYCE.

Next, Love was cast in the 1992-93 FOX series *Shaky Ground*, starring Matt Frewer, who remains better known as the computer-generated character Max Headroom, the basis of a short-lived 1987 series. In *Shaky Ground*, Frewer played Bob Moody, a white collar worker whose financial struggles and frustrations at work formed the basis of the comedy. Love played Bob's smart daughter, 13-year-old Bernadette. Airing on Sunday evenings opposite ratings giant *60 Minutes*, *Shaky Ground* received dismal ratings and was canceled after 17 episodes.

In 1993, Love joined Whoopi Goldberg for the screen comedy *Sister Act II: Back in the Habit*. Love appeared as street-smart Margaret, one of the Catholic school choir members led by Goldberg's "Sister" Mary Clarence. Love, who had always been billed as 'Love Hewitt', started using her full name professionally beginning with *Sister Act II*. She says that she had never made a conscious decision to omit the 'Jennifer'. "Since I was a little kid everyone's always called me Love, and for a long time I just didn't put it on the beginning of my name because I just didn't think about it," she said in a 1996 interview.

Love's next job took her to the tropical isle of Oahu, Hawaii. The ABC TV series *Byrds of Paradise* starred Timothy Busfield as Sam Byrd, a Yale ethics professor and father of three whose wife was killed in an ATM robbery. Wanting to start anew, he takes a job as headmaster at a tiny school in Hawaii. The plots revolved around the Byrd family's difficulties in adjusting to the culture and the locals, as well as Sam's relationship with a beautiful Hawaiian colleague. Love played Franny, Sam's rebellious 15-year-old daughter, whose bitterness over her mother's death leads her to act out her anger. Love found the role of Franny to be her most challenging, since she had little in common with her character. She told the *Hollywood Reporter*, "She was full of teen angst, smoking, yelling at people, driving her dad's car off a cliff. I am not like that."

Byrds of Paradise premiered in March 1994. The *Hollywood Reporter* hailed it as "a fresh, beautifully written, snappily acted, quality family drama." Despite such praise, the series was canceled after only three months on the air. Though it was short-lived, Love found the experience to be rewarding in that it helped her to grow. She told *Soap Opera Digest*, "I went there still the teenager who liked talking on the phone and was into New Kids on the Block. When I came back, I had a whole new perspective on life. My character was just such a grown-up, smart person that I learned a lot just by playing her."

Love also experienced her first kiss during the filming of *Byrds of Paradise*. Like her *Party of Five* costar Lacey Chabert, Love's first real kiss and her first screen kiss were one and the same. She recalled on *The Tonight Show with Jay Leno*, "The director came to us and he said, 'Now it's supposed to look like you guys have been kissing for a while, so go in the bushes and practice.' I had never kissed anybody before in my whole life and I was scared half to death . . . and my Mom was standing on the other side of the bushes! And the guy was like 19 years old and I was 14."

After *Byrds of Paradise* was canceled, Love jumped right into another series, *McKenna*. Filmed in Central Oregon, *McKenna* starred Chad Everett as widower Jack McKenna. After his son Guy dies in an accident, Jack's estranged son Brick (played by Eric Close) returns to help keep the family outfitting business afloat. Jack's teenaged daughter Cassidy was portrayed by Vinessa Shaw in the pilot episode, but Love took over the role beginning with the second installment. As in *Byrds of Paradise*, Love played a rebellious teen who had lost her mother. *McKenna* featured an interesting premise that allowed for some great action sequences set in the great outdoors. But white-water rafting and rock climbing wasn't enough to attract viewers. *McKenna* floundered in the ratings and was dropped from ABC's schedule after only a handful of episodes had aired.

After starring in three failed TV shows in quick succession, it would have been understandable if Love had shied away from future television series. Luckily for *Party of Five* fans, she had no such reticence when she was offered the role of Sarah Reeves.

Since she had been in Oregon filming *McKenna* when *Party of Five* debuted, Love had only seen one or two episodes of the series. After a busy day of auditioning and running errands, Love returned home to find sides (pages of dialogue) on her fax machine which said, "PO5" at the top. "What's P-O-5?" she wondered, not recognizing the abbreviation. Once she read the pages, she felt an immediate connection to the character of Sarah. She recalls, "I was like, 'Wow, this character talks exactly like me!' I knew how to play her instantly."

Since she felt that the character of Sarah was so much like her, Love decided to just be herself for the interview, dressing in jeans and a T-shirt and wearing minimal makeup. Pumped up prior to the audition, her optimism waned when she saw the other actresses trying out for the role. She recalls, "I walked in and there were 25-year-olds in little tight dresses with lots of makeup and hair. They were beautiful, tall and model-looking. I came in jeans and a little T-shirt and I looked ten next to them. I'm thinking, 'Oh, right! Like I stand a chance.'"

But Love's non-glamorous approach worked. The producers were so impressed with her audition that they changed the direction of the character to fit her personality. Co-executive producer Ken Topolsky says of Love, "She's probably the most talented young actress I've ever worked with. She has incredible instincts, she has incredible talent, she takes direction well. She's smart. She's a special actress." Love told fans on America Online that when she got the call offering her the job, she ran around her house screaming with excitement.

Though she has become a fan favorite, many female fans were initially antagonistic towards the character of Sarah because they didn't want Bailey to settle down with any girl. At a 1996 promotional event with the cast at Universal Studios, Love said, "I get a lot of hate mail about that. I do. I get a lot of mail that starts off 'we hate you'... but then by the end of it, it's like, 'But we're glad if he's going to have a girlfriend, it's you.' So it's kind of nice."

The girl who snagged Bailey calls her handsome costar, "one of the most adorable, sweet, honorable people you could ever meet." She says, "Every morning he takes time to make you feel special—whether it's giving you a hug, or saying, 'Wow, you look nice today.'" Frequently asked by fans what it's like to kiss Scott Wolf, she always answers, "It's great!" She told *People* magazine, "Sometimes I say, 'Wow, I'm the luckiest teenager alive—kissing an older man every day and getting paid for it!"

Shortly after her *Party of Five* debut, Love had another reason to celebrate: the release of her CD, *Let's Go Bang*. The Atlantic Records release features a mix of pop and rhythm and blues music, including one song co-written by Love, "Free to Be a Woman." The CD artwork features a heavily makeup Love in sexy, sultry poses. Love described the album as "very fun and funky."

Love's first hiatus from *Party of Five*, in the summer of 1996, was a hectic one. She rushed back and forth between a recording studio, where she was laying down tracks for her next CD, the self-titled *Jennifer Love Hewitt*, and the set of the MGM/UA feature film *House Arrest*. "It was definitely tough," she says of the grueling schedule. "I would record during the day and go to work at night or vice versa."

The album, which was released in the fall of 1996, features twelve songs, mostly romantic ballads. The album spawned a single, "No Ordinary Love," which received the following assessment from *Entertainment Weekly*: "[Hewitt] has a pleasant enough voice, but her earnest passion can't overcome the repetitive lyrics and forgettable melody of this mush. Even die-hard romantics will overdose on the syrupy sweetness." Also included on the album is "It's Good to Know I'm Alive," which she sang on the *House Arrest* soundtrack.

House Arrest starred Kevin Pollack and Jamie Lee Curtis as a couple contemplating divorce, who are locked in the basement by their children. Once word of their deed gets around school, other kids kidnap their parents and bring them to the same basement to work out their problems. Love played Brooke Figler, the most popular girl in school, who locks her mother away because she dresses and acts like a kid.

Love described her audition in an interview with *Entertainment Today*: "Originally they said I looked a little too old. The character is 13 and they were afraid I might be a little too mature-looking to play 13. So I came back with like no makeup on, my hair a little curly because curly tends to look younger, played down my clothes a bit, and I got the movie." For Love, part of the attraction of the role was working with Jennifer Tilly. She said, "I was really looking forward to working with Jennifer Tilly who plays my mom. As Brooke, I'm supposed to be embarrassed by her, but all I kept thinking was, 'My mom was nominated for an Oscar!'"

Also in the summer of 1996, Love filmed a romantic comedy for Warner Bros. opposite *Boy Meets World* star Will Friedle. Originally titled *Trojan War*, then *Rescue Me*, the film will most likely have another title when it is released in theaters in late 1997. Love describes her character, Leah, as "a closet romantic." In the film, Friedle's character pines for another girl but eventually realizes that his pal Leah is the girl for him. A similar story played out in real life, as Love and Friedle started out as friends and ended up dating in real life. Love's previous romance, with *Blossom* star Joey Lawrence, lasted a few months in early 1996.

Shortly after *Party of Five* wrapped its third season, Love flew to North Carolina to shoot *I Know What You Did Last Summer*, with Sarah Michelle Gellar (of *All My Children* and *Buffy the Vampire Slayer*). The suspense thriller was written by Kevin Williamson who also penned Neve Campbell's surprise hit, *Scream*.

Love lives with her mother in a penthouse apartment in Burbank, California. Her brother Todd, a chiropractor in Dallas, doesn't miss an opportunity to congratulate Love on her success. She says, "He calls after every show no matter what and says, 'You did a great job. I love you.'" The active actress works out with a personal trainer three to four times per week and likes to rollerblade and surf in her free time. When asked how she maintains such a high-energy lifestyle, she replied, "I am pretty hyped on life, I guess you could say. I'm very energetic and I owe it all to just pure energy, no caffeine!"

Love, who turned 18 as *Party of Five* was wrapping its third season, has finished with her on-set schooling. She would eventually like to attend college, and has mentioned Pepperdine, Stanford, and Boston University as her top choices. She wants to study journalism and creative writing, with an eye towards writing children's stories and poetry. For now, she is not looking ahead, but is taking time to appreciate the present. She says, "Somebody upstairs is looking out for me big time. There could never be a dream or a wish that would be as good as what it is right now. My life is fantastic."

Selected Credits

Feature Films

Munchie (1992) 'Andrea'
Little Miss Millions (aka *Home for Christmas*) (1993) 'Heather Lofton'
Sister Act II: Back in the Habit (1993) 'Margaret'
House Arrest (1996) 'Brooke Figler'
I Know What You Did Last Summer (1997) 'Julie'
Rescue Me (upcoming) 'Leah'
Telling You (upcoming) 'Kristen'

Television

Kids Incorporated (The Disney Channel, 1989-91) 'Robin'
Shaky Ground (FOX, 12/13/92 - 5/23/93) 'Bernadette Moody'
Byrds of Paradise (ABC, 3/3/94 - 6/23/94) 'Franny Byrd'
McKenna (ABC, 9/22/94 - 7/20/95) 'Cassidy McKenna'
True Tales of Teen Trauma (MTV Special, 1996) 'Host'
Senior Prom (ABC Special, 7/2/97) 'Host'

Recordings

Love Songs (Medlac Records, Japan, 1992)
Let's Go Bang (Atlantic Records, 1995)
Jennifer Love Hewitt (Atlantic Records, 1996)
House Arrest soundtrack (1996) (sings "It's Good to Know I'm Alive")

Video

Dance! Workout With Barbie (1991)

Commercials

Mattel Toys/Barbie, Mrs. Smith's Pies, L.A. Gear, Circuit City, Chex
   Cereal, Ross Department Stores, others

Writings

Love's essay, "Bright Heart," appears in *Chicken Soup for the Teenage
   Soul: 101 Stories of Life, Love and Learning* (Health Communications,
   1997)

Alexondra Lee
(Callie Martel)

Callie is not a bad girl. She's just misunderstood.
                    — Alexondra Lee, November 1996

Alexondra Lee's addition to the cast of *Party of Five* in the third season inspired passionate reactions from fans. As Callie, Bailey's free-spirited roommate, she portrayed the kind of character that fans either love or hate—and mainly the latter. Not only did Callie come between Bailey and Sarah, but she was instrumental in his descent into alcoholism. Alexondra, who is not afraid to take risks in her acting career, likened her character to Elisabeth Shue's role in the feature film *Leaving Las Vegas* (1996). "He's getting bombed and I'm the one pouring the drinks," she said in a February 1997 interview with *Axcess* magazine.

Alexondra (known to her friends as Alex) knew from the start that many fans would dislike her character. She told *Sassy* magazine, "Everyone loves Love [Hewitt] and I come in and break them up!" But she did not mind playing the girl-you-love-to-hate, because it was the first role to give her real exposure.

Twenty-one when she joined the cast of *Party of Five*, Alexondra had been preparing for a life in show business since a very young age. While growing up on the East Coast, Alexondra pursued the dual ambitions of becoming an actress and a dancer. She began studying ballet at the age of four, trained at the School of American Ballet in New York City at age seven, and performed principal roles in productions of *The Nutcracker Suite* and *A Midsummer Night's Dream.*

She also modeled and appeared in commercials. She recalls of her modeling career, "I was so young, I didn't really enjoy it. I liked being made up and having my hair done and all that, but I didn't really find it fulfilling for me at all."

At the age of 12, Alexondra was faced with choosing between her two career goals. If she decided to become a prima ballerina, the hours of intense training involved would require her to give up her acting. Instead, she chose to focus on acting, and she left ballet school behind. She told fans on America Online, "Acting was always my first love and I just really wanted to pursue that full time."

Alexondra Lee, as Callie, has Bailey in her clutches.
EVERETT COLLECTION.

She moved with her family to Los Angeles when she was 13. While attending high school, Alexondra found an agent and began making the rounds of auditions. She landed a guest spot on the ABC series *thirtysomething* due to her resemblance to series regular Melanie Mayron (Melissa). In the 1991 episode, which deals with Melissa's history with men, Alexondra appeared in flashback sequences as Melissa at 16. Later that year, she played a teenage rape victim on an episode of *L.A. Law*. She recalls, "Looking back, I don't really know how I got the part other than being able to cry on cue!"

That skill also served her well in her first film role, the 1993 psychological suspense thriller *The Road Killers*, with Craig Sheffer and Christopher Lambert. The movie follows a family that is terrorized by a gang of psychopaths while on a road trip through the desert. As Ashley, the teenage daughter of Lambert's character, Alexondra was chased, kidnapped, roughed-up, and nearly raped by the gang's ringleader, played by Sheffer. She says, "The film itself was very intense and basically the whole movie was me screaming and crying and looking terrified. Needless to say, that was pretty hard to pull off for my first movie." The attempted rape scene with Sheffer was particularly intense for Alexondra, who recalls, "I was terrified in and out of the scene, because he was playing a psycho and offcamera he would be in character, so to speak. So he was scaring me both in and out of the scene!"

Alexondra created a stir in a 1993 episode of the CBS drama *Picket Fences*, in which her character falls in love with her best friend, Kimberly Brock (series regular Holly Marie Combs). The episode featured a controversial kiss between Lee's character (Lisa Fenn) and Kimberly. As Kimberly questions her sexuality, her family reacts to the shocking discovery of their kiss.

During an America Online chat session, Alexondra described the experience as "very, very awkward." She said, "I didn't know anybody, and I was brought on specifically to, basically, make out with the star teenager on the show who was also very uncomfortable! And then afterwards there was a lot of controversy, and CBS ended up blacking it out in the end, so you didn't really see the kiss at all, which made it, I think, even more suggestive." Alexondra's *Picket Fences* character was brought back for another episode in the fall of 1993 when a drug raid on the high school campus results in her arrest.

When the January 1994 earthquake destroyed her Los Angeles apartment, Alexondra took the catastrophe as a sign that it was time to move back East. She felt that if she was going to become a serious actress, she needed professional training. She moved to New York City and enrolled at New York University. She studied drama and archaeology at NYU, and she also studied with acting coaches outside of the college.

That fall, Alexondra took a break from her studies to take a leading role in the feature film *Learning Curves*. Originally titled *Bad With Numbers*, *Learning Curves* is a coming-of-age story about a high school senior (played by Jason London) involved in a love triangle with his girlfriend

Alexondra Lee at the *Party of Five* sound-track release party in 1996. Photo by Brenda Scott Royce.

(Alexondra) and his voluptuous math tutor (played by Tia Carrere). To complicate matters, his tutor turns out to be his math teacher's wife. Problems at the distribution company, Savoy Pictures, caused *Learning Curves* to be shelved after filming wrapped. The film has yet to be released.

Though still apprehensive about the potential of another California earthquake, Alexondra returned to Los Angeles when she was offered the role of Callie on *Party of Five*. From hundreds of actresses screened for the part, she was one of about a dozen who were brought in to read with Scott Wolf. Scott told *Access Hollywood* that Alexondra immediately stood out from the pack: "They were all really good, but you're either right or you're wrong for it, and when Alex walked in the room, she was just right for this part. I guess she was right physically, but she also had a real calm sort of control over the material and over my character."

With a one-year contract on the show, Alexondra moved back to Los Angeles and transferred from NYU to UCLA. She took night classes while working on the series. From her first appearance, it was apparent that Callie (whom Sarah called "a nubile exhibitionist") was going to spell trouble for Bailey and Sarah. By her fourth episode, Bailey and Callie had slept together. In an interview with *Access Hollywood*, Alexondra discussed her kissing scenes with Scott Wolf: "It's funny because when it happens, you're actually thinking, for one split second, every young woman in America probably wants to be in my place right now, and it's a nice feeling, that's for sure."

She also has high praise for her costar's acting abilities. She told *Axcess* magazine, "I couldn't have asked for a better actor to work opposite. He's very professional, yet always willing to help me out. He's a really great guy, who also just happens to play one on TV. People always want some dirt on Scott, but he couldn't be more perfect."

Alexondra says that during the course of her run on the show, the reaction she received from fans was mainly positive. In a December 1996 interview, she said, "I can't help but think that people just like her a lot, even though she does some pretty interestingly bad things. The writers on the show can't possibly write a one-dimensional character if they tried. So no one is just 'bad' on the show. She's got a pretty interesting personality so you couldn't really just hate her."

Near the end of the third season, Bailey got his act together, quit drinking, and moved back in with his family. With her character written out of the show, Alexondra has gone back to college full-time while pursuing new acting assignments.

Selected Credits

Feature films

The Road Killers (1994) 'Ashley'
Learning Curves (aka *Bad With Numbers*) (1994; unreleased)

Television

thirtysomething ep. "Melissa and Men" (ABC, 1/8/91) 'Melissa Steadman at 16'
L.A. Law ep. "The Gods Must Be Lawyers" (NBC, 2/21/91) 'Laurie'
Picket Fences ep. "Sugar and Spice" (CBS, 4/29/93) 'Lisa Fenn'
Picket Fences ep. "Blue Christmas" (CBS, 12/17/93) 'Lisa Fenn'
Sisters
Saved by the Bell

Jeremy London
(Griffin Holbrook)

*Jeremy is the kind of actor that when he's onscreen, you don't see
anyone else. I wish I had some love scenes with him.*
— Jennifer Love Hewitt, February 1997

If you thought you recognized Jeremy London when he turned up
as *Party of Five*'s rebellious but sensitive Griffin Holbrook in the 1995-96
season, you may be right. In five brief-but-productive years in the business, he had piled up a number of television and film appearances,
including a lead role on the acclaimed series *I'll Fly Away*. But you may
be wrong. Jeremy has an identical twin brother, Jason, who has accumulated an equally impressive list of credits on his résumé. The two
are often mistaken for one another, and many fans have difficulty keeping track of who's who. Liked *Dazed and Confused?* That was Jason.
Mallrats? That was Jeremy. *The Man in the Moon?* That was Jason. Well,
mostly.

Jeremy and Jason were born 27 minutes apart (Jason is older), on
November 7, 1972, in San Diego, California. They spent their youth in
Oklahoma, where their father, Frank London, a construction worker,
still resides. Following their parents' divorce in 1977, the twins and their
younger sister, Dedra, were moved around quite a bit, as their mother,
Debbie, constantly sought to improve the family's living conditions.

By 1986, the family had settled in a trailer park in DeSoto, Texas, a
suburb of Dallas. In their new blue-collar surroundings, the London
boys realized something that hadn't been apparent before: they were
poor. In an *Us* magazine interview, Jeremy recalled, "We didn't know
how poor we were in Oklahoma, because everyone was poor and living
in trailers." Though their social standing initially invited their classmates' derision, the brothers eventually prospered in high school. Both
excelled at sports, performed in school plays, and competed for girls.
Jason told *Us*, "Jeremy always went out with the hottest girls at school."

Jeremy exhibited an interest in performing at an early age. He and
Jason staged plays in their living room and were always competing for
attention. But it wasn't until he played Professor Harold Hill in a high
school production of *The Music Man* that Jeremy began to think seriously about pursuing acting as a career. Serendipity struck when his

Jason and Jeremy London's senior yearbook photos from DeSoto High School in DeSoto, Texas, 1991. Seth Poppel Yearbook Archives.

mother, Debbie, a waitress, met a customer who suggested Jeremy try modeling. The customer, a model herself, recommended an agency in Dallas. Debbie brought Jeremy, Jason, and Dedra to the agency and all three were signed and enrolled in acting classes. Jeremy views this occurrence as a turning point in his family's fortune. "Before that, we were doomed to redneckhood," he told *People.*

Though all three London siblings signed with the agency, it was Jeremy who possessed a driving ambition to be an actor. In the spring of 1990, he heard that the producers of a feature film, *The Man in the Moon,* were conducting a ten-state talent search to cast three key teenage roles. Jeremy desperately wanted to try out, but he needed a ride to the audition. Jason had a car, but he also had a date that he didn't want to break. Eventually, Jeremy won out, and both brothers attended the casting call. The film, *The Man in the Moon,* is about a young farm boy who inspires a romantic rivalry in two sisters, 14-year-old Dani and 17-year-old Maureen. Over five thousand young performers read for the roles.

Ironically, the role which Jeremy coveted went to his reluctant chauffeur, Jason. Jason's indifference may have been what won him the part, as Jeremy recalled in a 1992 interview, "Jason didn't care at all about the part, so he just read. But it came out perfect! It was the weird-

Griffin and Julia in "Summer Fun, Summer Not." ARCHIVE PHOTOS.

est thing." Jeremy harbored no hard feelings toward his brother. He told the *Los Angeles Times*, "If I'm going to lose a role, there's only one person I would want to get it and that's my brother." Jeremy also recognized the value of someone in the family getting a foot in the door of show business.

The film, which also starred Sam Waterston, Tess Harper, and Reese Witherspoon, was filmed in Natchitoches, Louisiana, in the summer of 1990. Jeremy worked on the film after all—he was hired as Jason's stand-in and stunt double. You can see him in the scene where Court drives the truck wildly, trying to scare Dani. On the set, the twins enjoyed playing pranks on people who couldn't tell them apart. When the film was released in 1991, Jason's performance drew wide acclaim and led to more movie offers.

Jeremy's next acting opportunity came when the NBC television movie *In Broad Daylight* was being filmed in Austin, Texas. He and his sister, Dedra, both landed small roles in the 1991 telefilm, which starred Brian Dennehy as a sociopath who intimidates the residents of a small town. Another bit part followed in the CBS TV movie *A Seduction in Travis County*, with Lesley Ann Warren and Peter Coyote. In the story, which is reminiscent of the film *Fatal Attraction*, Warren played a deranged woman who is accused of murdering her husband and who then becomes obsessed with her married attorney.

Meanwhile, as Jeremy was aching to get a big break and leave bit parts behind him, Jason's career was thriving. As Jeremy had predicted, having a sibling in the business, especially one who looked just like him, would turn out to be a great advantage. When Jason had to turn down a role in the NBC series *I'll Fly Away* because he was already under contract for a FOX series, he suggested Jeremy as his replacement. Jeremy already had the look the producers wanted, so they gave him a screen test and he won the role of Nathaniel Bedford.

I'll Fly Away starred Sam Waterston (Jason's costar from *The Man in the Moon*) as a liberal attorney in the South during the late 1950s. Jeremy played Waterston's eldest son. The critically acclaimed series followed the lives of the Bedford family and their outspoken black housekeeper (played by Regina Taylor) as they faced the changes wrought by the changing racial climate in the South and the fledgling civil rights movement. *I'll Fly Away* was filmed in Atlanta, and his tenure on the series marked the first time Jeremy was away from his twin brother for any substantial period of time.

From its debut in October 1991, *I'll Fly Away* struggled in the ratings. Though the series ranked in the top 25 percent of all shows among adults over 40, its overall ranking was low. In an attempt to draw younger viewers to the show, the producers gave Jeremy's character a make-over in the second season. The formerly clean-cut varsity jock began sporting jeans, a leather jacket, and a bad attitude. Despite Nathaniel's hot new image, the show failed to attract a younger demographic and was canceled in its second season.

After *I'll Fly Away* was canceled, Jeremy quickly found another series, *Angel Falls*. The CBS serial drama, set in rural Angel Falls, Montana, focused on the intertwined relationships of three families, the Snows, the Harrisons, and the Larsons. Chelsea Field played Rae Dawn

Snow, once the town tramp, who moves back to Angel Falls to take over the family pool hall after the death of her father. Jeremy played Rae Dawn's teenage son, Sonny, who has difficulty adjusting to his new home and rumors of his mother's checkered past. Before long, Rae Dawn is sleeping with her now-married high school sweetheart (played by Brian Kerwin), and Sonny is squiring Kerwin's daughter (played by Cassidy Rae of *Models Inc.*). *Angel Falls* debuted in August 1993. In a review of the series, *Entertainment Weekly* wrote that Jeremy, "as he did on *I'll Fly Away*, exists primarily to have his innocence betrayed while looking handsome." Despite its titillating plots, *Angel Falls* failed to attract a following, and it was canceled after only six episodes.

While his innocence was being betrayed in *Angel Falls*, Jeremy lost the opportunity to reprise his role in a reunion TV movie of *I'll Fly Away*. The PBS network, which picked up the rights to rebroadcast the series, filmed an original two-hour movie that would wrap up the series. Since Jeremy was unavailable, Jason took over the role of Nathaniel— a role for which he had initially been cast two years earlier. Jason told *People* magazine that he would put his own spin on the character his brother had created. Jeremy was characteristically upbeat about his brother's good fortune: "I can't wait to see Jason working with all the people I've worked with these last two years."

By 1995, Jeremy had carved out more of a name for himself as an actor, rather than as one of the nearly interchangeable London twins. Instead of scraping for parts, he found himself in hot demand that year, appearing in two television movies, three feature films, and joining the cast of *Party of Five*. First up was a Hallmark Hall of Fame movie, *A Season of Hope*, which aired on CBS. He played a farmer's son who decides he wants more out of life than farming. *People* magazine opined, "Like most of its Hallmark cousins, the film is distinguished by an indelible sense of place, fine acting, and a strong emotional undertow." His next TV movie outing was not so well-received. *TV Guide* called *A Mother's Gift*, starring Nancy McKeon as a pioneer woman in post-Civil War Nevada, "a snoozer." Jeremy played McKeon's adult son, John Deal.

Jeremy starred opposite Alicia Silverstone in the R-rated 1995 psychological thriller, *The Babysitter.* Silverstone played a beautiful, all-American teen who becomes the unwitting object of the fantasies of three men. Jeremy played her boyfriend, Jack, whose jealousy and desire leads to tragic circumstances.

Jeremy London on the Salingers Restaurant set.
PHOTO BY BRENDA SCOTT ROYCE.

In the Gramercy Pictures release *Mallrats*, Jeremy and Jason Lee played best friends, dumped by their girlfriends on the same day, who seek solace, revenge, and redemption at a shopping mall. Jeremy was T. S. Quint, the least shiftless of the mall-dwellers who inhabit the movie. Working with a bigger budget than he had for his self-financed first film, the cult hit *Clerks*, writer/director Kevin Smith could afford bigger stars (including former *Beverly Hills 90210* denizen Shannen Doherty), and better settings, but *Mallrats* was criticized for lacking the originality of *Clerks*. The mixed reviews tended to praise the cast but pan the film, as in the case of *Magill's Survey of Cinema:* "London and Lee are appealingly idiotic, but saddled with too many gross-out jokes and tiresome come-back lines to really make an impression." *Boxoffice* magazine gave the film one of its most glowing reviews, calling it, "a surprisingly clever and hilariously bizarre take on the Gen-X teen experience [which] mostly transcends those trappings of teen flicks and works on a far more witty level of humor, generating many laugh-out-loud moments."

Jeremy's twin status caused some confusion on the set for actress Joey Lauren Adams, who had previously worked with Jason. She recalled, "After playing Jason's girlfriend in *Dazed and Confused*, it wasn't hard to play Jeremy's ex-girlfriend in *Rats*. The only thing hard was calling him Jeremy when he looks so much like Jason. Plus there were two other Jasons on set (Jason Lee and Jason Mewes), and I knew Jason first and so I guess Jeremy looks like Jason to me because I didn't meet Jeremy first because if I had, then Jason would probably look like Jeremy."

The same year, Jeremy starred in *Breaking Free*, a family film about a delinquent teen who gets a second chance working at a rehabilitation camp for the blind. He initially views his job as an easy way out of jail, but everything changes when he falls in love with a blind girl at the camp. Shown in limited release in theaters in 1995, *Breaking Free* was released on home video in 1996 and airs frequently on the Disney channel.

Unlike his brother, who has shied away from television work in favor of feature films, Jeremy says he will work in either medium when a good opportunity presents itself. In the summer of 1995, he was offered the role of Griffin Holbrook on *Party of Five*. The role had been introduced in the first season finale, with another actor in the part. James Marsden had since signed to do another series, *Second Noah*, forcing the producers to recast the role of Griffin. Jeremy, who has been described by *Party*'s casting director, Patrick Rush, as "the handsome bad-boy crossed with the boy next door" took over and made the part his own, soon achieving teen heartthrob status.

Jeremy could relate to his character because he, like Griffin, had a difficult upbringing, and had dealt with the tragedy of losing a sister. Dedra London was killed in a car accident in 1992, at the age of 16, only months after giving birth to a daughter. Enacting scenes in which Griffin spoke of his sister Jill's death dredged up painful memories for Jeremy. At a Museum of Television & Radio event, Jeremy spoke of his difficulty in reliving his sister's death, "I didn't think it was going to be so hard, but sometimes it was really tough. And sometimes I don't think

I was a very likable person because of it, because I would feel it, like a constant reminder."

After seven episodes, Jeremy was temporarily written out of the series, as Griffin was shipped off to military school and Julia reunited with her former boyfriend, Justin. Fans bombarded the shows' producers with letters and petitions begging for Jeremy's return. (One petition had 600 names, all in the same handwriting.) The show's writers had no intention of dumping Jeremy, but were planning stories that would bring Griffin into and out of Julia's life periodically, stirring things up and creating drama. Griffin's return at the end of the third season may have finally marked the end of his wanderlust, as he and Julia got married in the season finale.

In between his *Party of Five* appearances, Jeremy kept busy with film and television roles. He played an angel in the independent film *Levitation* and wrote a 30-minute film about the ill-effects of drugs. He was cast as a mental patient in the 1997 NBC television movie *On the Edge of Innocence*, opposite Kellie Martin, but had to drop out when he broke his arm. Ironically, his replacement was James Marsden, whom he had replaced on *Party of Five*!

One of the questions he is most frequently asked by fans is, "What is it like being a twin?" to which he responds, "I don't know what it's like not to be a twin." Despite their close bond, he doesn't live with his brother. He told *Seventeen* magazine, "We've tried being roommates twice, but if we want to remain friends, we shouldn't be living together. I mean, when you're in a room with yourself, you'll go crazy, right?" The brothers have more in common than their looks and their acting talent: each has a tattoo on his upper left arm (Jeremy's tattoo is a Cherokee tribal elder, while Jason's is a scorpion), and both are aspiring musicians. They were jointly named by *People* magazine as among the World's 50 Most Beautiful People in 1996. Sam Waterston, who worked with both brothers, says, "I think, of the two, Jeremy is the gentler soul. They both impress me because their background was pretty rough and they've had to mature faster than most. They both have tremendous steel."

When life gets him down, Jeremy reflects on his good fortune. "I remind myself that I'm not out there digging with my nails like my parents did," he said in a 1997 *Us* interview. "I say, 'You get to act for a living. You're fortunate. So act like it.'"

Selected Credits

Feature films

The Man in the Moon (1991) 'stunt double'
Mallrats (1995) 'T. S. Quint'
The Babysitter (1995) 'Jack'
Breaking Free (1995) 'Rick'
Levitation (1997) 'Bob'
The Red Lion (upcoming)
Prairie Fire (upcoming)

Television

In Broad Daylight (NBC, 2/3/91) 'Teenager'
A Seduction in Travis County (CBS, 5/19/91) 'Delivery Boy'
I'll Fly Away (NBC, 10/7/91 - 2/5/93) 'Nathaniel Bedford'
Angel Falls (CBS, 8/26/93 - 9/30/93) 'Sonny Snow'
A Season of Hope (CBS, 1/8/95) 'Mickey Hackett'
A Mother's Gift (CBS, 4/16/95) 'John Deal (adult)'
Perversions of Science (HBO, 6/7/97)

Recordings

Mallrats soundtrack (1996) (features dialogue from the movie)

chapter eight

Recurring and Supporting Characters

Mitchell Anderson
(Ross Werkman)

Prior to landing the recurring role of Ross, Claudia's gay violin teacher on *Party of Five*, Mitchell Anderson was best known for his two-year stint on *Doogie Howser, M.D.* (1989-91), where he played the womanizing Dr. Jack McGuire. The role of Ross is much closer to Mitchell's heart than Jack was—he left *Doogie* in the middle of the show's successful run to pursue more satisfying roles.

Born in Jamestown, New York, the fourth in a family of six children, Mitchell studied drama at Williams College and Julliard. He made his acting debut in *On Shilo Hill* at the Ford Theatre in 1984. Shortly afterward, he moved to Los Angeles to find work in film and television. He appeared in episodes of *Hill Street Blues*, *Cagney and Lacey*, and *Highway to Heaven*, and made his film debut in the comedy *SpaceCamp* (1986). Next up was a role in *Jaws: The Revenge* (1987), in which he was the killer shark's first victim.

Veteran director Roger Corman gave him his first leading role, in the low-budget horror film *Deadly Dreams* (1988). Mitchell played Alex, a young man whose parents were murdered ten years earlier. Plagued by nightmares about the killer, he tries to unravel the mystery, which is tied to a conspiracy to steal his inheritance.

Mitchell portrayed singer Richard Carpenter in the television movie *The Karen Carpenter Story* (1989), which recounted the story of Karen

129

Mitchell Anderson between takes on the set of *Party of Five.*
PHOTO BY BRENDA SCOTT ROYCE.

Carpenter's career and her losing battle with anorexia and bulimia. The real Richard Carpenter was on the set during filming and coached Mitchell with his performance. Mitchell says, "It was a very interesting experience to be creating a role with the person right there." He feels that the production rose above the quality generally associated with the genre. "TV biographies generally aren't very good, but this one was excellent."

The following year he played an adult Huck Finn in the Disney Channel television movie *Back to Hannibal: The Return of Tom Sawyer and Huckleberry Finn.* He had a supporting role in the humorous mystery thriller *All-American Murder* (1992), in which he was one of many suspects in the murder of a campus queen played by Josie Bissett. In a memorable 1993 episode of *Melrose Place*, he played a male model who poses in the buff for Jo (Daphne Zuniga).

Mitchell enjoys working on *Party of Five*. He and Matthew Fox had crossed paths before *Party of Five*—they both auditioned for the same role on a soap opera, and neither got the role. Of costar Scott Wolf, Mitchell has said, "He's absolutely the nicest. He's a great guy. He's so cute, and so talented, and so nice that you just want to punch him in the face."

Mitchell's only frustration with his role on *Party of Five* is the limited amount of screen time given to his charac-

Mitchell Anderson on the night he publicly announced that he is gay. PHOTO COURTESY OF GLAAD.

ter. In an effort to expand the size of his role, Mitchell has suggested potential story lines for his character, including Ross' adoption of a baby in the first season finale. He was disappointed when the adoption story line wasn't explored further in the following season. In a December 1996 online interview, he said, "That's a sore spot for me. I feel like they dropped the ball on that story line."

In fact, in the show's second season, the producers decided to have Claudia give up the violin, virtually eliminating Mitchell's role on the series that year. Amy Lippman says she hadn't thought about how Claudia's decision to quit would impact Mitchell until the table reading for the script ("Hold On Tight," 1/10/96). She says Mitchell approached her afterwards and asked nervously, "What do you mean she gives up the violin?!" Mitchell says jokingly, "I was hoping my mortgage company wasn't reading the script."

Though he is always hoping to expand his role, Mitchell understands the writers' dilemma. "They say they have lots of other stories to tell. There are four main characters, and the real challenge of the show is how to bring other stories in and still have them revolve around the four main characters." In an interview in *The Advocate*, he said, "I have a great job on *Party of Five* but it's not feeding me completely. It's not making me full. So you look elsewhere."

To that end, Mitchell is very active in the theater. He has appeared in Los Angeles stage productions of *South Pacific, Streamers, The Dybbuk,* and *Therese Raquin,* and directed Christopher Durang's *Laughing Wild.* In 1996, he appeared in a Los Angeles production of Terrence McNally's *Love! Valour! Compassion!* The play is set at a summer home in the country, where eight gay men convene over several weekends. Mitchell portrayed Bobby Brahms, a blind man. (A feature film version of *Love! Valour! Compassion!* was released in 1997, with Justin Kirk in the role of Bobby.) In the play, Mitchell appeared on stage completely naked. The uninhibited actor wasn't nervous about baring all in front of a live audience every night. He says, "People ask me how I could do it, but I didn't really think about it until the first night. The only time I had trouble with it was when my agent, who is a little younger than my parents, came to see it. That made me a little uncomfortable."

Though he plays an openly gay character on *Party of Five*, Mitchell was not yet publicly open about his own sexuality when he began working on the series. But in March 1996, he stunned the audience at the Gay and Lesbian Alliance Against Defamation's Annual Media Awards in Los Angeles by announcing that he is gay. After taking the stage to present an award, Mitchell told the crowd of approximately 1,200 members of the entertainment industry, that he had just been asked by a reporter how it felt to be a straight man playing a gay role on television. He said he felt that it was a good time to correct the reporter's assumption: he is a gay man playing a gay role. GLAAD managing director William Waybourn recalls, "The crowd went wild and gave him a standing ovation. He was the highlight of the evening and was swarmed afterward. It was a scene of high drama." Mark B. Perry, a co-executive producer on *Party of Five,* said, "I've always loved Mitchell, and I was particularly proud to be associated with him that night."

Prior to that evening, Mitchell's family and friends knew that he was gay, but professionally, he had remained in the closet. He says, "Conventional wisdom, and fear, told me be gay in private, but don't bring it to work." However, when he began to get involved in politics and fought for various gay rights issues, he realized that to have a real voice, he would have to come out.

Mitchell didn't consult anyone about his decision to declare his sexual orientation publicly. He told *The Advocate,* "If I would have talked to my manager, he might have said, 'You know what? I don't know if it's a good idea.'" As a result of his surprising announcement, Mitchell received a flurry of media attention and several requests for public appearances and speaking engagements. He has also received more film offers, although primarily for gay roles. While he is happy with the offers, he told *The Advocate* that he hopes to also be considered for straight roles, and to be given the opportunity to disprove the Hollywood myth that the public won't accept a homosexual in a straight role. "In some ways it would be great to get a rampantly heterosexual role now that I'm out, and prove them all wrong," he said. "If the world can accept and fall in love with Robin Williams in a gay role [*Birdcage*], I don't think it's too unreasonable to assume that they can accept a gay man in a straight role."

In January 1997, the *National Enquirer* reported that 35-year-old Mitchell, who had ended an 11-year relationship in December 1996, was dating Jason Gould, the 30-year-old son of Barbra Streisand and Elliott Gould. In a June 1997 cover story in *Genre* magazine, Mitchell stated that the story was untrue and expressed his surprise at the tabloid's treatment of the rumor. He said, "It was completely false, but the interesting thing about it was that there was no scandal implied. It was like, 'Isn't it nice that these two people are together?'"

If tabloid attention and dubious casting directors are a downside of his revelation, Mitchell is proud to say that he has opened the door for others. "The letters I have received from people in different parts of the country tell me I did the right thing. There's not a moment or a second that I regret it."

Tom Mason
(Joe Mangus)

Tom Mason just might hold a show business record. He has had regular roles on six television series, all of which were one-season wonders (canceled after one season or less). He jokes, "I'm the one the networks seem to call when they have a good show that they want to put in a bad time slot." His first series, *Grandpa Goes to Washington* (1978-79), had the misfortune of being scheduled opposite *Happy Days* and *Laverne and Shirley* when they were the two top-rated shows on television. Next, he was Tim "Freebie" Walker in *Freebie and the Bean* (1980-81), which CBS scheduled opposite the high-rated *Love Boat*. His 1983 series *Two Marriages* lasted less than a month in head-to-head competition with *Magnum, P.I.* His 1985-86 drama, *Our Family Honor*, was defeated by *Remington Steele* and *Miami Vice*, and *D.E.A.* (1990–91) lost viewers to the Friday night youth-oriented comedy line-up on ABC.

The most memorable of his defunct series was ABC's *Jack and Mike* (1986-87), in which he was paired with ex-*Charlie's Angels* star Shelley Hack. He played a restaurateur married to Hack, a newspaper columnist. In the series, which was patterned after *Moonlighting*, the couple has difficulty balancing marriage with the demands of busy careers.

Tom was born in Brooklyn, New York, and raised on Long Island. He attended college in Maine, then furthered his acting studies at the Herbert Berghof Studio (which Scott Wolf later attended) in New York City. He began his acting career with Trinity Square Repertory Company in Providence, Rhode Island, where he appeared in productions of *Troilus and Cressida*, *The Crucible*, *That Championship Season*, and *Long Day's Journey Into Night*. He then appeared in the New York Shakespeare Festival's *Kid Champion*, which led to film and television roles.

In addition to his numerous series, Tom also appeared in several failed television pilots. One of the more far-fetched was *The Aliens Are Coming*, in which he played an astrophysicist battling aliens (one of the creatures was played by Max Gail of *Barney Miller* fame).

Tom has appeared in numerous feature films and made-for-TV movies during his career, often playing politicians or police officers. One of his earliest roles was a supply sergeant in Francis Ford Coppola's epic *Apocalypse Now* (1979). His other film credits include *Crimes of the Heart* (1986), *Mississippi Burning* (1988), *FX:2* (1991), and *Greedy* (1994).

Carroll O'Connor
(Jacob Gordon)

Television icon Carroll O'Connor is so identifiable from his role as Archie Bunker in the long-running, pioneering sitcom, *All in the Family* (1971-79), and its spin-off, *Archie Bunker's Place* (1979-83), that many

TV veteran Carroll
O'Connor joined the
cast of *Party of Five*
in 1996 as Jake Gor-
don, the kids' long-
lost grandfather.
PHOTOFEST.

viewers have difficulty accepting him in another role. Even Neve Campbell says that when she was first introduced to the actor who would play her long-lost grandfather, she squealed, "Oh, my God, it's Archie Bunker!"

Of Irish Roman Catholic background on both sides of his family, Carroll was born on August 2, 1924, in New York City. He attended University College of Dublin in Ireland, making his acting debut at Dublin's Gate Theatre. When he returned to New York, he supported himself by working as a substitute teacher while trying to find acting work. He made his Broadway debut in *Ulysses in Nighttown* in 1958, and his first film, *A Fever in the Blood*, was released in 1961. Character parts in dozens of films followed: *Cleopatra* (1963), *In Harm's Way* (1965), *Hawaii* (1966), and *Kelly's Heroes* (1970). On television, he appeared in episodes of such series as *The Rifleman*, *Bonanza*, *Voyage to the Bottom of the Sea*, *I Spy*, *That Girl*, and *Gunsmoke*.

Carroll's big break came when Mickey Rooney turned down the role of "lovable bigot" Archie Bunker in a sitcom Norman Lear was developing, *Those Were the Days*. After two failed pilots, the series finally made it to CBS's prime-time line-up in 1971 as *All in the Family*. Ground-breaking and controversial, *All in the Family* marked a radical departure from the situation comedies the American public had been exposed to. It trod on topics formerly considered taboo on television, and had as its centerpiece a loud-mouthed, uneducated, working-class hero with a wide repertoire of racial epithets, which he used unsparingly.

The role of Archie Bunker earned Carroll O'Connor four Emmy Awards over the show's long run. He added a fifth Emmy to his mantle for his next television series, *In the Heat of the Night* (1988-94), in which he played Bill Gillespie, a Southern police chief partnered with Virgil Tibbs (played by Howard Rollins, Jr.), the first black on Sparta's police force. (O'Connor and Rollins recreated the roles originated by Rod Steiger and Sidney Poitier in the 1967 feature film of the same name.) In a development that would have shocked Archie Bunker, Chief Gillespie romanced and married a black councilwoman during the series' run.

Costarring in the series as a deputy was Carroll's adopted son, Hugh, who committed suicide in March 1995, after a 16-year-long battle with drug addiction. Enraged at his son's death, Carroll took an active role in crusading for the arrest and ultimate conviction of his son's drug dealer.

In a December 1995 interview with the *New York Post*, the actor said, "You never get over losing your kid. You go on." For Carroll, moving on meant returning to work. He accepted the recurring role of the Salinger kids' wayward grandfather after screening an advance copy of *Party's* pivotal episode, "The Wedding." He told the *Post*, "It's a very well-written show and the young people are great actors."

The show's stars, especially Lacey Chabert, were delighted at his addition to the cast. Lacey had never seen *All in the Family*, so she was not as awestricken as her castmates were upon meeting the TV legend. But she quickly formed a bond with him, saying, "He is so incredible! He's like a grandfather, he is such a happy spirit, telling stories and doing funny voices. He's always making us laugh. I love him!"

The *Party of Five* producers were thrilled when Carroll's first episode ("Benefactors," 1/31/96) resulted in a boost in the show's sagging ratings. Amy Lippman says that his ratings-draw definitely influenced the decision to cast O'Connor over an unknown character actor. The day after the ratings were posted for Grandpa Jake's first appearance, Lippman says she approached Carroll on the set and said excitedly, "Did you see the ratings? Isn't it great!?!" To which he replied with a smile, "Sweetheart, that's what you're paying me for."

In 1996, Carroll took on another recurring TV role, as Helen Hunt's father on the NBC sitcom *Mad About You*. He has an autobiography in the works and hopes to bring Archie Bunker back to television.

Tamara Taylor (Grace Wilcox)

Prior to joining the cast of *Party of Five*, Toronto-born Tamara Taylor was best-known as the AT&T spokesperson in a series of commercials urging consumers to dial "1-800-CALL-ATT." Though many viewers already knew her face from the popular ads, Tamara was a relative new-comer to show business. *Party of Five* was her first real acting job, unless you count her one-line bit part in the 1993 Marlee Matlin thriller, *Hear No Evil*. She doesn't.

Tamara's first foray in front of the cameras came after she dropped out of high school and tried to launch a modeling career. She soon found that she wasn't cut out for modeling. "I was horrible. I wasn't tall enough, exceptional-looking enough. I wasn't enough of anything," she told *People* magazine.

A few trips to Los Angeles to visit her best friend, actress Cree Summer of *A Different World* (NBC, 1988-93), convinced Tamara to make the move herself. She says, "I would visit Cree's set. It seemed like a lot of fun. Being that acting was sort of my biggest fear, I figured let's jump in with both feet and see how we fare."

Tamara moved to Los Angeles in 1993. She took acting classes, and within six months of her arrival, she appeared in her first commercial, a spot for the California Lottery. Other commercials quickly followed, including the AT&T contract. (She appeared in 17 AT&T commercials between 1993 and 1996.) Commercial work paid the bills and allowed her to enjoy her leisure time, but she was aching to get a chance to do some real acting.

After auditioning unsuccessfully for dozens of film and television roles, Tamara was beginning to get discouraged. When she first read for *Party of Five*'s producers, she was just going through the motions. She recalls, "The day I auditioned was the day I didn't care." Despite her

Charlie's relationship with Grace Wilcox (Tamara Taylor) ended when he learned she didn't want children. Everett Collection.

waning enthusiasm, Tamara read well enough to get called back for a second, third, and fourth audition. As the producers pared down the list of contenders for the role of Grace Wilcox, Tamara kept making the cut. In her final call back, she read opposite Matthew Fox, who would be her onscreen love interest. The decision to cast Tamara came down to chemistry, according to Chris Keyser. He told *People* magazine, "The real issue when casting a love interest is if there's a spark between the characters. From the time Tamara read with Matthew, she had it."

Tamara wasn't an avid watcher of *Party of Five* prior to joining the cast, but she had seen enough episodes to know that it was a quality show. In a *People* magazine interview, she described her reaction upon learning she got the role: "I laughed. I cried. I literally had hot flashes." She admits that she was apprehensive about joining the established cast, but says that her costars quickly put her at ease. "Everyone was so warm and welcoming that I was fine after the first few minutes," she said in an America Online chat session.

The exotically beautiful 26-year-old actress, who calls herself an "Africanadian", was pleased with *Party of Five*'s depiction of an interracial relationship. Herself a product of an interracial marriage (her mother, a property manager, is white; her father is a black musician), Tamara was glad that the show did not make their racial differences the

Tamara Taylor on the set of *Party of Five,* PHOTO BY BRENDA SCOTT ROYCE.

focus of Grace and Charlie's relationship. She told fans on America Online, "As a black woman, it's very important to me that this issue is dealt with intelligently and with honesty...I am happy to say the writers handled it well." As for her own feelings about interracial romance, she said, "I'm black, you're white; now let's celebrate the differences and move on to the love part."

Tamara calls herself "slightly warmer" than her character, the politically-minded Grace Wilcox. Though she wished her alter ego would lighten up, she found plenty to admire in her character. "I like that Grace is very straightforward. She's fairly opinionated and is truly concerned about the well-being of others. I like that. I dislike that sometimes, she can appear a little cold. That's probably the only thing that I don't like about Grace. She's a little controlled."

Originally signed for nine episodes, Tamara's stay on the show was extended to fifteen episodes during the 1996-97 season. Tamara had hoped that Charlie and Grace would get married, but the writers placed insurmountable roadblocks in their path. Rather than race, what came between the couple was kids. He was already guardian to his younger siblings and wanted children of his own; she didn't want any at all.

Though Grace and Charlie separated in the third season finale, Tamara still has ties to the Salinger gang. A few months after she got the *Party of Five* gig, she learned that she and Neve Campbell are distantly related through marriage. She says, "Lord knows how the family tree works, but it's there!"

After leaving *Party of Five*, Tamara was cast as the female lead in the Miramax comedy *Senseless*, opposite David Spade and Marlon Wayans.

Megan Ward
(Jill Holbrook)

The youngest of four children, Megan Ward was born on September 24, 1969, in Los Angeles. Her family moved to Honolulu, Hawaii, when she was four. Megan got her first glimpses of show business at a young age by observing her parents, who were both actors, as they worked in Hawaii-based television productions such as *Hawaii Five-O* and *Magnum, P.I.* Her parents also owned an acting school in Honolulu and, as a child, Megan performed in plays that they produced.

Her decision to become an actress came at a young age, when she realized that the career came with limitless possibilities. She says, "Everyone wanted to be something very specific growing up. I didn't know if I wanted to be a doctor, a housewife, a nurse, a lawyer, whatever. Then I realized that as an actress, I could be all of those things."

Megan began modeling at age nine. She started with local department store commercials and was soon appearing in national and international magazines. At the age of 15, she made the first of several trips to Japan for a modeling assignment. She had learned to speak Japanese in school, and the skill served her well, as she became somewhat of a celebrity in Japan. She got the lead in a Japanese film, *Bosho's Journey*, and hosted a Japanese TV talk show. She told the *Los Angeles Times*, "I was the Japanese Vanna White."

Though she made good money, she didn't enjoy modeling and quit once she graduated from high school. Back in the States, she landed her first professional acting role, battling androids in the 1990 sci-fi film *Crash and Burn*. From that point on, she worked steadily in feature films, often in the sci-fi/horror genre. Her films include *Trancers II* and *III* (1990, 1992), *Amityville 1992: It's About Time* (1992), *Encino Man* (1992), and *Freaked* (1993).

She turned to television in 1993, with a lead role in the 1993 FOX series *Class of '96*. The series followed the lives of six college freshmen at Havenhurst College, a fictional Ivy League school in the Northeast. Megan played Patty Horvath, an aspiring actress. The low-rated series was canceled after five months on the air.

Megan Ward as Jill distracts Bailey from his studies. PHOTOFEST.

Her next project, the prime-time soap opera *Winnetka Road,* had an even shorter run. The NBC drama, set in Oak Bluff, Illinois, was canceled after one month. In the series, Megan was pitted against Paige Turco for the attentions of Josh Brolin.

Megan relished her role on *Party of Five* as Jill Holbrook, Bailey's drug-addicted girlfriend in the series' first season. She described her character as "the exact opposite of me" in a *TV Guide* interview. She said, "It's fun to be the bad girl, especially when you get to seduce the top teenage heartbreaker on TV. My friends say, 'How could you act like such a slut?'—and then they want to know if Scott Wolf is a good kisser." Her answer to that oft-asked question is "yes!" although the sparks between Bailey and Jill did not carry over offscreen. Megan married Mattel executive Michael Shore in 1996.

She followed *Party of Five* with the science-fiction period drama, *Dark Skies* (1996–97), which tracked the spread of aliens as they altered historical events. Megan played Kimberly Sayers, a woman trying to stop the alien invasion of Earth with her fiancé John Loengard (Eric Close, who played Jennifer Love Hewitt's brother in *McKenna*). When asked why she chose the role, Megan responded, "It offered me the opportunity to play a strong woman who gets to shoot a gun, be in love with a man, and change the future."

Perhaps unsurprisingly, the actress—who was implanted with alien tendrils on *Dark Skies* and covered with cockroaches in *Joe's Apartment* (1996)—names *Party of Five* as her favorite acting experience. Not long ago, Megan said, "I've loved something about every job I've had, but Jill in *Party of Five* was the most satisfying. I never knew what she was going to do next."

chapter nine

First Season (1994-95)

First Season Regular Cast

Scott **Wolf** as Bailey Salinger

Matthew Fox as Charlie Salinger

Neve Campbell as Julia Salinger

Lacey Chabert as Claudia Salinger

Paula Devicq as Kirsten Bennett

Scott Grimes as Will McCorkle

Brandon and Taylor Porter as Owen Salinger

First Season Technical Credits

Executive Producers: Amy Lippman and Christopher Keyser

Co-Executive Producer: Ann Lewis Hamilton

Supervising Producers: Ken Topolsky, Mark B. Perry

Consulting Producer: Peter O'Fallon

Co-Producer: Susannah Grant

Associate Producers: Bruce J. Nachbar and Valerie Joseph

Executive Story Editor: W. K. Scott Meyer

Story Editor: Susannah Grant

Executive Consultant: Richard Pearce

Unit Production Managers: Edward E. Vaughan, Stephen Lillis

Directors: See Episode Credits for Director of Each Individual Episode

1st Assistant Directors*: Eric Jewett, Vicki Jackson Lemay, Scott Printz

2nd Assistant Director: Carla Brand Breitner

Director of Photography: Roy H. Wagner

Production Designer: Steve Wolff

Original Production Design: Brandy Alexander

Editors*: Stephen Potter, Richard Freeman, Millie Moore, Elsa Sanchez-Short, David Dworetzky

Costume Designer: Scilla Andreen-Hernandez

Music Composer: Stephen Graziano

End Credit Music: Steven Cahill

Music Supervision: John McCullough

Casting: Patrick Rush, Liberman/Hirschfield Casting

Camera Operator: Gary Huddleston

Gaffer: Brian Crane

Key Grip: Dale Alexander

Sound Mixer: Steve Cantamessa

Script Supervisors*: Theresa Eubanks, Paul Tinsley

Set Decorator: Marty Price

Property Master: Gregory R. Wolf

Makeup*: Anna Dolan, Susan "Sam" Mayer

Hair Stylist: Doreen Schultz

Bullseye the Dog's Trainer: David McMillan

Original Casting: Mary V. Buck and Susan Edelman

Production Coordinator: Carol Kravetz

San Francisco Liaison: Jennifer Thomas

Location Manager: Rosa-Lee Pierce

Production Auditor: Hilton Smith

Transportation Captain: Steve Salzman

Assistants to Producers: Rick Draughon, Molly Whelan, Guinevere Shaw

Music Editor: Don Sanders

Sound Supervisor: Bob Redpath

Assistant Editors*: Merry Tigar, David Dworetzky, Jane Kass

Re-recording Mixers: R. Russell Smith, Greg Orloff, Tony D'Amico

* = different episodes

Publicity still from the first season of *Party of Five*. PHOTOFEST.

First Season Overview

Party of Five's first season was characterized by enormous struggle, both onscreen and off. As *Party of Five* teetered on the brink of cancellation, ranking at the bottom of the Nielsen charts week after week, the Salinger family was battling bill collectors, social workers, and each other, in an effort to get through their first year on their own.

During its premiere year, *Party of Five*'s plot lines centered mainly around the Salinger family's struggle to come to terms with the loss of their parents. Nick and Diana Salinger were killed in an automobile accident by a drunk driver, Walter Alcott, in March 1994, approximately six months prior to the pilot episode. Each character deals with their parents' deaths in a different way. Charlie, age 24, feels burdened by the responsibility of caring for his siblings, who don't view him as much of an authority figure to begin with, due to his history as a perennial screw-up. He matures as the season progresses, eventually making perhaps the biggest sacrifice of his career by giving up a lucrative job in Seattle because his siblings don't want to move.

Bailey, age 16, a junior at Grant High School, assumes responsibility for the younger children, balancing the checkbook, caring for the baby, and making sure the family gets together for family dinners. The ever-dependable Bailey gets a taste of the wild life when he meets a carefree waitress who turns out to be addicted to drugs. Bailey's caretaking tendencies shift from his family to Jill, whom he loves but ultimately cannot help.

Julia, age 15, a tenth-grader who has been an A-student all her life, decides to change her image. Her grades slip, and she drops her bookish friend Libby in favor of a popular party girl, Nina. She lies about her age in order to get a job waitressing in a seamy nightclub, and dates the club's much-older owner. Eventually she realizes that her actions could jeopardize her family's tenuous living situation, quits her job, and starts to pay more attention in school. Things change again for Julia when she falls in love for the first time with her childhood friend, Justin.

Claudia is 11 years old and in the fifth grade at the start of the series. Her priorities revolve around her violin. Her music is her connection to her late mother, who was a concert violinist. Claudia dreams of a career with a major symphony orchestra. She also feels responsible for keeping her family together, as the fear of being separated presents more of a threat to her than to her older siblings. In an early episode she searches for her long-lost grandfather in an attempt to bring some stability into their lives. Claudia often feels neglected by her siblings, who are too wrapped up in their own lives to notice when she is missing. Claudia's quirks include a proclivity for sleeping in unusual places. Rather than share a bedroom with Julia, she lives in a tent in the dining room. After an earthquake leaves her shaken, Claudia sleeps in a shower stall, and later persuades the whole family to spend the night in Charlie's pickup truck.

Joe Mangus provides a paternal presence in the Salingers' lives during the first season. Joe was Nick Salinger's partner in Salingers Restaurant. After Nick's death, Joe took over management of the restaurant. He hires Charlie as a bartender in the hopes of training him to take over the business one day, as Nick would have wanted.

The major turning point of the first season occurs during the "Thanksgiving" (11/14/94) episode, in which the Salinger siblings confront the drunk driver who killed their parents. Though they jointly agree that they will not speak to him, one by one they each seek him out for their own reasons. Confronting Walter Alcott with their questions, accusations, and grief enables the kids to let go of some of their anger and begin to look forward instead of dwelling on the past.

Ads for the first season finale of *Party of Five* teased: "A new life...an untimely death...and the most romantic moment two people can share." Many viewers naturally suspected that the new life referred to an unplanned pregnancy resulting from Bailey and Jill's careless attitude toward sex. Few expected the shocking turn of events when Jill dies of a drug overdose early in the episode. The new life springs from Claudia's gay violin teacher, Ross, who adopts a baby girl. The "most romantic moment" is shared by Kirsten and Charlie, who become engaged.

By the end of the first season, the characters have grown to a point that they no longer define themselves as victims of their parents' deaths. Their methods of dealing with tragedy has changed, so that when they are faced with another death, they cope differently. At a panel on "Creating Television" at the Museum of Television & Radio in Los Angeles, Christopher Keyser explained the evolution of the show's inaugural season: "If you look at the construction of the first season, it's book-ended by two deaths. The interesting thing that happened in the course of the season is how the family reacts to those two. The pilot is all about a family that doesn't talk to each other. By the end of the season, when Jill dies, everybody's talking to everyone about everything, and there's a scene at the end of that episode, where Charlie says to Bailey, 'I love you,' and it's one of the first times that anyone in the family says 'I love you' to somebody else. So the whole first season was conceived as a way of taking them through the process of becoming a real family and taking care of each other, and dealing with their emotions."

Offscreen, this unglamorous series on the fourth network, with a cast of unknowns and unproven creators, faced an uphill battle from the beginning. Only the faith of the FOX network, which saw breakout potential in its stars, kept the series afloat.

FOX initially scheduled *Party of Five* on Monday nights at nine, opposite football on ABC, *Murphy Brown* and *Love & War* on CBS, and made-for-television movies on NBC. The pilot episode of *Party of Five* was beaten in its time slot by its competition on the big three networks. Still, its 8.9 rating placed it 56th out of 84 shows for the week, a fairly respectable showing for a FOX show. (The network has fewer affiliate stations than the big three networks, which means fewer potential viewers, so even its hit shows are rarely in the top 20.) The ratings dropped to 6.9 in the series' second week, and 5.4 in its third. It ranked in the bottom ten each week for the rest of 1994.

Ratings improved slightly when the series moved into its new time slot on January 4, 1995, Wednesday nights at nine p.m., following *Beverly Hills 90210*. The long-established, youth-oriented *90210* was a much more compatible lead-in for *Party of Five* than the steamy *Melrose Place*. However, the competition in the Wednesday night slot was formidable: *Party* now went up against two hit sitcoms, *Roseanne* and *Ellen*, on ABC, *Dateline with Diane Sawyer* on NBC, and special programming on CBS. *Party of Five* hovered in or around the bottom ten for the rest of the season, with the exception of the season finale on March 15, 1995. The much-hyped finale garnered an 8.0 rating, the series' highest rating since its debut.

As viewers said good-bye to the Salingers at the end of the first season, the future of *Party of Five* was uncertain. The series, which ended the season ranked 124th out of 142 shows, was placed on hiatus while FOX decided its fate. The sci-fi drama *Sliders* took its place, significantly outperforming *Party* in the Nielsen ratings. Getting "creamed" in the ratings by *Sliders* (per the *Hollywood Reporter*) did not augur well for *Party*'s renewal chances. Critics predicted it had been dealt its death blow.

But *Party* didn't go down for the count. As fans bombarded the network with letters and petitions, the critics pleaded its case in the media. John Martin of the *New York Times* wrote, "Think hard FOX. *Party of Five* may not be a ratings hit—don't forget it's opposite *Roseanne*—but it's a show you can be proud of." In *TV Guide*'s fourth annual "Save Our Shows" issue, *Party of Five* was one of four endangered shows profiled (along with *My So-Called Life*, *Earth 2*, and *Under Suspicion*). *Party of Five* won the magazine's poll, with approximately 28,000 readers casting their votes in support of the show. FOX heard the outcry and ordered 13 new episodes for the 1995-96 season. It was the only one of the four shows in *TV Guide*'s "Save Our Shows" poll to be renewed.

During its first year, *Party of Five* did not have a consistent opening theme song—and sometimes it didn't have any theme song at all. Following a trend started by ABC, the FOX network had decided to cut down on the use of themes and opening title sequences, to reduce the opportunity for channel surfing. The networks experimented with theme-less programming, as well as "seamless programming" (leading from one program directly into the next, without a commercial break) and "living credits" (credits running alongside or underneath a tag scene, bloopers, or outtakes), in an effort to keep viewers glued to their couches between shows. Producers were urged to run the opening credits under the first scene, rather than under a title sequence. The *Party of Five* producers played the network's game—at least for the first half dozen episodes.

Amy Lippman says, "We complied with that until we realized that every show other than ours had a main title. We went back to FOX and explained that it is important that we use visuals and the name of the show so that the audience knows the show is beginning. Then the thought was to try to put hip, new music under the main title sequence. We rotated five pieces of music until we found "Closer to Free" by the BoDeans, which says everything lyrically of what this show is about." The other songs used as opening themes during the first season are "Come to My Window" by Melissa Etheridge, "Hold My Hand" by Hootie & the Blowfish, "Climb On (A Back That's Strong)" by Shawn Colvin, and "Sun's Gonna Rise Again" by Sass Jordan.

By summer of 1995, even ABC, the network that started the trend, had realized that the moratorium on theme songs was a bad idea. TV theme songs create awareness of a show, and have always played a part in the insinuation of programs into popular culture. Part of what helped *Friends* skyrocket into popularity was its catchy theme song, played on radio stations nationwide. Most viewers who grew up watching *Gilligan's Island* and *The Brady Bunch* can easily recite the words to those series' memorable themes.

First Season Episode Descriptions

1. "Pilot"

Original Airdate: September 12, 1994   *NR/AS: 8.9/13
Writers: Amy Lippman and Christopher Keyser
Director: Richard Pearce

---

*NR stands for Nielsen Rating and AS stands for Audience Share. One ratings point equals 954,000 households, or 1% of the nation's 95.4 million TV-viewing homes in the 1994-95 season. "Share" is the percentage of television sets in use which are tuned in to a particular show.

Guest Cast: Tom Mason (Joe Mangus), Mitchell Anderson (Ross Werkman), Johnny Whitworth (P. K.), Maxine Miller (Mrs. Kelleher), Kevin McNulty (Plumber), Byron Lucas (Doug), Sandy Tucker (Mrs. Elleson), Susan McLennan (Nanny), Jay Brazeau (Pawnbroker), Delores Drake (Mrs. Pick), Suzy Joachim (Janet), Alan Lysell (Teacher), Zachary and Alexander Ahnert (Owen)

Six months after their parents were killed in a car accident involving a drunk driver, the five Salinger orphans are struggling to make ends meet and keep their family together. Sixteen-year-old Bailey assumes most of the responsibility for the family, which in the pilot episode includes finding a replacement for Owen's 65-year-old nanny, Mrs. Kelleher, who quits suddenly.

Fifteen-year-old Julia turns her back on family commitments when a classmate, P. K., shows an interest in her, but when her heart gets broken she longs for her mother's advice and comfort. Eldest sibling Charlie, 24, shocks the family by revealing that he has lost $12,000 of their money in a bad real estate investment. Joe, his father's partner in Salingers Restaurant, loans Charlie enough money to tide them over on the condition that Charlie work at Salingers as a bartender, a job which Charlie accepts very reluctantly.

Taking her family's financial problems to heart, 11-year-old Claudia pawns her violin and announces that she'd rather be a regular kid than a child prodigy. Ross, her violin instructor, reminds her that she has a rare gift and encourages her to stick with it. Claudia later retrieves her violin from the pawn shop. Charlie decides that he should take more responsibility for his younger siblings, so he moves back into the house, but his brother and sisters have a tough time viewing Charlie as an authority figure.

Bailey thinks he has solved the family's nanny problem when Kirsten Bennett appears at the doorstep to apply for the job. But his decision to hire her on the spot may have more to do with her beauty than her qualifications.

Highlight: Julia and Bailey have a conversation in the park in which they talk about the loss of their parents and why they never speak about them. They agree about the importance of remaining together as a family.

Notes: The pilot episode was filmed in Vancouver, British Columbia, Canada. When the series was picked up, the show found a permanent home on the Sony Pictures studio lot in Culver City, California, where the sets were reconstructed. Note the differences in the set design of Salingers Restaurant in the pilot compared to the rest of the series.

The character of P. K. was named after writer P. K. Simonds. Simonds, a friend of creators Keyser and Lippman, joined the *Party of Five* writing staff in 1995. His prior writing credits include *Doogie Howser, M.D.* and *Earth 2*.

2. *"Homework"*

```
Original Airdate: September 19, 1994          NR/AS: 6.9/10
Writers: Christopher Keyser and Amy Lippman
Director: Richard Pearce
Regular Cast Changes: Scott Grimes, who did not appear in the
pilot, joins the regular cast as Bailey's best friend and class-
mate, Will McCorkle. He is featured in the opening credits until
the third season, when Will goes off to college. (In real life,
Scott Grimes left to do another series, Goode Behavior). Twins
Brandon and Taylor Porter take over the role of baby Owen,
played in the pilot by Zachary and Alexander Ahnert.
Guest Cast: Alan Young (Jack Gordon), Bryn Erin (Libby Dwyer),
Cari Shayne (Nina), Laura Innes (Liz), Freda Foh Shen (Miss
Minor), Brittany Murphy (Abby), Graham Heywood (Alan Tisk),
Lorna Scott (Government Clerk), Tara Charendoff (Lorna)
```

Her siblings try to discourage Claudia when she decides to search for their long-lost grandfather. Claudia locates a man with her grandfather's name, but the man denies being the same Jack Gordon who abandoned their mother 30 years before. Bailey has a crush on the new nanny, Kirsten, but she is only interested in his older brother, Charlie. When Bailey asks Charlie to back off, he does, although he knows Bailey doesn't stand a chance with Kirsten due to their age difference. Julia desires to shed her bookish image and hang out with the cool kids in school. She chooses partying over studying, but when a struggling Bailey needs her help, she skips the party to help him with his assignment.

Familiar Faces: Alan Young is best known as Wilbur Post, sidekick to talking horse *Mister Ed* (CBS, 1961-65). Laura Innes' TV roles include Lowell's ex-wife, Bunny, on *Wings* (NBC, 1991-93) and Dr. Kerry Weaver on *ER* (NBC, 1995-).

Notes: This episode remains one of Lacey Chabert's favorites, in that it shows Claudia's spunk and independence, and sets the tone for her character.

3. "Good Sports"

Original Airdate: September 26, 1994   NR/AS: 5.4/8
Writer: W. K. Scott Meyer
Director: Steve Robman
Guest Cast: Bobby Jacoby (Adam), Stephen Root (Coach), Cari Shayne (Nina), Brittany Murphy (Abby), Lorinne Dills Vozoff (Principal Stickley), Larry Poindexter (George Lewis), David Sheinkopf (Jason), Brett Donowho (Greg), Nikki Tyler (Receptionist), Annie O'Donnell (Mrs. Peterson), Christian Frazell (Grunge Kid), Kenneth Lloyd Bowers (Mr. Harlan)

Bailey witnesses a fight between one of his teammates and some members of an opposing team. When he refuses to name the teammate who was involved in the incident, Bailey is suspended from the football team. Though Charlie advises him to protect himself and his future, Bailey sticks to his guns and refuses to squeal. Wanting to be "cool", Julia offers the Salingers house as a party pad to her new-found friends, who quickly abuse her generosity, trashing the house and showing up uninvited when the family is heading out for dinner. Julia eventually gets the courage to stand up to them and is surprised when Nina, the queen of cool, still wants to be friends.

When Kirsten starts dating a lawyer, Charlie regrets not making a move when he had the chance. Then he learns that Kirsten's boyfriend lied about his profession, and spills the beans. Kirsten dumps George, but isn't interested in Charlie and his games.

Familiar Faces: Stephen Root went on to play radio station owner Jimmy James in NBC's *NewsRadio* (1995–). Larry Poindexter would return in a different role in episode 48 ("Mixed Signals," 9/18/96).

4. "Worth Waiting For"

Original Airdate: October 3, 1994   NR/AS: 5.5/8
Writer: Susannah Grant
Director: Steven Cragg
Guest Cast: Michael Goorjian (Justin Thompson), Cari Shayne

(Nina), Jennifer Blanc (Kate Bishop), Shirley Prestia (Demanding Customer), Jean Sincere (Older Woman), Susan Mohun (Lisa), Ladd York (Drew), Cynthia Lynch (Bartender)

Everybody's thinking about sex, but no one will answer Claudia's questions on the subject. After her friend Nina goes all the way, Julia decides it's time she "get it over with," too. She comes on to her friend Justin, but then backs off, admitting that she's not in love with him. Charlie and Kirsten finally make a date, but just as their romance is heating up, she learns that he used one of his tried-and-true pick-up lines on her. Charlie smoothes things over and they sleep together. Bailey is blue when he learns that Kate, the pretty customer he met at the shoe store, already has a boyfriend. He decides to just hang around Kate until she falls for him. Claudia thinks it's a sure bet that Kate will eventually realize what a great guy her brother is. Why? She explains, "Duh! He's Bailey."

Familiar Faces: Prior to her eight-episode stint on *Party of Five*, Jennifer Blanc had played Tiffany in the NBC comedy series, *The Mommies* (1993-94). She starred opposite Shannen Doherty and Jason London in the 1997 made-for-TV thriller, *Friends 'Til the End.*

Notes: This episode marked Michael Goorjian's first appearance as Justin, Julia's childhood friend. He was added to the regular cast in the second season.

5. "All's Fair"

Original Airdate: October 10, 1994   NR/AS: 5.8/9
Writer: Ann Lewis Hamilton
Director: Peter O'Fallon
Guest Cast: Susan Diol (Rebecca), Cari Shayne (Nina), Jennifer Blanc (Kate Bishop), Mitchell Anderson (Ross Werkman), Tom Gallop (Mike), Doug Hutchison (Loren), David Drew Gallagher (Tom), Barbara Allyne Bennet (Judge), Zach Luna (Richard)

A visiting ex-girlfriend, Rebecca, turns to Charlie for comfort over her failing marriage, and they end up sleeping together. Soon Charlie is telling lies to two women—his girlfriend, Kirsten, and his ex-flame, Rebecca, whom he assumes wants to resume their relationship. However, Rebecca wanted a friend, not a commitment, and she points out that Charlie hasn't changed as much as he may have thought. Kate's

Bailey tries to impress Kate (Jennifer Blanc) in "All's Fair." PHOTOFEST.

boyfriend, Tom, is so darn nice that Bailey almost feels bad trying to win Kate over. But try he does, and he eventually succeeds. As Julia tries to pass for 18 to get a job waitressing in an after-hours club, Claudia pretends to be younger so she can gain advantage in a violin competition.

Notes: The club where Julia gets a job is named Stage 18, after the soundstage that houses the sets for the Salinger home on the Sony lot.

Familiar Faces: Susan Diol is best-known for her roles in the daytime TV dramas *One Life to Live* and *Days of Our Lives.* Doug Hutchison portrayed Eugene Victor Tooms, a mutant killer who eats human livers, on two memorably creepy first season installments of *X-Files* (FOX, 1993-94).

Familiar Places: The house used for exterior shots of the Salingers' home is located in San Francisco, on Broadway between Fillmore and Steiner Streets. Built in 1895, the 6,705-square-foot house has five bedrooms, three-and-a-half bathrooms, and full views of the Golden Gate Bridge and the San Francisco Bay.

6. "Fathers and Sons"

Original Airdate: October 17, 1994   NR/AS: 5.6/8
Writers: Amy Lippman and Christopher Keyser
Director: Ellen S. Pressman

Guest Cast: Tom Mason (Joe Mangus), Johnny Whitworth (P. K.), Geoff Pierson (Elliot Bishop), Jennifer Blanc (Kate Bishop), Rick Fitts (Police Officer), Annabella Price (Eileen), Richard McGonagle (Emmett), Doug Hutchison (Loren), Tom Simmons (Customer), Patti Tippo (Sharon Bishop), Brogan Roche (Gil), Billy Burke (Guy in Club)

While working at Stage 18, Julia runs into P. K., who later turns up on her doorstep sporting a black eye and seeking refuge from his abusive stepfather. The family shelters P. K. until the police come looking for the missing youth. Her siblings tell Julia that hiding P. K. could get them in trouble with social services, so he must go. P. K. won't take her advice to report his stepfather, but he does take the $100 she presses on him—all her tips from waitressing at the club.

Joe promotes Charlie from bartender to night manager, but Charlie isn't interested. He doesn't want to follow in his father's footsteps and resents being constantly compared to him and coming up short. Joe reveals that he has been pushing Charlie to learn the restaurant business because he hopes that one day Charlie will take over the reins, like Nick would have wanted.

Bailey's efforts to impress Kate's stern father are futile. To make matters worse, Bailey has painted Charlie as an ultra-responsible guardian, but when Mr. Bishop meets him, Charlie is in over his head at the restaurant and snaps at his customers and his family. Mr. Bishop imposes a curfew on Kate to curtail her relationship with Bailey, but she insists they will find a way to be together.

Highlight: Bailey tells Kate what it would have been like if he had taken her home to meet his parents. During a CompuServe forum, Amy Lippman revealed that the scene was based on her own life. She said, "Chris's wife and my husband both lost parents early on. And we have both used some of their experiences in the show. Since I never met my husband's father, I imagined what it would have been like to meet him. So while that moment was about Bailey's dad, it was also a little about my own life."

Familiar Faces: Kate's father is played by Geoff Pierson, best-known for his role as Frank Ryan on the daytime drama *Ryan's Hope*, a show he starred in for three years. He also played the recurring role of Grace's ex-husband, Jimmy, on *Grace Under Fire*, and starred in the Warner Bros. network series *Unhappily Ever After*.

7.   "Much Ado"

Original Airdate: October 24, 1994   NR/AS: 5.7/8
Writer: Hollis Rich
Director: Ken Topolsky
Guest Cast: Mitchell Anderson (Ross Werkman), Jennifer Blanc
(Kate Bishop), Zachary Throne (Danny), Jane Lynch (Dr. Pennant),
Darin Heames (Martin), Marie Barrientos (Clerk), Cynthia Avila
(Nurse), Christa Miller (Theresa), Cynthia Lynch (Nicole), Ingo
Neuhaus (Bouncer)

Kirsten finds out about Charlie's infidelity with Rebecca and ends
their relationship. His siblings are upset that Charlie's cheating ways
cost them the best nanny they ever had. Charlie sees Julia at the club
where she works and assumes she is there partying. When he tries to
lecture her about drinking, Julia brings up his own party-boy past and
refuses to listen to his counsel. Jealous of the time Bailey is spending
with Kate, Claudia gives Kate the wrong message so she'll miss a date
with Bailey.

Owen is rushed to the hospital with a high fever and doctors fear he
may have meningitis. Ross brings Claudia to the hospital to wait with
the rest of the family but she won't go in—she hasn't stepped foot in the
hospital since the night of her parents' accident. Owen's illness brings
everyone closer together, including, for a time, Kirsten and Charlie.
Kirsten helps Charlie through the crisis, but she can't forgive him for
cheating. Bailey apologizes to Claudia for neglecting her, but explains
that Kate is his first girlfriend and he wants to spend time with her. He
promises if she ever needs him, Claudia will come first. Just as they get
the news that Owen will be fine, Claudia arrives at the hospital, where
she plays the violin at her baby brother's bedside.

Familiar Faces: Christa Miller plays Kate on the ABC sitcom, *The
Drew Carey Show*, which debuted in the fall of 1995.

8.   "Kiss Me Kate"

Original Airdate: November 2, 1994   NR/AS: 6.6/10
Writer: Susannah Grant
Director: Richard Pearce
Guest Cast: Mitchell Anderson (Ross Werkman), Eric Pierpoint
(Bruce Curran), Christine Healy (Margaret), Cari Shayne (Nina),
Jennifer Blanc (Kate Bishop), Lorinne Dills Vozoff (Principal

Stickley), Zachary Throne (Danny), Kathleen Freeman (Mona), Michael Kaufman (Mr. McQuilkin), Robin Pearson Rose (Dr. Weeks), Allen Williams (Douglas), Christopher Carroll (Dan Barton), Cynthia Lynch (Nicole)

Bailey is shocked when his girlfriend, Kate, reveals she plans to remain a virgin until she marries. His inability to accept her decision and her unwillingness to change her mind lead to their breakup. Julia has been keeping late hours at the coffeehouse, where she teams up with a songwriter to put her poetry to music. Julia's teachers are concerned over her falling grades and unexcused absences, but she shrugs off their advice. When Charlie intercedes, she promises to keep up in school but refuses to stop hanging out at the coffeehouse, explaining what it means to have someplace to go where people don't look at her with pity.

After Claudia is named one of the Bay area's most gifted young musicians, she begins acting like a prima donna, refusing to do household chores, and demanding to be treated like a star. Charlie underbids on a construction job so he can get the job and impress the owner of the company. But when nanny problems impede his progress, Charlie turns to his siblings for help in completing the project on time.

Highlight: Danny sings "Most Like Me," a song Julia wrote about Owen.

Familiar Faces: Charlie's construction client is portrayed by Eric Pierpoint, who played alien detective George Francisco on the FOX series *Alien Nation* (1989-90). Among veteran character actress Kathleen Freeman's most memorable TV roles are Gertrude Burkhalter on *Hogan's Heroes* (CBS, 1965-71) and Flo Shafer on *The Beverly Hillbillies* (CBS, 1969-71).

Notes: FOX aired this episode in *Models Inc.*'s 9 p.m. time slot on Wednesday night in an attempt to bring new viewers to the show. Though the episode picked up the series' third highest Nielsen rating (6.6) to date, it still ranked in the week's bottom ten.

9. "Something Out of Nothing"

Original Airdate: November 7, 1994   NR/AS: 5.7/8
Teleplay: Susannah Grant
Story: Amy Lippman and Christopher Keyser
Director: Steven Robman
Guest Cast: Mitchell Anderson (Ross Werkman), Gates McFadden

(Greer Erikson), Darrell Larson (Ed Brighton), Cari Shayne
(Nina), Sarah Lassez (Cynda), Catherine Lloyd Burns (Jeannie),
Carol-Ann Plante (Heather), Jessica Hecht (Amanda)

When family friend Greer Erikson visits, her well-meaning interference causes problems for the Salingers. Greer tries to bolster Julia's
confidence by sending her to a fashion photographer who convinces
her she could have a future as a model. But the $800 she spends on the
photo session gets Julia in hot water with Charlie. Greer tries to get Bailey over his breakup with Kate by fixing him up on a blind date, but the
date is a bust and Bailey develops an attraction for Greer instead. Greer
tells Bailey that the attraction is mutual, but that they shouldn't act on
it. When Charlie exposes several of Greer's lies, both Julia and Bailey
question her motives. But after she leaves, they realize that she did help
them to feel better about themselves.

Ross's revelation that he is gay affects his relationship with Claudia.
She admits to being uncomfortable with him and skips their lessons. Ross

Star Trek star
Gates McFadden guest-
starred in "Something
Out of Nothing,"
which the creators
name as the series'
worst episode.
PHOTOFEST.

is hurt by her reaction until he learns the real reason behind it—Claudia had always hoped that when she grew up Ross would want to marry her.

Not wanting to repeat the mistake he made with Kirsten, Charlie sets out to find a nanny that he won't be tempted to get involved with romantically. He finally hires the only candidate he isn't attracted to—a guy named Bill.

Familiar Faces: Gates McFadden is best-known as Dr. Beverly Crusher from *Star Trek: The Next Generation* (Syndicated, 1987-88, 1989-94). Jessica Hecht costarred in the first season of *The Single Guy* (NBC, 1995-96), and plays the recurring role of Ross's ex-wife's lover on *Friends* (NBC, 1994-).

Notes: The character of Ross was not initially conceived as a gay role. Actor Mitchell Anderson says that after his fourth or fifth appearance on the show, the producers approached him and asked how he would feel about portraying a homosexual character. Mitchell, who is openly gay in real life but did not publicly come out of the closet until March 1996, said, "I think it's a great idea." Amy Lippman says that in contrast to other actors who auditioned for the role of Ross, Mitchell approached the relationship between Ross and Claudia as one of equals rather than adult and child. Mitchell says, "The neat thing about the character and the relationship that he has with Claudia is that it's really always about them teaching each other something. In the episode where Ross comes out, it's really not necessarily about Ross's homosexuality, it's about Claudia learning how to be a better friend, and I think that's the beauty of the show and the beauty of that relationship."

Executive producer Chris Keyser names "Something Out of Nothing" as the worst episode of *Party of Five*. He says, "It's the one where Julia is worried about not being pretty." Why is it the worst episode? He explains, "Because she *is* pretty. And Bailey's story line is that he is concerned no one will ever want to sleep with him!"

10. "Thanksgiving"

Original Airdate: November 14, 1994   NR/AS: 6.2/9
Writers: Amy Lippman and Christopher Keyser
Director: Michael Engler
Guest Cast: Tom Mason (Joe Mangus), John Rubinstein (Walter Alcott), Kelli Williams (Annie), Jennifer Blanc (Kate Bishop), Richard McGonagle (Emmett)

After confronting the drunk driver who killed their parents, the Salingers sit down to enjoy a belated Thanksgiving dinner in "Thanksgiving."

As Thanksgiving approaches, the kids decide they're not ready to celebrate the first major holiday since their parents died. The family's lawyer, Emmett, informs them that Walter Alcott, the drunk driver who killed their parents, has been released from prison after serving only half of an 18-month sentence. Alcott wants to see the Salingers, but they agree as a family that they will have nothing to do with him. However, one by one, each of the Salinger children seeks out Walter Alcott for his/her own reasons.

Claudia just wants to see what he looks like, since she was too young to attend the trial. Bailey wants Walter to suffer like they have, and is bitter and resentful that Walter has returned to a seemingly normal life. After an explosive confrontation with Walter, Bailey shows up at Kate's house. They reconcile, and Kate helps Bailey let go of his anger. Julia tells Walter that she will try to forgive him, and she lets him know that they will be O.K.

Charlie is the last to talk to Walter, and when he does, he reveals that he feels guilt over his parents' deaths. He was supposed to baby-sit for Owen while they attended a concert, but he was late. If he had been on time, his parents would have been in their seats at the concert at the time the accident occurred. Walter assures Charlie that he is not responsible and that he, in fact, is the hero in this story. The next day, having dealt with the feelings raised by Walter Alcott's re-appearance in their lives, the family sits down to a belated Thanksgiving dinner.

Highlights: In an episode filled with emotional scenes, the confrontation between Charlie and Walter Alcott stands out as the most evocative. Amy Lippman told journalist Mike Hughes, "Matthew only did two takes. They were so powerful we actually sat in our office and cried."

Familiar Faces: John Rubinstein's extensive list of credits includes starring roles in the television series *Family* (ABC, 1976-80) and *Crazy Like a Fox* (CBS, 1984-86). The son of famed classical concert pianist Artur Rubinstein, and a gifted composer in his own right, he wrote music for *Family*, *China Beach*, and other TV series.

Awards: Chris Keyser and Amy Lippman won a 1995 Humanitas Prize for writing this episode, which the judges cited for its "luminous declaration that we can forgive other people only when we have first gotten in touch with our own need for forgiveness." The Humanitas Prize honors film and TV scripts that enrich the public.

Notes: Keyser and Lippman wanted to write this episode from the earliest planning stages of *Party of Five*. They always knew they needed to have the characters confront the person responsible for their parents' deaths so that they could begin to heal and move on. While the Salingers had been forced by circumstances to be selfless, once they got past this hurdle, they could begin to be more human and pursue their individual desires.

At a Museum of Television & Radio event held in Los Angeles in October 1996, Amy Lippman revealed another reason this episode is special in the progress of the series. "It's the episode in which we realized just what an extraordinary cast we had. We knew they were good. We knew they were attractive. But until this episode, I don't think Chris and I really realized the extent of their commitment to the show and their understanding of the characters." At the same event, several of the cast and crew named this episode as being among their all-time favorites.

11. "Private Lies"

Original Airdate: November 21, 1994   NR/AS: 6.3/9
Writer: W. K. Scott Meyer
Director: Peter O'Fallon
Guest Cast: LaTanya Richardson (Jane Gideon), Peter Dobson
(Morgan), Doug Hutchison (Loren), Michael Shulman (Artie Baum),
David Burke (Bill), Harry Johnson (Professor Dwight), Nicole
Sullivan (Terry), Bob Kane (Police Officer), Erik Palladino
(Customer), Lauren Kenny O'Fallon (Dana), Beth Colt (Molly)

A surprise visit from the family's social worker, Mrs. Gideon, brings
all their secrets out into the open. Charlie's late hours and odd behavior lead Bailey to suspect he has a drug problem, but Charlie has been
taking classes at Berkeley and didn't want anyone to know in case he
failed. Julia has to wear a "figure-flattering" uniform to keep her job at
the club. Meanwhile, her siblings believe she works at a burger joint. Bailey is failing two courses and is on the verge of academic probation. And
everyone is too busy to pay attention to Claudia until she's missing.

When Mrs. Gideon returns for a re-evaluation, the family is on its
best behavior, and even Kirsten helps out by filling in for nanny Bill,
who has been called for jury duty. Mrs. Gideon isn't fooled by their charade and implies that if they don't straighten up, the family could be
separated. Julia quits her job at the club even after the revealing uniforms are dropped, but she keeps the door open for a possible romantic
involvement with Morgan, the club owner. Bailey and Julia take an
active interest in Claudia's life, while Charlie and Bailey urge each other
to stick with school. Claudia pleads her family's case to Mrs. Gideon and
returns home with the news that the family can stay together as long as
they follow the rules. They are gathered together celebrating when they
witness Owen taking his first steps.

Familiar Faces: Peter Dobson starred in the short-lived 1993 CBS
series *Johnny Bago*, as a small-time hustler on the run in a Winnebago,
trying to clear his name of false murder charges. Nicole Sullivan is one
of the stars of FOX's late night sketch show, *Mad TV*, which has spoofed
Party of Five on a few occasions.

Notes: Michael Shulman makes his first appearance as Claudia's
friend, Artie Baum. Shulman and Lacey Chabert were old friends, having worked together in *Les Miserables* on Broadway.

12. *"Games People Play"*

Original Airdate: November 28, 1994   NR/AS: 6.8/10
Writer: Susannah Grant
Director: Michael Engler
Guest Cast: Peter Dobson (Morgan), Christine Healy (Margaret),
Cari Shayne (Nina), Jennifer Blanc (Kate Bishop), Geoff Pierson
(Elliott Bishop), Michael Shulman (Artie Baum), David Burke
(Bill), David Cowgill (Sanchez), John Ducey (Ice Cream Guy)

Kirsten turns to Charlie for comfort when she discovers she may
have cancer, but pulls away from his advances, saying she needs a
friend, not a lover. After having some time to think, Charlie comes back
to her bearing gifts and declares that he wants to take care of her and be
her friend. By then Kirsten has learned that she doesn't have cancer, she
has a malformation of her fallopian tubes and can never have children.
When she sobbingly tells Charlie, he holds her while she cries.

Kate is accepted into an out-of-state boarding school and tells Bailey she wants to sleep with him before she leaves. They sneak away on
a camping trip but Bailey realizes that Kate isn't really ready for sex,
and they decide to wait. Julia dates Morgan, who assumes she is in college, when she isn't even old enough to drive. Then she learns that he
has been keeping secrets, too: he has a young daughter. Claudia uses
Julia's unknowing advice to get Artie's attention, but he becomes
annoyed with her games and starts avoiding her. She wins his friendship back by being herself. Julia decides to tell Morgan the truth about
her age, but before she gets the chance, the club receives a surprise
inspection. Underage Julia is the first one asked to produce her I.D.

Notes: Michael Engler's prior directing credits include *Dream On*,
Sisters, and *My So-Called Life.*

13. *"Grownups"*

Original Airdate: December 12, 1994   NR/AS: 5.9/9
Writer: Ann Lewis Hamilton
Director: Ellen S. Pressman
Guest Cast: Megan Ward (Jill Holbrook), Peter Dobson (Morgan),
Leslie Hope (Meg), Doug Hutchison (Loren)

Passion takes over when Bailey meets Jill, a fun-loving waitress
who wastes no time with small talk in getting Bailey into bed. Bailey is

a more-than-willing lover, but afterwards he feels that their relationship progressed too quickly and wishes they had spent more time getting to know each other. He asks her on an old-fashioned movies-and-burgers date so that they can start all over.

Morgan turns to booze after his club is closed down and he is forced to pay a fine. Julia feels responsible, but Morgan won't accept her apology or the $250 she offers him to help pay the fine. Julia eventually realizes that she isn't to blame for all of Morgan's problems and there's nothing she can do to help him.

When Claudia gets her first period, no one is home but Bailey, who is ill-at-ease helping her shop for feminine hygiene products. Claudia, who still likes to watch *Sesame Street* once in a while, isn't sure she's ready for womanhood, but she is comforted by sisterly advice from Julia.

Kirsten's family urges her to return home to Chicago while she deals with the news that she can't have children. Charlie offers her another alternative: "Let's get married." Kirsten impulsively accepts, but later decides she is not emotionally ready for such a big decision. While Kirsten grapples with her options, Charlie invites her to move in with him, explaining that while she can't have kids, he somehow ended up with four of them. "So why don't you share mine?" he asks. She takes his hand and they go inside the Salinger home.

Notes: Lacey says that when she first read her script for this episode, her mouth dropped open when she discovered that it dealt with her character getting her period. She recalled on MTV's *Party of Five @ 5*, "I think that was probably the most embarrassing episode ever. You know, it's pretty embarrassing to grow up in front of like 15 million people." She was so mortified at the prospect of enacting the script that she didn't show up for the table read. The supermarket scene between Bailey and Claudia remains one of Scott Wolf's favorites. The scene in which Charlie invites Kirsten to move in is one of co-creator Chris Keyser's personal favorites.

14. "Not Fade Away"

Original Airdate: January 4, 1995   NR/AS: 7.1/10
Writers: Amy Lippman and Christopher Keyser
Director: Peter O'Fallon
Guest Cast: James Sloyan (Avery Baltus), Megan Ward (Jill Holbrook), Tom Mason (Joe Mangus), Michael Shulman (Artie Baum),

Paul Hayes (Mr. Thurman), Dennis Napolitano (Guard), Joyce Kurtz (voice of Diana Salinger)

Kirsten moves into the Salinger house, upsetting Julia, who worries that what traces were left of her mother are fading away. Julia finds her mother's journal, which leads her to suspect that her mother had an affair with a colleague, Avery Baltus. Julia tracks down Avery, who admits that he was in love with Diana, but insists that they did not have an affair. Kirsten and Julia reach an understanding when Kirsten insists she is not trying to take their mother's place.

Bailey shoplifts a pair of sunglasses to impress Jill, but he is caught. Bailey isn't impressed by Charlie's lecture since Charlie's own record isn't so clean. Bailey is tired of being ultra-responsible and would rather be carefree, like Jill. As Artie prepares for his bar mitzvah, Claudia considers converting to Judaism. She eventually decides not to convert, because she wants to go to the same heaven as her parents.

Familiar Faces: TV veteran James Sloyan's roles include starring opposite Madeline Kahn in the ABC sitcom *Oh Madeline* (1983-84) and a recurring role on *Murder, She Wrote* (CBS, 1990-91).

Notes: The voice of Diana Salinger on the recordings played in this episode sounded so similar to Julia's voice that many fans believed that Neve Campbell's own voice was used. But the voice belonged to actress Joyce Kurtz, whose voice-over work includes the ABC live-action series *Dinosaurs.*

15. "It's Not Easy Being Green"

Original Airdate: January 11, 1995   NR/AS: 6.4/10
Writer: Susannah Grant
Director: Michael Engler
Guest Cast: Megan Ward (Jill Holbrook), Michael Goorjian (Justin Thompson), Louis Mustillo (Mr. Parker), Michael Shulman (Artie Baum), David Burke (Bill), Bryn Erin (Libby Dwyer), Mark Moses (Ben Atkins), Cristan Crocker (Eliza), Mary Scheer (Ms. Shaver)

The green-eyed monster invades the Salinger household. Charlie is jealous when Kirsten spends time with her dissertation advisor, Ben Atkins. Claudia is envious when Artie lands the title role in the school production of *Oliver!* When Julia is teamed with Justin in driver's education class, she finds herself attracted to him. Then she learns that he's dating her friend Libby, and decides to flirt with him anyway. Will is bothered by Bailey's relationship with Jill, whom he calls a juvenile delinquent. When he uses test answers Jill stole and defends her actions, Bailey loses his best friend. Later, Bailey doesn't see Jill hide drugs in her locker.

After Kirsten learns that Ben is interested in her romantically, and Charlie's jealousy nearly drives him into the arms of another woman, they realize they need to learn to trust one another. Just as Julia comes to terms with Justin's relationship with Libby, Justin kisses her. Claudia turns Artie away in a storm, and he gets sick and can't perform. Claudia lands the role of Oliver, but she feels so guilty she tries to make herself sick. She goes on after all and makes her family proud.

Familiar Faces: Mark Moses played Jonathan Silverman's married neighbor on *The Single Guy* (NBC, 1995-96), but was written off the show after one season.

16. "Aftershocks"

Original Airdate: January 18, 1995   NR/AS: 7.3/11
Writers: Mark B. Perry and Ann Lewis Hamilton
Director: Ken Topolsky
Guest Cast: Michael Goorjian (Justin Thompson), Megan Ward (Jill Holbrook), Bryn Erin (Libby Dwyer), Mia Korf (Gwen), David Burke (Bill), Pat Cronin (Salesman), Jeff Doucette (Repairman), Richard Ryder (Delivery Man)

An earthquake rattles everyone's nerves and leaves Jill more jumpy than ever. Charlie accuses Jill of being on speed but Jill denies it. Bailey believes Jill, until her increasingly bizarre behavior makes him suspicious, and he finds a bag of pills in her purse. Jill promises to stay clean, but later steals pain killers from the Salingers' medicine cabinet. Bailey pressures her to admit she has a substance abuse problem and agrees to help her overcome it.

Julia and Justin fight their attraction to one another for Libby's sake, but when an aftershock traps them in a darkroom together, they end up locked in a passionate embrace. Thereafter, Justin breaks up with Libby, and Libby turns to Julia for comfort, not realizing that Julia was the cause. When Libby discovers the truth, she feels doubly betrayed. Justin and Julia's happiness at being together is tempered by the guilt they feel over deceiving and hurting Libby.

The Salingers before we knew them

Did you know...

Bailey threw up on his first day of kindergarten when he forgot the alphabet.

Julia was a cheerleader in school for "about ten minutes," until she learned she had to smile all the time, and quit.

In high school, Charlie drilled a peephole in the girls' locker room and set the boys' bathroom on fire.

Charlie dropped out of college at the University of California at Berkeley and was planning to re-enroll when his parents were killed.

When the Salinger siblings were younger, they would gather on rainy nights to play the board game Chutes and Ladders.

Kirsten loans Charlie $7,000 so he can go into business with a furniture designer, Gwen. But he regrets taking the loan when Kirsten begins making management suggestions. Their disagreement boils over into other household decisions, and they finally reach peace when Charlie gets a bank loan and returns Kirsten's money.

17. "In Loco Parentis"

Original Airdate: February 1, 1995   NR/AS: 7.4/12
Writers: Amy Lippman and Christopher Keyser
Director: Ken Topolsky
Guest Cast: Michael Goorjian (Justin Thompson), Jane Kaczmarek (Helene Thompson), Megan Ward (Jill Holbrook), Michael Shulman (Artie Baum), David Burke (Bill), Julia Ariola (Mrs. Holbrook), Bruce Nozick (Dr. Baum), Robert Fieldsteel (Howard), Harry S. Murphy (Pete), Langdon Bensing (Barry), Deborah Offner (Mrs. Baum), Keith Bogart (Tim Dwyer)

Bailey suspects Jill is using drugs again, but once more she denies it. When she is injured in a car accident and refuses to go to the hospital, he realizes it is because she is high. Bailey goes to Jill's mother, who won't accept that her daughter has a drug problem. Fed up with Bailey's interference, Jill leaves town.

Justin's mother is thrilled to learn that her son is dating Julia. But Justin is bothered when Julia shares too much personal information with his mother. Julia explains that without a mother to turn to, she just wanted someone with whom to talk about her love life. Justin later encourages his mom and Julia to spend time together.

Charlie is having difficulty bonding with little Owen, who has learned to say the nanny's name but not Charlie's. Charlie struggles to act like a father to Owen, who eventually calls him "da da." Claudia learns that the reason Artie has been hanging around the Salingers' so much is that he doesn't want to go home to his parents' constant fighting. Claudia and Artie arrange for his parents to meet at Salingers, in the hopes that candlelight and violin music will lead to a reconciliation. The plan fails, and Claudia convinces Artie to stop trying to fix his parents' relationship and start learning to deal with it.

Familiar Faces: Jane Kaczmarek played Lacey Chabert's mother in the 1995 ABC AfterSchool Special *Educating Mom* and had a starring role on the ABC legal drama *Equal Justice* (1990-91).

18. "Who Cares?"

Original Airdate: February 15, 1995   NR/AS: 6.5/10
Writer: Susannah Grant
Director: Ellen S. Pressman
Guest Cast: Megan Ward (Jill Holbrook), Zachary Throne (Danny),
Mia Korf (Gwen), Cari Shayne (Nina), Michael Shulman (Artie
Baum), Charlotte Booker (Lady Jane), Tim Wrightman (CHP Offi-
cer), Betsy Zang (Mary Elizabeth), Lynn A. Henderson (Andrea),
Brett Marx (Hippie), Lonna Montrose (Vendor)

Claudia's 12th birthday is approaching, but her siblings are too busy to notice. Charlie's new furniture company is taking off, with a buyer wanting eight hand-crafted tables by the first of the month. Julia learns that her friend Danny is HIV-positive. Danny wants to leave a mark on the world through his music and asks Julia to be his songwriting partner. Julia agrees, but she finds writing lyrics difficult, especially while trying to keep up with her schoolwork. She finds a way to show Danny that he'll be remembered when he's gone.

Bailey heads to L.A. to find Jill and convince her to come home. He begs for another chance and promises not to judge her. Jill agrees and they head back to San Francisco, but Jill's reckless behavior on the trip leads to a fight and she leaves him. Bailey returns home in time for Claudia's birthday party at Salingers. He gives her a charm for her bracelet—a family tradition she thought everyone forgot.

Inside Jokes: In one scene, Julia teases her brother, "That Bailey, they always say he's a party animal." Journalists had, in fact, been overusing that catch phrase to describe the male stars of *Party of Five*, who happened to have canine last names. ("Party Animals," *Entertainment Weekly*, 9/9/94; "Fox & Wolf: Party Animals," *TV Guide*, 12/10/94.)

From the earliest articles written about him, Scott Wolf has been compared to Tom Cruise. In this episode, as Bailey walks around Venice, California, a couple from Wisconsin follow him around taking pictures, believing him to be Cruise!

19. "Brother's Keeper"

Original Airdate: February 22, 1995   NR/AS: 5.9/9
Writer: Mark B. Perry
Director: Richard Pearce
Guest Cast: Michael Goorjian (Justin Thompson), Mitchell Anderson (Ross Werkman), Mia Korf (Gwen), Debra Mooney (Gloria Metzler), Shareen Mitchell (Monica Phelps), David Purdham (Tom Cullen), David Cromwell (Gronemeyer), Cayce Callaway (Ms. Byrd), Wendle Josepher (Lori)

Charlie and Gwen are elated when a furniture manufacturer wants to hire them to mass produce their line of fine furnishings. Charlie's $65,000 salary would mean an end to the family's financial problems. But the family stops celebrating when they learn that the job is Seattle-based and they will have to relocate. Only Kirsten is supportive of Charlie. Bailey and Julia flatly refuse to move to Seattle. Claudia fears that her family will be split up.

Tensions in the Salinger house rise even higher when Julia is assigned to tutor Bailey in geometry. Julia would rather spend time with Justin, and Bailey is resentful that his sister has both good grades and a stable relationship. Ross tells Claudia that she has surpassed his

talents as a music instructor and she needs a better teacher. He
arranges an interview with Gloria Metzler, but Claudia purposely plays
below her level because she doesn't want to lose Ross as a teacher. She
insists that if she has to move, she'll quit the violin.

After all the sacrifices he has made for his family, Charlie begs them
to give him this one chance to do something for himself. Julia and
Justin try to convince his parents to let her move in with them, but the
answer is no. Just as his siblings come to the realization that they will
have to go with Charlie if he takes the job, Charlie announces that he
sold his share of the company to Gwen.

Notes: Charlie takes it all off! This is the first episode in which Charlie appears clean-shaven.

20. "The Trouble With Charlie"

Original Airdate: March 1, 1995   NR/AS: 6.0/9
Writers: Amy Lippman and Christopher Keyser
Director: Ken Topolsky
Guest Cast: Megan Ward (Jill Holbrook), Jennifer Blanc (Kate
Bishop), David Burke (Bill), Michael Kaufman (Mr. McQuilken),
Jennifer Rhodes (Carolyn Prousky)

Charlie is feeling increasingly resentful of his family, after having
given up his big career opportunity because of them. Claudia disobeys
his rules and Bailey goes behind his back to give Bill a raise after Charlie said no. Kate pays a surprise visit to Bailey. She senses that something is wrong, but Bailey denies it. Then Jill reappears and tells Bailey
she is in rehab. Bailey rejects Jill to be with Kate, but he can't get Jill off
his mind. Before she returns to boarding school, Kate suggests that they
see other people. Bailey goes back to Jill and gives her another chance;
he doesn't want to love her, but he can't help it.

Julia's prize-winning story is printed in a magazine, and her siblings
are angry at the way they are depicted. Charlie is especially hurt as he
feels it is one more indication that his siblings don't respect him or
appreciate the sacrifices he makes for them. He announces that he is
moving out of the house.

Notes: This episode marked David Burke's last appearance as nanny
Bill, although Bill remained an offscreen presence until midway
through the second season, when Owen begins nursery school. While

Bill was offscreen tending to baby Owen, Burke was working on the short-lived FOX sitcom, *The Crew*, which debuted in the fall of 1995. He played Paul, one of four young flight attendants whose antics formed the premise of the series.

The editor at fictional *SF Magazine* is named after the publicist at FOX who handles *Party of Five*, Carolyn Prousky.

21. *"All-Nighters"*

Original Airdate: March 8, 1995 NR/AS: 6.0/9
Writers: Susannah Grant and Mark B. Perry
Director: Steven Robman
Guest Cast: Michael Goorjian (Justin Thompson), Megan Ward (Jill Holbrook), Tim Conlon (Dudley), Michael Shulman (Artie Baum), Vernee Watson-Johnson (Officer Windlan), Brent Jennings (Mr. Fountain), Rick Zieff (Public Defender), Robin Mary Florence (Kiki Nash), Senta Moses (Madeline), J. Gordon Noice (Man)

Charlie takes an apartment in his friend Dudley's building and tries to relive his carefree partying days. Kirsten understands Charlie's need to get away from the kids, but thinks he is making a mistake leaving them on their own, especially when Claudia starts having nightmares after witnessing a convenience store robbery.

Jill organizes a school dance marathon, but Bailey thinks she has taken on too much and tries to run interference. Jill tells Bailey he has to stop trying to fix her problems so that she can learn to take care of herself. Julia finds a condom in Justin's wallet and assumes he wants to have sex. When she tells him she's not ready, Justin assures her he will wait.

Claudia's nightmares continue even after the robber is captured. Charlie realizes that the nightmares aren't about the robber after all, they are about Charlie leaving. Realizing that his siblings still need him, Charlie decides not to take the apartment. Though he sometimes resents the responsibility his family entails, he recognizes that living up to those responsibilities has made him a better person.

Familiar Faces: Vernee Watson-Johnson played Verna Jean on *Welcome Back, Kotter* (ABC, 1975-77) and Lucille on *Carter Country* (ABC, 1977-79). Stand-up comedian Tim Conlon starred in the short-lived 1994 FOX series *Wild Oats*.

22. *"The Ides of March"*

Original Airdate: March 15, 1995   NR/AS: 8.0/13
Writers: Christopher Keyser and Amy Lippman
Director: Ellen S. Pressman
Guest Cast: Michael Goorjian (Justin Thompson), Megan Ward (Jill
Holbrook), Mitchell Anderson (Ross Werkman), Jimmy Marsden
(Griffin Holbrook), Maud Winchester (Kendra Erhardt)

Bailey is stunned when Jill dies suddenly from a cocaine overdose.
As his family and friends try to comfort him, Bailey pushes everyone
away, vowing never to love anyone again because it hurts too much to
lose them. Julia sees Jill's brother Griffin at the funeral. She buys him
the jacket that Jill had planned to buy him to replace one she left
behind in L.A. Julia has a hard time getting through to Griffin, who
doesn't want to be pitied. She explains that she knows what it's like to
lose a loved one, and he accepts the coat.

Charlie decides to propose to Kirsten, who beats him to it. Con-
gested due to an allergic reaction to Thurber, the family dog, she asks,
"Will you bury me?" Charlie agrees to both bury and marry her, and
gives her his mother's engagement ring. Ross announces that after over
a year on a waiting list, he's adopting a baby girl. But when he tells the
case worker that he's gay, his application is suddenly held up by red
tape. Bailey goes to the agency and makes an impassioned plea on
Ross's behalf. When the adoption goes through, Ross celebrates with the
Salingers and thanks Bailey for quite possibly being the reason he got
the baby, whom he names Tess.

Highlights: Kirsten's allergies provide a moment of levity in an hour
of intense drama. When she announces that she's allergic to Thurber
and that the family will have to choose between them, Charlie dead-
pans, "Kirsten, where will you go?" The family gives Thurber to Ross,
but by "Change Partners and Dance" (11/1/95), the pooch is back in the
Salinger household, and it is never explained why.

Notes: James [Jimmy] Marsden originated the role of Griffin Holbrook, but with the fate of the series up in the air, he accepted a role in
the ABC drama *Second Noah.* He played teenage father Ricky Beckett in
the series, which debuted in February 1996. With Marsden unavailable
when *Party of Five* resumed production, the role of Griffin was filled by
Jeremy London. Ironically, Marsden would later replace London when

a broken arm forced London to drop out of the 1997 NBC television movie *On the Edge of Innocence.*

The story line concerning Ross's adoption of the baby was suggested to the writers by actor Mitchell Anderson. Amy Lippman told fans during a CompuServe conference, "It was a wonderful idea, and I think a really compelling and relevant story to tell about a gay character." The story line marked a television "first," in that Ross was the first gay man on network television to adopt a child. The Gay & Lesbian Alliance Against Defamation lauded *Party of Five* for this milestone. Mitchell Anderson recalls that when he first read the script, he cried. "I remember thinking at that moment that if I never did another hour of television, I will have done something that I am incredibly proud of."

This episode also marks a milestone in the emotional development of the Salinger siblings according to co-creator Amy Lippman. At a 1995 event honoring the show, she explained why they chose to wait a full season before having any of their characters say "I love you" to one another. "It's really easy to have characters say 'I love you' to each other and to really wring some tears out of it. And in writing the show we put that statement in a few episodes and then Chris and I would look at each other and say 'not yet.' I think that was a good decision to make because when we did it, we did it with a lot more power and force—that we actually waited 22 episodes to have the two men of the show acknowledge what they feel for each other." Since it combined the tragedy of Jill's death with life-affirming events (Charlie and Kirsten's engagement, the adoption of the baby), Lippman calls "The Ides of March" the quintessential *Party of Five* episode.

chapter ten

Second Season (1995-96)

Second Season Regular Cast

Scott Wolf as Bailey Salinger
Matthew Fox as Charlie Salinger
Neve Campbell as Julia Salinger
Lacey Chabert as Claudia Salinger
Paula Devicq as Kirsten Bennett
Scott Grimes as Will McCorkle
Jennifer Love Hewitt as Sarah Reeves
Michael Goorjian as Justin Thompson
Brandon and Taylor Porter as Owen Salinger (9/95-11/95)
Steven and Andrew Cavarno as Owen Salinger (12/95-)

Second Season Technical Credits

Executive Producers: Amy Lippman and Christopher Keyser
Co-Executive Producers: Lisa Melamed, Mark B. Perry, Ken Topolsky
Producers: P. K. Simonds, Paul Marks
Co-Producer: Bruce J. Nachbar
Associate Producer: Valerie Joseph
Executive Consultant: Susannah Grant

Unit Production Manager: Paul Marks
Directors: See Episode Credits for Director of Each Individual Episode
1st Assistant Directors*: Eric Jewett, Vicki Jackson Lemay
2nd Assistant Directors*: Carla Brand Breitner, Violet Caranjian
Directors of Photography: Roy H. Wagner, Gary Huddleston (finale only)
Production Designers*: Steve Wolff, Bill Eigenbrodt
Editors*: Stephen Potter, Richard Freeman, Robert Frazen, David Dworetzky
Costume Designer: Scilla Andreen-Hernandez
Music Composer: Stephen Graziano
Music Supervision: John McCullough
Casting: Patrick Rush, Liberman/Hirschfield Casting
Camera Operators: Gary Huddleston, Steven H. Smith (finale only)
Gaffer: Brian Crane
Key Grip: Dale Alexander
Sound Mixers*: Steve Cantamessa, Gary Thomas
Script Supervisors*: Theresa Eubanks-Richland, Anne Nelville, Suzanne Gundlach, Joanna Yearsley, Jesse H. Long
Set Decorator: Marty Price
Property Master: Gregory R. Wolf
Makeup*: Anna D. Dryhurst, Emily Katz, Michelle Bari Ross
Hair Stylist: Doreen Schultz
Bullseye the Dog's Trainer: David McMillan
Original Casting: Mary V. Buck and Susan Edelman
Production Coordinator: Carol Kravetz
San Francisco Liaison: Jennifer Thomas
Location Manager*: Rosa-Lee Pierce, Donna Gross
Production Auditor*: Hilton Smith, Vince M. Rotonda
Transportation Captain*: Steve Salzman, Walt Riley
Assistants to Producers: Rick Draughon, Guinevere Shaw, Peter Wyse
Music Editor: Don Sanders
Sound Supervisor: Jeremy Gordon
Assistant Editors*: Merry Tigar, David Dworetzky, Dana Devorzon, Robert E. Seidenglanz II
Main Title Editor: Brian Dollenmayer

Construction Coordinator: Larry Libecap
Re-recording Mixers: Neil Brody, Gary Rogers, Tony D'Amico
* = different episodes

Second Season Overview

The second season opener introduces a new character, Sarah Reeves, an old friend of Julia who has spent the summer working at Salingers Restaurant and nursing a crush on Bailey. Michael Goorjian, who appeared in several first season episodes as Julia's boyfriend, Justin, is added to the opening credits as a series regular. Jeremy London takes over the recurring role of Griffin Holbrook, introduced in the first season finale. In December 1995, twins Andrew and Steven Cavarno take over the role of Owen from Brandon and Taylor Porter.

The series officially adopted a theme song in the second season. The BoDeans' "Closer to Free" was one of five songs that had been used for the opening sequence during the first season. The song, which was first released on the band's 1993 album, *Go Slow Down*, had never gotten much airplay until it was selected by *Party*'s producers as their theme. By March 1996, the song became a Top 20 radio hit that spawned a single and a music video featuring the *Party of Five* cast. The video was directed by *Party of Five* cinematographer Roy Wagner. Staged on the Salingers Restaurant set, the video features the cast dining at their usual table while the band plays.

In its second season, *Party of Five*'s plot lines focus less on the parents' deaths and more on the characters' relationships. Charlie and Kirsten prepare to marry, but when the day comes, Charlie can't go through with the wedding. Charlie, at 25, feeling overburdened by his responsibilities and resentful at having his entire life planned for him, balks, and Kirsten, after giving him a "now or never" ultimatum, walks. Charlie then reverts to his womanizing ways, engaging in a string of unfulfilling relationships. After a scorned TV producer exacts revenge on him by trying to shut down Salingers, Charlie realizes that he made a mistake by letting Kirsten go. In the finale, he wins her back, moments before she is set to marry another man.

In his senior year of high school, Bailey struggles to establish his own identity. Try as he might to distance himself from his family, Bai-

Publicity still from the second season of *Party of Five*. PHOTOFEST.

ley still feels responsible for taking care of them. He even feels guilty over Charlie's near infidelity on the night of his bachelor party. After spending his senior year trying to get into an Eastern college, he turns down his one opportunity in order to save the family restaurant.

Julia's romance with Justin is threatened by her growing attraction to Jill's brother, Griffin. Justin breaks up with her when he discovers she has been secretly seeing Griffin. Desperate to get away from an unhappy home, Griffin steals money from Salingers Restaurant and is sent away to military school as punishment. Julia and Justin drift back together, jumping into a sexual relationship that leads to tragic consequences when Julia gets pregnant. After deciding to have an abortion, Julia miscarries. Julia and Justin are unable to get their relationship back on track after the miscarriage, and they separate.

Twelve-year-old Claudia enters junior high school and feels out of place. When an injury forces her to temporarily give up the violin, she discovers that she enjoys being a "regular kid," not distinguished by her special talent. She gets involved with a bad girl at school, Jody, under whose influence Claudia experiments with smoking and drinking.

As *Party of Five* entered its second season, public awareness of the show was increasing, but the viewing audience, according to the Nielsen ratings, was still small. It no longer ranked in the bottom ten, due at least in part to the addition of two new networks' (UPN and WB) shows to the Nielsen race. With only a 13-episode commitment from the FOX network, *Party of Five* had a lot to prove.

Returning in its Wednesday night 9:00 time slot, *Party of Five* was positioned against the sitcoms *Grace Under Fire* and *The Naked Truth* on ABC, *Dateline* on NBC, and *Central Park West*, a new serial from *Melrose Place* creator Darren Starr, on CBS. Though it lagged far behind its ABC and NBC competition, *Party of Five* garnered higher ratings than the much-hyped *Central Park West*, which was replaced midway through the season by the Montel Williams drama *Matt Waters*. *Matt Waters* fared no better in the time slot, and was soon canceled.

Though viewership was increasing, *Party of Five* was still perceived as a show no one was watching. Amy Lippman said in an interview that she was getting tired of hearing her series referred to as "critically acclaimed but low-rated." The show took a jab from Jon Stewart, host of the *Billboard Music Awards*. The awards special, which aired Wednesday, December 6, 1995, pre-empted both *Beverly Hills 90210* and *Party of Five*. In his opening remarks, Stewart apologized to the millions of *90210* fans who would miss their favorite show that night. He then apologized to the fans of *Party of Five*, reading three names from a piece of paper.

Party of Five's surprise win for Best Drama Series at the Golden Globes in January 1996 (beating out such formidable competition as *ER*, *NYPD Blue*, and *Chicago Hope*) increased the series' visibility and gave the network an added incentive to stand by the show. The statuette brought a token of prestige to a network whose trophy case wasn't exactly full.

The addition of TV veteran Carroll O'Connor to the cast in a recurring role as Jacob Gordon, the kids' grandfather, provided a ratings boost. The episode that introduced his character received the series' second highest rating of the season. The remainder of the season saw a steady climb in ratings, and on February 29, FOX renewed the series for a full third season. Fans of the series could watch the season finale without wondering if it would be their last chance to *Party*. Cast and crew could go on hiatus without worrying about their show's future. In an interview with *USA Today*, Lacey Chabert said, "It felt great to say 'See you after the hiatus,' and being sure of it."

23. *"Ready or Not"*

Original Airdate: September 27, 1995   *NR/AS: 6.9/11
Writers: Amy Lippman and Christopher Keyser
Director: Peter O'Fallon
Guest Cast: Jeremy London (Griffin Holbrook), Sara Mornell
(Pamela Rush), Monica Creel (Holly Blanchard), Tim Halligan
(Patron at Salingers), Monet Mazur (Erica, Griffin's Girl-
friend), Stephanie Siemiller (Will's Cousin Sharon),
David Correia (Building Super)

Charlie and Kirsten's wedding plans are interrupted by the arrival of Charlie's old girlfriend Pamela, who claims that he fathered her four-year-old son, Spencer. Charlie balks at first, but eventually takes responsibility for Spencer and wants to be a part of his life, emotionally as well as financially. However, Pamela takes Charlie's money and runs.

Will plays matchmaker for Bailey, but it's too soon after Jill's death and Bailey isn't ready to date. He is oblivious to the fact that his friend Sarah is head over heels in love with him. Justin returns from a summer in Europe and Julia learns he spent much of his trip sightseeing with a female friend, Allison. Julia doesn't tell him that she spent her summer days getting to know Jill's brother, Griffin.

Notes: The beginning of the episode recaps what happened in the first season finale. Since the character of Griffin had been recast, some footage from the first season finale was reshot for this montage.

---

* NR stands for Nielsen Rating and AS stands for Audience Share. One ratings point equals 959,000 households, or 1% of the nation's 95.9 million TV-viewing homes in the 1995-96 season. "Share" is the percentage of television sets in use which are tuned in to a particular show.

24. *"Falsies"*

Original Airdate: October 4, 1995   NR/AS: 6.0/9
Writer: Mark B. Perry
Director: Ellen S. Pressman
Guest Cast: Jeremy London (Griffin Holbrook), Allison Smith
(Keri), Lorinne Dills Vozoff (Principal Stickley), Sara Mornell
(Pamela), Kymberly Kalil (Receptionist), Mari Weiss (Ms. Stemp-
son), Monet Mazur (Erica), Darla Haun (Stewardess), Phillip
Dawkins (Donald Gross)

Claudia feels out of place in junior high school, where the girls are
more developed physically than she. But she isn't ready for the kind of
attention she attracts when she stuffs her bra. Bailey tags along when
Will checks out an Eastern college. Far from home, Bailey invents a new
history for himself while romancing a pretty student. But Will spoils
things by revealing the truth of his recent tragedies. Bailey returns
home intent on improving his grades so that he can get accepted into
an out-of-state school where he can get a fresh start.

Julia and Justin take action when a new rule prohibits kissing in
school. They organize a protest and convince Principal Stickley to mod-
ify the rules. But when kissing is legal again, it's Griffin—not Justin—
whom Julia kisses. Charlie tracks down Pamela, who reveals that
Spencer isn't his son—she was desperate for the money and assumed
Charlie would pay her to get out of town. Seeing Charlie's disappointment, Kirsten wonders if he'll be happy with her, knowing she can
never have children. Charlie admits he wants children, but he wants to
be with Kirsten more. They decide to adopt Owen.

Familiar Faces: Allison Smith played the title role in *Annie* on Broadway (1980-82), and Jennie Lowell on *Kate and Allie* (CBS, 1984-89).

Notes: Lacey Chabert told MTV audiences on *Party of Five @ 5* that
one of her most embarrassing moments occurred during filming of this
episode. When Claudia decides to revert to her natural state, she enters
the girls' room full-chested and exits moments later, minus the padding.
She said that she had only a second in the stall to rip the silicone falsies
out of her bra and exit. During one take, she tossed one of the falsies
aside and it landed in the toilet. She recalled, "I come out of the stall, and
I'm rolling on the floor laughing, and the director is going, 'What happened, get back in there,' and I'm like, 'I can't, my boob fell in the toilet!'
I have to say, that's like the most embarrassing thing that's happened."

Awards: Mark B. Perry's script was nominated for a Writers Guild Award for Outstanding Achievement in Television, along with episodes of *Law & Order*, *Murder One*, *NYPD Blue*, and *The X-Files*. An *NYPD Blue* episode, "Girl Talk," nabbed the trophy.

25. "Dearly Beloved"

```
Original Airdate: October 18, 1995        NR/AS: 6.0/10
Writer: Lisa Melamed
Director: Michael Engler
Guest Cast: Jeremy London (Griffin Holbrook), Tim Conlon (Dud-
ley), Lance Guest (Mr. Peck), Venus DeMilo Thomas (Gail), Skye
McKenzie (Groom-to-Be), Curtis Anderson (Paul)
```

Kirsten is irritated by the family's interference in her wedding plans, so she and Charlie decide to run off to Reno and elope. The rest of the family is furious when they discover the couple's absence. Despite the happy couple's disappearance, Charlie's friend Dudley continues to plan their engagement party, calling it a casual reception.

To beef up his college transcripts, Bailey decides to run for class vice president. Sarah volunteers to be his campaign manager as a way to spend time with him. But Sarah does all the work and Bailey pays little attention, until she blurts out her real reason for helping him, "I'm in love with you, you jerk." Julia lies to Justin in order to spend time with Griffin. When both guys show up at Charlie and Kirsten's engagement party, Justin guesses the truth and demands that Julia tell Griffin to leave. When Julia refuses, Justin leaves instead.

Kirsten and Charlie arrive at the party and reveal they are still single. When the justice of the peace said, "dearly beloved," they realized they couldn't get married without the family present.

Highlights: A lachrymose Claudia explains why she is upset that Charlie and Kirsten have apparently eloped. "We're always together for the sad stuff," she says. "Just once, why couldn't we be together for something happy?"

26. "Have No Fear"

```
Original Airdate: October 25, 1995        NR/AS: 6.9/10
Writer: Melissa Gould
Director: Rodman Flender
Guest Cast: Jeremy London (Griffin Holbrook), Tom Mason (Joe
```

Mangus), Cari Shayne (Nina), Vicellous Reon Shannon (Andy Hughes), Bradford English (Coach), Esther Scott (Mrs. Hughes)

When Joe suffers a heart attack, Charlie takes over management of Salingers. The transition is hardly smooth: Joe has a tough time relinquishing control, and Charlie fears he won't live up to his father's reputation. Julia assumes Griffin will want a sexual relationship with her, but when he asks to sleep with her, it turns out he literally wants to sleep. He later reveals he doesn't want to be her first lover because he's not into big deals.

Bailey injures a teammate during football practice, and the boy may never walk again. Though the boy recovers, Bailey is haunted by the incident and what might have happened. Even though he has treated her badly, Sarah is there for Bailey when he needs comfort.

Notes: Director Rodman Flender is married to creator/executive producer Amy Lippman. Flender's directorial credits include the sci-fi/horror films *The Unborn* (1991) and *Leprechaun 2* (1994), as well as episodes of the TV series *Tales from the Crypt*, *Dark Skies*, and *Chicago Hope*.

27. *"Change Partners and Dance"*

Original Airdate: November 1, 1995   NR/AS: 6.3/10
Writer: Susannah Grant
Director: Ken Topolsky
Guest Cast: Jeremy London (Griffin Holbrook), Mitchell Anderson (Ross Werkman), Sam McMurray (Thomas), Bette Ford (Miss Corso), Julie Hayden (Ms. Grey), Steve Fitchpatrick (Rocky), David Fabrizio (Policeman), Christopher Maleki (Guy with Guitar), Philip Barney (Movie Patron), Scotty Morris (Singer)

Claudia breaks her arm while ice skating and Ross fears the injury may affect her future as a musician. Sarah is confused by Bailey's impulsive behavior until she realizes that he is trying to relive his relationship with Jill. She breaks off their relationship because she doesn't think he is over Jill's death yet.

Julia persuades Charlie to give Griffin a job at Salingers, but Griffin's lackadaisical attitude quickly gets him fired. Griffin resents Julia's attempts to change him, while Julia mistakes Griffin's inability to express emotion for indifference. A psychic's prediction sends Kirsten and Charlie to dance class, where Charlie's lack of rhythm leads to a fight about their future. Later, Julia explains to Charlie why a woman dreams of dancing at her wedding, and teaches him the steps their father once taught her.

Familiar Faces: Comedic actor Sam McMurray was a regular on *The Tracey Ullman Show* (FOX, 1987-90).

Notes: You might think that wearing an itchy cast for eight weeks of filming would have been a drag for Lacey Chabert. Actually, she loved it. She squealed with delight when she revealed the upcoming plot development to fans at a Viewers for Quality Television luncheon: "I get to break my arm! And I get to wear a cast for a really long time and everyone signed it. I got to go to the hospital to get four [casts] made, and it was like the most exciting day of my life!" She admitted, "I've always wanted to break something. My next big thing is crutches."

28. "Analogies"

Original Airdate: November 8, 1995   NR/AS: 7.7/12
Writers: Amy Lippman and Christopher Keyser
Director: Ellen S. Pressman
Guest Cast: Jeremy London (Griffin Holbrook), Kathleen Noone (Ellie Bennett), Nicholas Pryor (Gene Bennett), Stacy Galina (Maggie)

Kirsten's parents show up unexpectedly, and their visit gives Charlie an uncomfortable glimpse of what might lie ahead for him and Kirsten. He bristles when Ellie compares him to her husband, Gene, a dreamer who never gets to live out his dreams. Kirsten also resents being compared to her mother, a fussy perfectionist who always bursts her husband's bubble. As Kirsten insists they won't turn out like her parents, Charlie fears that getting married may have to mean giving up his dreams.

Julia tries to put an end to Claudia's bratty behavior toward Griffin. Yet, when Griffin and Claudia make friends and start spending time together, Julia gets angry. Griffin reveals that being with Claudia reminded him of what it was like when his little sister, Jill, was alive. Frustrated with his low SAT scores, Bailey decides to quit trying to get into a good school and settle for SF State, where "all you need to do is sign your name" to get in. However, when his pretty teacher, Maggie, offers to tutor him, Bailey decides to give it another try.

Familiar Faces: Kathleen Noone had long-running roles on the daytime drama *All My Children* (1977-89) and the nighttime soap, *Knots Landing* (CBS, 1990-93). Among Nicholas Pryor's many television credits is the recurring role of Chancellor Arnold on another FOX drama, *Beverly Hills 90210.*

29. "Where There's Smoke"

Original Airdate: November 15, 1995   NR/AS: 6.5/10
Writer: Mark B. Perry
Director: Daniel Attias
Guest Cast: Jeremy London (Griffin Holbrook), John M. Jackson (Major Holbrook), Richard Fancy (Sam Arborgast), Marla Sokoloff (Jody Lynch), Dale Raoul (Miss Bullock), Kate Zentall (Judge Faulkner), Monté Russell (Theo), Zina Bethune (Ballet Teacher), Mailon Rivera (Officer Stempski), Susan D. Moore (District Attorney), Bryan Rasmussen (Public Defender)

Charlie is suspected of arson after a fire breaks out at Salingers. The investigator believes that Charlie set the fire to claim the insurance money and offset the restaurant's recent losses. As circumstances mount that suggest he did it, even Kirsten begins to suspect Charlie is guilty. Charlie steadfastly maintains his innocence and, in the absence of proof, the insurance company gives him half of the settlement he's entitled to.

When $1,200 in cash is stolen from the restaurant, Julia suspects Griffin, who is desperate to get away from his abusive father. Her suspicions prove correct and Griffin is arrested for grand theft. Charlie refuses to help her get the charges dropped, so Julia turns to Major Holbrook. She pleads with him to stop taking his anger over Jill's death out on Griffin. The major enlists an Army lawyer to help with the case, and Griffin is sent to military school instead of prison. Before leaving, he tells Julia that he loves her, but he doesn't plan to write.

Bailey gives Will permission to date Sarah, but when he sees them together, he is jealous. Claudia meets a trouble-making classmate, Jody, who abuses Claudia's position in the attendance office and tempts her into smoking a cigarette.

Familiar Faces: Marla Sokoloff has had recurring roles on *3rd Rock from the Sun, Step by Step,* and *Full House.*

Familiar Places: The exteriors for Griffin's apartment were filmed in front of an apartment building located at 607-613 Burnside Avenue in Los Angeles.

Taking it all off

In the early days of *Party of Five*, programming executives at FOX thought that the show's lagging ratings might benefit by exposing some of the show's hidden assets, namely the studly physiques of its male leads, Matthew Fox and Scott Wolf. Amy Lippman revealed in a 1994 interview that she often received instruction from the network to have the actors appear oncamera shirtless. She said, "We have these very handsome boys on the show, and the note would come from the network, 'Play them without their shirt. Have them sorting laundry without a shirt on.' They feel it brings viewers, and I feel compromised by it. I think it is sensationalistic. And I have been on the set with these kids, and Scott Wolf, who works out all the time, is there without his shirt, and I think 'I hate myself, what have I done, how have I let this happen?'" She particularly objects when such exposure is gratuitous, and not intrinsic to the scene. "I don't mind doing it if you play a scene where someone's in the bathroom and he's just come out of the shower, and there's a line to get into the bathroom."

Whether for legitimate plot purposes or to appease network execs, the *Party* guys appear bare-chested in the following episodes:

Bailey:
"Good Sports" (9/26/94)
"Much Ado" (10/24/94)
"Change Partners and Dance" (11/1/95)
"Before and After" (2/21/96)
"Deal With It" (9/11/96)
"Gimme Shelter" (11/13/96)
"I Do" (11/27/96)
"Significant Others" (1/15/97)
"MYOB" (2/5/97)

Charlie:
"Homework" (9/19/94)
"Worth Waiting For" (10/3/94)
"It's Not Easy Being Green" (1/11/95)
"The Trouble With Charlie" (3/1/95)
"Where There's Smoke" (11/15/95)

30. "Best Laid Plans"

Original Airdate: November 22, 1995   NR/AS: 5.8/10
Writer: Lisa Melamed
Director: Rodman Flender
Guest Cast: Tim Conlon (Dudley), Julia Campbell (Monica), Angela
Dohrmann (Honey), Robin Thomas (Marshall Thompson), Robert Bauer
(Leo), Dean Cameron (Neil)
Special appearance by: Sophie B. Hawkins

As Charlie struggles to write his marriage vows, Dudley and Bailey organize his bachelor party. The party is a bust: the bachelors get trapped in an elevator, the stripper wins at strip poker, and Charlie never shows up. The groom-to-be spends the evening comforting a distraught woman who caught her husband cheating. Though tempted, Charlie turns down her invitation to spend the night, having realized that Kirsten is the only woman he wants. Kirsten's sister cancels their pre-wedding plans, and Claudia tries to fill in, but everything she plans goes awry.

Julia tries to patch up her friendship with Justin, but he isn't interested. They spend an uncomfortable evening together at a concert they had purchased tickets for while they were dating. Also at the concert is Justin's father, cozying up to a woman who is not Justin's mother. When he needs a friend to talk to about his father's infidelity, Justin turns to Julia. As the hours wind down to his wedding day and he is still filled with apprehension, Charlie decides to flip a coin to decide whether or not he should marry Kirsten.

Notes: Los Angeles deejays Rick Stacy and Leah Brandon (KYSR-FM Star 98.7) had cameos in this episode. Stacy ushered Julia to her seat, and Brandon played Mr. Thompson's date. The episode was tied into a radio contest sponsored by American Dairy Farmers, hence the placement of their slogan, "Got Milk?" into the episode. Sophie B. Hawkins performs "As I Lay Me Down" in the concert scene, which was filmed at the Hard Rock Cafe in San Francisco.

31. "The Wedding"

Original Airdate: December 13, 1995   NR/AS: 7.9/12
Writers: Amy Lippman and Christopher Keyser
Director: Steven Robman
Guest Cast: Tom Mason (Joe Mangus), Mitchell Anderson (Ross
Werkman), Tim Conlon (Dudley), Kathleen Noone (Ellie Bennett),

Nicholas Pryor (Gene Bennett), Philip Abrams (Photographer),
Suanne Spoke (Caterer), John Carlos Frey (Server)

On their wedding day, Charlie tells Kirsten he isn't ready to get married. He loves her, but he feels as though his entire life has been mapped out for him at age 25. Kirsten gives him an ultimatum—get married today or say good-bye forever. As they wait to find out if the wedding will take place, Julia and Justin kill time with a bottle of champagne and end up in bed together. Will steps aside when he realizes that Sarah and Bailey still have feelings for each other. Bailey and Sarah kiss. Faced with Kirsten's ultimatum, Charlie agrees to go through with the wedding, but then Kirsten is the one who calls it off. She is afraid that if they get married, Charlie will regret it. She gives Charlie's ring back and leaves for Chicago with her parents. While the others express their disappointment in Charlie for screwing things up with Kirsten, Bailey tells his brother he's on his side.

Notes: Though the vast majority of viewers were rooting for Charlie and Kirsten to make it down the aisle, the decision to split them up was inevitable from the writers' perspective. As staff writer and co-executive producer Lisa Melamed explained at a Museum

Charlie and Kirsten's ill-fated wedding. PHOTOFEST.

of Television & Radio seminar, "If Charlie and Kirsten are together and happily married, they are effectively the parents. And it really takes away from the struggle of the show."

Amy Lippman described Charlie's dilemma in a *Los Angeles Times* interview: "He lives in his father's house, takes care of his father's children. His life has been set for two years now, and he's thinking, 'How do I define my life? What responsibility do I have to myself? I've been responsible to kids almost over 30 episodes and I'm on the brink of this marriage and putting on the brakes.'"

Though the couple didn't wed, Paula Devicq remained in the opening credits as a regular cast member for the next four episodes, causing viewers to speculate that the breakup may have only been temporary.

Julia's alcohol-influenced decision to have sex with Justin began a plot line which would dominate the remainder of the season. When questioned how she felt about her character's actions, Neve Campbell replied that she was happy with the way the story was scripted. "I did not want Julia to be like Tori Spelling [on *Beverly Hills 90210*]—spend 13 episodes worrying [about going all the way]." She is glad that the characters are allowed to make mistakes and that they—and the audience—can learn from those mistakes.

32. *"Grand Delusions"*

Original Airdate: December 20, 1995   NR/AS: 7.0/11
Writer: Susannah Grant
Director: Ken Topolsky
Guest Cast: Brooke Langton (Courtney), Alyson Reed (Mrs. Reeves), Jonathan Hernandez (Enrico), Carol Bruce (Sarah's Grandmother), Robin Thomas (Marshall Thompson), Elizabeth Norment (Dr. Sullivan), Judy Kain (Woman on Airplane), Robert Covarrubias (Concierge), Walter D. Morris (Coffee Guy)

In the wake of the wedding-that-wasn't, Charlie decides to get away to think. He takes Claudia to Mexico on what would have been his honeymoon trip. Claudia is resentful and barely speaks to Charlie on the trip. While Charlie romances a beautiful tourist, Claudia finds a love of her own, Enrico, with whom she shares her first kiss.

Sarah discovers that she was adopted and begins to question who she is and where she belongs. Julia and Justin enjoy exploring their new-found sexuality, but they quickly learn that separating sex from emotion isn't as easy as they thought. They decide to date again, and agree to take things slowly.

Familiar Faces: Brooke Langton joined the cast of FOX's *Melrose Place* in 1996 as Samantha. Carol Bruce played Mama Carlson on *WKRP in Cincinnati* (1979-82).

Notes: Claudia's first kiss was Lacey Chabert's first real-life kiss, as well, and she was quite nervous about having to experience this milestone in front of a gaggle of cast and crew members. She told *TV Guide* how she tried to turn the situation to her advantage, telling her producers, "I'm looking for a boyfriend anyway, so just cast somebody cute." On *The Tonight Show with Jay Leno*, she told Jay that they filmed about 17 takes of the scene, adding, "My lips were chapped the next day, that's for sure."

33. *"Unfair Advantage"*

Original Airdate: January 3, 1996   NR/AS: 7.3/11
Writers: Mark B. Perry and Lisa Melamed
Director: Michael Engler
Guest Cast: Lance Guest (Mr. Peck), Julie Bowen (Shelly), Alyson Reed (Mrs. Reeves), Lorinne Dills Vozoff (Principal Stickley), Mark Metcalf (Mr. Reeves), Marla Sokoloff (Jody Lynch), Marco Sanchez (Parker), Charlie Heath (Jason), Alexandra Boyd (Ms. Esser), John Ducey (Ice Cream Guy), Robyn Johanna (Administrative Assistant)

Sarah goes on a spending spree, making Bailey uncomfortable and upsetting her parents, who feel Sarah is trying to punish them for not telling her she is adopted. Charlie makes a pass at a waitress, and when she turns him down, he cuts back her hours. When Julia's teacher makes a pass at her, she wonders if she is responsible. As Charlie explains to Julia that the teacher used his authority to take advantage of her, he realizes that he did the same thing to his waitress. Charlie apologizes to the waitress, and Julia decides to report her teacher.

Jody persuades Claudia to steal liquor and cigarettes from Salingers. When he finds them drunk in her tent, Charlie forbids Claudia to see Jody any more. With limited funds, Bailey struggles to find the perfect birthday gift for Sarah. His romantic gesture of naming a star after her captures Sarah's heart and impresses her more than any of her expensive gifts.

Familiar Faces: Lance Guest played Michael Romanov on *Life Goes*

On (ABC, 1992-93) and was a regular in the 12th season of *Knots Landing.* Marco Sanchez played Chief Miguel Ortiz on *seaQuest DSV* (NBC, 1993-95).

34. "Hold On Tight"

Original Airdate: January 10, 1996　　　　NR/AS: 6.9/11
Writer: Melissa Gould
Director: Oz Scott
Guest Cast: Mitchell Anderson (Ross Werkman), Marla Sokoloff (Jody Lynch), Chris Douridas (Record Store Clerk), Steven Basil (Waiter), Lonna Montrose (Movie Theatre Patron), Jack Hawkins (Usher)

Charlie is heartened when Kirsten calls saying she needs him, but she just needs his help with a tax problem. After their date with the IRS, they end up in bed together. But they soon realize that they are not ready to get back together, they are simply trying to hold on to the past. Bailey and Julia battle over who gets to move into the attic. Their rivalry escalates into war when Bailey encourages Sarah to audition for a singing gig Julia wanted, and Julia coaches Justin into interviewing for Bailey's dream job. When Julia learns that Bailey has been accepted into a college in the East, she realizes how much she will miss him, and she lets him have the attic room.

Claudia's cast comes off but she isn't eager to resume her violin lessons. She enjoyed being a normal kid, having a best friend and doing regular kid stuff. Despite the protests of Ross and her family, she quits her lessons, trades in her classical CDs for alternative music, and packs her violin away in the basement.

Highlights: The scene in which Bailey and Julia fight over the attic is reminiscent of the *Brady Bunch* episode in which Greg and Marcia have a similar dispute. Julia and Bailey are not amused when Sarah and Justin point out their Brady-like behavior.

Notes: Chris Douridas hosts *Morning Becomes Eclectic,* a popular radio show on KCRW-FM in Los Angeles.

The set for the interior of Kirsten's apartment was constructed inside the set used for Charlie's bedroom. The band Sarah joins, the Nielsens, was named after the Nielsen ratings.

35. "Poor Substitutes"

Original Airdate: January 17, 1996   NR/AS: 7.5/12
Writers: Amy Lippman and Christopher Keyser
Director: Davis Guggenheim
Guest Cast: Patricia Heaton (Robin), Poppy Montgomery (Allison),
Alyson Reed (Mrs. Reeves), Marietta DePrima (Nursery School
Teacher), Douglas Sills (Michael), Billy Burke (Gil), Alison
Martin (Woman), Whitney Taubman (Frannie)

Julia makes fast friends with Justin's visiting friend, Allison, but
Allison shocks Julia by revealing she'd like to be more than just friends.
Julia declines Allie's advances and makes matters worse by revealing
Allie's sexual preference to Justin. A stranger's comment prompts Sarah
to search for her birth mother. Bailey finds the woman first, but she
doesn't want to meet Sarah. Bailey lies to Sarah to protect her feelings
and Sarah decides to stop looking.

Claudia learns that Kirsten is dating someone new, and contrives to
get her back together with Charlie. When that fails, she agrees to stay out
of Kirsten's personal life. Then she learns that Kirsten's new boyfriend
has a young daughter, and she fears Kirsten is trying to replace her.
Kirsten tearfully explains that she has to move on and find someone else
to love, and if she finds someone with kids, so much the better.

Highlights: Charlie's efforts to potty train Owen provide some of the
series' most hilarious moments.

Familiar Faces: Patricia Heaton starred in the sitcom *Room for Two*
(ABC, 1992-93), opposite Linda Lavin, and plays Ray Romano's wife on
the CBS sitcom *Everybody Loves Raymond* (1996-). Australian-born
Poppy Montgomery dropped her accent to play San Franciscan Jennifer
Lukens on ABC's *Relativity* (1996-97).

Notes: In an interview with *Genre* magazine, Neve Campbell said
that she would not have shared Julia's uneasy reaction to Allison's
admission that she's a lesbian. "It was actually kind of weird for me to
flip out about it. I felt like slapping Julia and saying, 'Relax!' Actually,
one of my girlfriends came out after she and I had been friends for a
couple of years. And it was really funny because she was so nervous
about telling me, and when she told me I was like, 'O.K., you got a beer?
It doesn't change who you are to me.'"

36. "Strange Bedfellows"

Original Airdate: January 24, 1996   NR/AS: 6.5/10
Writer: Mark B. Perry
Director: Steven Robman
Regular Cast Changes: Paula Devicq is no longer featured in the opening credits
Guest Cast: Jane Kaczmarek (Helene Thompson), Bess Meyer (Emily Schrader), Robin Thomas (Marshall Thompson), Alanna Ubach (Gina), Marla Sokoloff (Jody Lynch), Daniel Hagen (Mr. Trimble), Dan Klass (Bob), Dean Lemont (Tony)

Justin's parents discover that he and Julia are sleeping together and lecture them about the possible consequences. Mrs. Thompson knows all too well about unplanned pregnancies, having just learned that she is expecting unexpectedly. Justin and Julia don't think such a thing could happen to them, since they always practice safe sex.

Charlie is called to the school when Claudia is caught smoking and he becomes smitten by Claudia's teacher, Miss Schrader. Claudia begs Charlie to back off, and offers him a deal: she won't smoke, if he won't date her teacher. Charlie breaks the deal and Claudia comes to realize that if her brother is keeping the teacher happy, math class could get easier.

Bailey and Sarah can't stand Will's new girlfriend, Gina. Will dumps Gina, on Bailey's advice, then regrets his mistake and tells Bailey to butt out. Will wins Gina back, and Sarah and Bailey try to make her part of their circle.

Familiar Faces: Will's gabby girlfriend is played by Alanna Ubach, who plays Josie on the CBS Saturday morning show, *Beakman's World.* Ubach also appeared along with Jennifer Love Hewitt and Whoopi Goldberg in *Sister Act II: Back in the Habit* (1993).

Notes: One of the songs used as background music in this episode is "Saturday Night" by cast member Scott Grimes' band, Scott Grimes and the Misdemeanors.

37. "Benefactors"

Original Airdate: January 31, 1996   NR/AS: 7.8/12
Writer: Susannah Grant
Director: Daniel Attias
Guest Cast: Carroll O'Connor (Jacob "Jake" Gordon), Brenda Strong (Kathleen Eisley), Bess Meyer (Emily Schrader), Richard

Speight, Jr. (Miller West), Daniel Hagen (Mr. Trimble), Michael Mantell (Mr. Rosenthal), Dan Cashman (Martin)

Bailey is stunned when he learns that he has been selected to receive a full college scholarship from a mysterious donor, Garrett Williams. After meeting his benefactor, Bailey deduces that the man is really his grandfather, Jacob Gordon. Thirty years after abandoning his daughter, Jake returns to San Francisco and discovers that she had died, leaving five orphans behind. Jake wants to help them financially, but doesn't want the responsibility of the kids. He asks Bailey to keep his secret, but Bailey refuses to lie to his siblings.

Charlie tires of Emily's "let's-take-things-slow" approach and jumps into bed with Kathleen, an attractive TV producer. Claudia discovers Charlie cheated on her teacher and her only concern is how it will affect her math grade. A nerdy classmate tutors Julia in computer class in exchange for a date. When she passes her test, she reluctantly holds up her end of the bargain. Her date with Miller turns out to be more fun than she expected. As the family sits down to dinner at Salingers, Jake approaches their table and introduces himself as their grandfather.

Familiar Faces: Brenda Strong appeared in a few memorable episodes of *Seinfeld* as Sue Ellen Mishke, aka "The Bra Lady."

38. *"Comings and Goings"*

Original Airdate: February 7, 1996   NR/AS: 8.2/13
Teleplay: Lisa Melamed
Story: Melissa Gould
Director: Ken Topolsky
Guest Cast: Carroll O'Connor (Jacob Gordon), Patricia Heaton (Robin), Brenda Strong (Kathleen Eisley), Bess Meyer (Emily Schrader), Richmond Arquette (Salesman), Walter D. Morris (Coffee Guy)

Claudia is excited to have her grandfather in her life, but Julia does not trust him. After Claudia invites Jake to move in, Julia sends him away. Later, Julia has a change of heart. Though she believes her mother never would have forgiven Jake for abandoning her, she would have wanted him to know his grandchildren. Jake moves into Bailey's old room.

Charlie juggles relationships with two women at once, and finds himself in a sticky situation when they come face to face. Emily breaks

Julia is torn between her feelings for Justin (Michael Goorjian, left) and Griffin (Jeremy London, right) in "Valentine's Day." EVERETT COLLECTION.

up with Charlie, but Kathleen persuades him to give up his little black book and commit to a more serious relationship.

Sarah's fears of abandonment are compounded when she learns that Bailey is planning to go to college in Boston and her biological mother, Robin, is leaving on a six-month tour, days after coming back into her life. Bailey decides to apply to a state college to remain near Sarah, but she tears up his application and gives him her blessings to go to Boston.

39. "Valentine's Day"

Original Airdate: February 14, 1996   NR/AS: 6.9/11
Writer: P. K. Simonds
Director: David Semel
Guest Cast: Jeremy London (Griffin Holbrook), Brenda Strong (Kathleen Eisley), Ivan Sergei (Sean), Aaron Lustig (Terrell)

Sarah is not impressed by Bailey's idea of a romantic Valentine's date—the monster truck show. She'd rather spend time with her worldly neighbor, Sean. Jealous Bailey assumes that Sean's love poems were written for Sarah and punches him, further illustrating to Sarah that Bailey has a misguided idea of romance.

Kathleen enlists a celebrated chef to revamp Salingers. As she helps

Charlie to become more success-oriented, her own career takes a nose dive. She becomes dependent on Charlie, who balks when she brings up the L-word.

Julia is surprised by Griffin's sudden reappearance. He is on a three-day leave from military school and plans to run away. Against Justin's objections, Julia agrees to help him. However, when he realizes that running away would mean he'd never see Julia again, Griffin decides to go back to school. Julia climbs in Justin's bedroom window at dawn and breaks some shocking news—she's pregnant.

Familiar Faces: Aaron Lustig joined the cast of *The Young and the Restless* in 1996 as Dr. Tim Reid, earning a 1997 Emmy nomination as Outstanding Supporting Actor in a Daytime Drama.

40. *"Before and After"*

Original Airdate: February 21, 1996   NR/AS: 8.3/13
Writers: Amy Lippman and Christopher Keyser
Director: Steven Robman
Guest Cast: Carroll O'Connor (Jacob Gordon), Elizabeth Norment (Doctor), Dee Freeman (Mom), Edith Varon (Clinician), Susanne Wright (Girl)

Julia's pregnancy is confirmed. She makes an appointment to have an abortion without discussing it with Justin. But when her name is called, she leaves the clinic, realizing she needs more time to consider her options. As Julia agonizes over her decision, she shuts out Justin, who is angry that no one is taking his feelings into consideration. He offers to marry Julia, but she decides that the only right decision for her is to terminate the pregnancy.

Bailey and Sarah plan to have sex for the first time, but Sarah has second thoughts after learning of Julia's predicament. When Julia needs a friend to talk to, Sarah says she can't help her because she does not agree with her decision. Claudia also has difficulty accepting Julia's choice and asks her sister to explain how abortion is different than murder. Hours before she is scheduled to have an abortion, Julia suffers a miscarriage. Even though the decision was taken out of her hands, Julia knows that she will suffer the consequences for a long time.

Highlights: Bailey and Sarah's anticipation of their first sexual encounter provided some humorous exchanges. When Sarah asks if he has "protection," Bailey says, "Got it covered. So to speak."

Awards: The Environmental Media Association awarded *Party of Five* its Turner Prize for this episode. The Turner Prize is given each year in recognition of the television show that best deals with the issue of population growth. This episode was also nominated for a Humanitas Prize.

Notes: As originally scripted, this episode concluded with Julia going through with the abortion. It was a bold decision, and one which Keyser and Lippman discussed with Neve Campbell weeks before the script was written. Neve was excited about the opportunity to portray the issue. The network was less delighted about the prospect. Fearing they would lose advertisers, FOX executives told Keyser and Lippman that they could not go forward with Julia's abortion. FOX's decree should not have come as a surprise. In 1994, the network excised a kiss between two gay man on *Melrose Place* because of pressure from advertisers. When criticized for the move, FOX entertainment president Sandy Grushow countered, "The bottom line is that we're a business. It's show business, but it's still a business, and we just couldn't afford to take that kind of financial hit."

Keyser and Lippman were filming "Valentine's Day" when they got the call from the network saying that they could not go through with the plot line of Julia's abortion. As they had not yet filmed the scene in which Julia tells Justin she's pregnant, they considered dumping the story altogether. After much debate, they proceeded with a revised story, in which Julia suffers a miscarriage.

Keyser admits that having Julia miscarry was a cop out, but they decided that the story would stimulate discussion and debate. Neve was extremely upset when she heard about the plot revisions. She says, "Miscarriage was an easy way out. I thought it was just silly."

Keyser and Lippman gave the network one stipulation: that Julia clearly state that she would have had an abortion. Lippman says, "There was no way we would have gone ahead with that story had she not definitively said 'this would have been the right choice for me.' And she does say it."

But a few hours after they filmed the scene in which Julia makes that declaration, they received another call from the network asking them to re-shoot the line. They wanted Julia to say, "I *think* I would have done it," a revision which Lippman calls "a horrible, horrible copout." Neve Campbell was so troubled by the network's edict that she sabotaged her own performance on the retakes, as she later revealed to audiences at a Museum of Television & Radio event in Los Angeles. Exhausted from performing the emotionally draining scenes, she found it difficult to get the emotion back to the same level as when the scene was originally shot. She said that she made a subconscious decision not to match her performance from the other takes, so that the continuity of the scene would be off and they would not be able to use the new footage.

At the same Museum event, Amy Lippman revealed that although they shot the line both ways, they only put the original version on the reel they sent to the network, so that FOX would think they didn't have a choice. Though Julia was not allowed to become the first regular character on a prime-time drama to have an abortion, her intentions were very clear.

41. "Altered States"

Original Airdate: February 28, 1996   NR/AS: 7.0/11
Writer: Susannah Grant
Director: Michael Engler
Guest Cast: Jeremy London (Griffin Holbrook), Brenda Strong (Kathleen Eisley), Danny Masterson (Matt), Robin Polk (Agent), Christopher Jon Jaynes (Guy #1), Scott Ferguson (Guy #2)

Still troubled by her miscarriage, Julia isn't ready to return to school. Lying to Justin and her family, she flies to New Orleans to see Griffin. Having made mistakes he wishes he could undo, Griffin understands Julia's feelings and helps her cope with her pain. When she returns, Justin discovers that she lied but doesn't press her about where she was because he can see that it helped her.

Bailey is bothered by Sarah's sexy new stage persona. When he gets her band a gig at Salingers, he tries to dictate how Sarah should dress and what she should sing. Sarah resents his judgmental attitude. Bailey doesn't want Sarah to change, but she explains that, at 16, she's just finding herself.

Feeling pressured by Kathleen for a commitment, Charlie ends their relationship. But when she takes an overdose of pills, he rushes to her side. He decides to give the relationship another chance.

Familiar Places: The David Lean building on the Sony studio lot in Culver City was used for the exterior shots of Kathleen's apartment building.

42. "Happily Ever After"

Original Airdate: March 20, 1996   NR/AS: 6.9/11
Teleplay: P. K. Simonds and Melissa Gould
Story: Lisa Melamed
Director: Rodman Flender
Guest Cast: Carroll O'Connor (Jacob Gordon), Brenda Strong
(Kathleen Eisley), Susan Egan (Lauren Gordon), Aaron Lustig
(Terrell), Woody L. Bryant (Waiter)

Justin is frustrated by Julia's apparent indifference to their relationship. He writes a folk story that parallels their difficulties, except the fable ends happily, while Julia and Justin can't seem to find their way back to each other.

Bailey learns that Jake has a grown daughter from another marriage. Bailey fears that Jake will repeat his past pattern of abandoning his loved ones. He asks Jake to move out before Claudia grows too attached to him. Jake admits that he has a penchant for leaving when things get tough. He moves on, but promises to keep in touch with the kids.

Kathleen wins a local news award and, in her televised acceptance speech, says, "Charlie, I love you." Not wanting to hurt her feelings, Charlie tells Kathleen that he and Kirsten are reuniting. Kathleen learns that Charlie lied and decides to retaliate—by buying the building that Salingers Restaurant is in and terminating the lease.

43. "Spring Breaks, Parts 1 & 2"

Original Airdate: March 27, 1996 [two hours]   NR/AS: 8.0/13
Writers: Mark B. Perry (Part 1), Amy Lippman and Christopher
Keyser (Part 2)
Directors: Daniel Attias (Part 1), Steven Robman (Part 2)
Guest Cast: Carroll O'Connor (Jacob Gordon), Paula Devicq
(Kirsten Bennett), Tom Mason (Joe Mangus), Mitchell Anderson
(Ross Werkman), Brenda Strong (Kathleen Eisley), Danny Masterson
(Matt), Marla Sokoloff (Jody Lynch), Gabriel Olds (Ian Mathers),
Douglas Sills (Michael), Kate Hudson (Corey), Freda Foh Shen
(Miss Minor), Christopher Miranda (Derrick), Ramsay Midwood
(Mugger), J. Skylar Testa (Jim Trowell), Niecy Nash (Nurse),
Aaron Michael Metchik (Othello), Thomas Wagner (Bartender)

When they learn that Salingers will close down due to Charlie's romantic blunder with Kathleen, his siblings are furious. Joe returns but is unable to stop the sale of the building. Charlie's desperation leads him first to a bar, then a jail cell, then to Kirsten's doorstep. Losing everything else made him realize that he wants her back. Kirsten says it's too late, she is marrying someone else.

Bailey is obsessed with Sarah's safety after she is mugged. Sarah feels smothered and begs for some space, which Bailey gives her amply by breaking up with her. Julia and Justin drift further and further apart. While Justin spends time with a pretty co-worker, Julia finds herself attracted to a classmate in her photography class. Though they still love each other, Julia and Justin can't get past what happened and they decide to end their relationship. Boy-crazy Jody has little time for Claudia, who realizes that she may have given up too much when she quit the violin.

Desperate to save Salingers, Charlie asks for Jake's help. Jake tells Bailey he can either save the restaurant or pay Bailey's tuition. Bailey struggles with the decision, but in the end decides to save the family restaurant. He will attend a state college so he can be near his family and Sarah. As the family celebrates this good news, they get more— Kirsten and Charlie announce they are getting back together.

Notes: Kate Hudson is actress Goldie Hawn's daughter from her marriage to singer Bill Hudson.

"Spring Breaks" was originally planned as two separate episodes, until the producers learned that the network planned to pre-empt the series for a few weeks in between the two. Since the episodes were closely tied together, the producers were insistent that they air no more than one week apart, so viewers would not forget what had happened. A creative solution was reached when it was decided to conjoin the episodes and air them as the series' first two-hour episode.

The network sent advance copies of this episode to reviewers bundled with a package of tissues. Home viewers had to provide their own hankies.

Matthew Fox admits that his character has made a lot of mistakes, but he doesn't think Charlie is to blame for the Kathleen incident. He told *Entertainment Weekly*, "The whole thing with him losing the restaurant was in no way his fault! He simply started bedding a woman who was a totally vindictive bitch!"

A matter of opinion...

Which of the critics backed *Party of Five* from the beginning and which changed their opinion of the series over the years? The following chart gathers review excerpts from four major periodicals, year by year.

	Season One (1994-95)	Season Two (1995-96)	Season Three (1996-97)
Hollywood Reporter	"Aside from a talented cast of performers, *Party of Five* fails to deliver much in the way of interest."	"This FOX signature show continues its appeal with an opening surprise that will grab fans and give them a shaking up."	"The excellent script for this season debut centers around issues of misconduct, forgiveness and loyalty."
New York Daily News	"*Party of Five* comes up a bit short... as parties go, this one is a little too upfront with its moralizing."	"With hackneyed, predictable plot developments and woefully stunted acting performances... *Party of Five* is little more than a teeny-bopping soap opera."	"If *90210* is marshmallow fluff, and *Melrose Place* is pure cream puff, *Party of Five* is the one substantive meal on the [FOX] menu."

	Season One (1994-95)	**Season Two** (1995-96)	**Season Three** (1996-97)
TV Guide	"This is a well-made series built on an awful premise...I still don't like the idea behind *Party*—which makes it all the more amazing that I find myself liking the show."	"This beauti-fully written show offers no pronounce-ments, only conversa-tions—the meandering, inconclusive things real peo-ple say to each other."	"While most nighttime soaps involve sex and scan-dal, *Party of Five* has won a loyal following with its emo-tional story-lines."
USA Today	"*Party of Five* is recommended to any emotional masochist looking for a multiple hanky good cry."	"Week to week, *Party of Five* manages a rare trick: keeping alive the dying tradition of first-rate con-temporary family drama while doling out sexy soap opera with sub-stance."	"With its poignant storylines beautifully played by a poster-perfect cast, this show transforms soap-opera contrivances into deeply felt quality drama."

chapter eleven

Third Season (1996-97)

Third Season Regular Cast

Scott Wolf as Bailey Salinger

Matthew Fox as Charlie Salinger

Neve Campbell as Julia Salinger

Lacey Chabert as Claudia Salinger

Jennifer Love Hewitt as Sarah Reeves

Steven and Andrew Cavarno as Owen Salinger

Alexondra Lee as Callie Martel*

(*featured in the opening credits from 11/6/96 to 3/19/97)

Third Season Technical Credits

Executive Producers: Amy Lippman and Christopher Keyser

Co-Executive Producers: Lisa Melamed, Mark B. Perry, Ken Topolsky

Producers: Paul Marks, Steven Robman

Consulting Producer: Susannah Grant

Supervising Producers: Michael Engler, P. K. Simonds

Co-Producer: Bruce J. Nachbar

Associate Producer: Valerie Joseph

Executive Story Editor: Catherine Butterfield

Unit Production Manager: Paul Marks

Directors: See Episode Credits for Director of Each Individual Episode

1st Assistant Directors*: Eric Jewett, Janet Knutsen, Vicki Jackson Lemay, Jules Lichtman
2nd Assistant Directors*: Bob Acosta, David Darmour, Michael Pendell, Kim Shulman
Director of Photography: Charlie Lieberman
Production Designer: Bill Eigenbrodt
Editors*: David Dworetzky, Richard Freeman, Stephen Potter, Merry Tigar
Costume Designer: Scilla Andreen-Hernandez
Music Composers*: Stephen Graziano, Christopher Klatman, Danny Lux
End Credit Music: Stephen Graziano
Music Supervision: John McCullough
Casting: Patrick Rush, Liberman/Hirschfield Casting
Camera Operator: Steven H. Smith
Gaffer: Brian Crane
Key Grip: John Hatchitt
Sound Mixers*: Steve Cantamessa, James LaRue
Script Supervisors*: Theresa Eubanks-Richland, Suzanne Gundlach, Carol Banker
Set Decorator: Marty Price
Property Master: Gregory R. Wolf
Makeup*: Nadia DiPaolo, Michelle Bari Ross
Hair Stylists*: Doreen Schultz, Patricia Vecchio
Bullseye the Dog's Trainer: David McMillan
Original Casting: Mary V. Buck and Susan Edelman
Production Coordinator: Carol Kravetz
Location Managers*: Donna Gross, Katherine Kallis
San Francisco Liaison: Jennifer Thomas
Production Auditor: Vince M. Rotonda
Transportation Captain: Steven Salzman
Assistants to Producers: Rick Draughon, Debbie Fisher, Guinevere Shaw, Peter Wyse, Kerry Derzius, Scot Abrahamson
Music Editor: Don Sanders
Sound Supervisors*: Jeremy Gordon, Rich Tavtigian
Assistant Editors*: Merry Tigar, Dana Devorzon, Rob Seidenglanz II
Main Title Editor: Brian Dollenmayer
Construction Coordinator: Larry Libecap

Re-recording Mixers: Neil Brody, Gary Rogers, Tony D'Amico, Michael Dilman, Carlos deLarios, Bill Freesh

* = different episodes

Third Season Overview

The third season brought new women into the lives of the Salinger men. Alexandra Lee joined the cast as Callie, Bailey's college roommate, and Tamara Taylor played Grace Wilcox, a black woman who works for the Harvest Program in San Francisco, gathering food for the homeless. Grace and Charlie clash when she assumes he is from a privileged background and never had to struggle. Eventually, they patch up their differences and begin dating. Scott Grimes and Michael Goorjian were no longer featured in the opening credits, but both made a few appearances during the TV year.

Charlie and Kirsten are living together at the start of the season, to the dismay of her disapproving parents. They have no plans to wed but have realized that they belong together. After Kirsten suffers a major career setback, she falls into a deep depression and Charlie learns that it's not the first time—after he called off their wedding she was treated for clinical depression. As he watches Kirsten's mental condition deteriorate, Charlie is powerless to help her and he lets her parents take her home to Chicago. After an unsuccessful attempt to win her back, Charlie moves on with his life and begins dating Grace.

Having spent her summer interning at a San Francisco publishing house, Julia enters her senior year of high school already preparing for college. But when Stanford, her first-choice school—and her mother's alma mater—grants her an early acceptance, she balks, suddenly unsure of her goals. The once practical-minded Julia questions what she wants out of life and decides she is content to drift rather than follow a predetermined plan. Creator Amy Lippman describes Julia's behavior as "essentially a mid-life crisis that happened in her late adolescence, as she questions the path that she's on."

Griffin re-enters Julia's life twice during the TV year. The first time, she is troubled by his lack of direction in life and he leaves town to make something of himself. When he returns, she is the one who wants to be carefree, while he wants to settle down and be responsible. In the

The Salingers (minus Owen) from the third season of *Party of Five*. PHOTOFEST.

interim, Julia also dates Cooper, a college man who couldn't accept her decision not to have sex, and Sam, a roofer who was seven years her senior. In the season finale, recently reunited Julia and Griffin sneak off to Nevada and get married.

Bailey starts his freshman year at state college. Hoping to distance himself from his family, he moves out of the house and into an apartment, which he shares with Callie, a free-spirited older woman with whom he eventually has an affair. Bailey spends more time drinking than studying, but while he insists he is just indulging in normal college partying, those around him can tell that he has a drinking problem. He refuses to accept his family's help and pushes everyone away, until an accident in which he nearly kills Sarah forces him to accept responsibility for his actions.

Hints of Bailey's emerging drinking problem appear early in the season, and the story line unfolds very slowly during the year's run—an unusual approach for series television. In a review of "Intervention" (2/19/97), in which Bailey's family confronts him about his alcoholism, *Chicago Tribune* reviewer Steve Johnson wrote, "On its own, this is a superb hour of TV, but it is especially special for the way the series has respected its audience by laying the groundwork throughout the season, instead of just sticking a beer in the character's hand a couple of episodes prior, and by not wrapping a pretty bow around the problem once it is confronted." Amy Lippman told journalist Mike Duffy, "We've tried to be very true to the progression of alcoholism in his life, so that you don't see it emerge in a single episode." In fact, seeds of Bailey's behavior can be found as far back as the first season finale, "The Ides of March" (3/15/95), in which Bailey deals with Jill's death by getting drunk, driving while intoxicated, and trying to push everyone who cares about him away.

Scott Wolf explained his character's metamorphosis from the family caretaker to the one who needs to be taken care of in a *New York Daily News* interview: "He is a good, kind soul who, when given the option of trying to find an identity for himself, chooses to be the person who would take care of everyone. What is happening now is that the pressures and the neglect of himself for the past couple years are catching up with him." He was thrilled that instead of letting his character stagnate, the producers chose to take him in this unexpected direction. He said, "There's only so long you can look at one dynamic of a human being and have it stay interesting. And the great thing about what they do with all of our characters is move us around. Just when you can predict this is the guy you can count on and this is the guy who's going to screw it up, they swap."

Indeed, Charlie, the guy who could be counted on to screw things up during the series' previous two seasons, emerges as the most responsible member of the family this year. When he realizes that his girlfriend, Grace, doesn't want to have children of her own, and doesn't want to nurture a relationship with Claudia or Owen, he makes the difficult decision to end the relationship.

Party of Five began its third season early. In an effort to drum up ratings, FOX premiered it in August, while most other shows were still airing reruns. The show returned in its Wednesday night slot, positioned against *Grace Under Fire* and *The Drew Carey Show* on ABC, movies on NBC, special programming on CBS, *Star Trek: Voyager* on UPN, and *The Wayans*

Brothers and *The Jamie Foxx Show* on WB. The first half of the season saw a steady climb in the ratings, particularly among the 18-to-34 age group.

As the season progressed, the series received more press coverage than ever, with cover stories in *People* and *Entertainment Weekly* helping to build the buzz. When her feature film *Scream* topped box office charts, Neve Campbell became the series' new breakout star. She hosted *Mad TV* and *Saturday Night Live* and was featured on several magazine covers, including *TV Guide*.

In February 1997, FOX launched a $15 million promotional campaign, with sponsors Dr. Pepper and Express clothing stores. In the most elaborate advertising campaign in the network's history, the show was touted on 110 million soda containers, with a blizzard of print and broadcast ads supporting it. The promotion offered viewers a chance to win *Party of Five* merchandise, trips to Hollywood, and even a Jeep.

The increased publicity and promotion paid off when the show's ratings increased dramatically, as Bailey's alcoholism took center stage. "Intervention" (2/19/97) garnered an 8.9 rating, the highest in the series' history, until the following week, when "Hitting Bottom" (2/26/97) beat it with a 9.6. In an interview on CNN, Chris Keyser said, "We're getting like a million more people watching every week. It's been remarkable." The show celebrated another milestone when the season finale ranked in the week's top 30 rated programs for the first time.

Not surprisingly, FOX renewed the series in March 1997, ordering a full 22 episodes for the fourth season.

An end of season tally placed *Party of Five* 83rd out of 157 shows based on average ratings for the 1996-97 season. Nestled snugly in the middle of a listing that ranged from *ER* (#1) to *Savannah* (#157), *Party of Five* posed no immediate threat to *Friends* (#3), but it ranked higher than such popular shows as *Dave's World* (#93), *NewsRadio* (#95), *Murder One* (#117), and *Married With Children* (#115), and wasn't too far behind FOX's soapy staples, *Melrose Place* (#66) and *Beverly Hills 90210* (#64).

44. "Summer Fun, Summer Not"

Original Airdate: August 21, 1996   *NR/AS: 6.9/12
Writers: Amy Lippman and Christopher Keyser
Director: Steven Robman
Guest Cast: Paula Devicq (Kirsten Bennett), Scott Grimes (Will McCorkle), Jeremy London (Griffin Holbrook), Kathleen Noone

(Ellie Bennett), Alanna Ubach (Gina), Rider Strong (Byron), Dennis Fimple (Mechanic)

Bailey plans a guys-only "rite of passage" road trip to Mexico, but Will invites Sarah and Gina, who don't share Bailey's vision of adventure. The trip goes from bad to worse when Bailey's Jeep is stolen. Will eventually discovers that what's bugging Bailey is not the disastrous trip, but that Will is leaving for college and Bailey is staying behind.

Kirsten's mother shows up on the Salingers' doorstep with shocking news: her marriage is ending because of an affair she had eight years ago. Kirsten is angry and unforgiving, but Charlie lends a sympathetic ear to Ellie, who eventually comes to understand why Kirsten loves him.

Julia is surprised to run into Griffin, who is in town on shore leave from the merchant marines. She wants to resume their relationship, but Griffin keeps his distance. Eventually he reveals that he is afraid of screwing things up, now that there are no other obstacles in their way. Nonetheless, he decides to stay in town to be with Julia.

Claudia returns from summer camp with tales of her new boyfriend, Byron. The others assume that Claudia is making it all up, until Byron shows up on their doorstep.

Familiar Faces: Teen heartthrob Rider Strong stars as Shawn on the ABC series *Boy Meets World.* Though this wasn't her first screen kiss (see "Grand Delusions," 12/20/95), Lacey admits she was still nervous about kissing Rider. Coincidentally, both Rider and Lacey got their start in show business at age nine, in the musical *Les Miserables.* Lacey played Cosette on Broadway, while Rider played Gavroche in a San Francisco production.

45. "Going, Going, Gone"

Original Airdate: August 28, 1996   NR/AS: 7.0/12

Writers: Mark B. Perry and P. K. Simonds

Director: Michael Engler

Guest Cast: Paula Devicq (Kirsten Bennett), Scott Grimes (Will

---

* NR stands for Nielsen Rating and AS stands for Audience Share. One ratings point equals 970,000 households, or 1 percent of the nation's 97 million TV-viewing homes in the 1996-97 season. "Share" is the percentage of television sets in use which are tuned in to a particular show.

McCorkle), Jeremy London (Griffin Holbrook), Rider Strong
(Byron), Peter Simmons (Tucker), Dennis Lipscomb (Mr. Conklin)

Kirsten gets a fabulous job offer at Cal State Monterey. She accepts
the position, despite the fact that the long hours and commute mean
that she and Charlie will have less time together. Charlie doesn't like the
arrangement, but Kirsten doesn't want to sacrifice the opportunity to
advance her career.

Bailey's last days with Will are strained by the presence of Tucker,
Will's new college roommate, whom Bailey dislikes. Feeling that everyone is moving on but him, Bailey decides to move out of the house.

Claudia is heartbroken when her new boyfriend, Byron, develops a
crush on Julia. Julia, meanwhile, is frustrated at Griffin's irresponsible
behavior and lack of goals for the future. Griffin leaves town to rejoin
his ship, but promises to come back when he has more to offer her.

Notes: Jennifer Love Hewitt's song, "No Ordinary Love," from her
album *Jennifer Love Hewitt* (Atlantic Records, 1996), plays in the background of a scene between Julia, Claudia, and Byron.

46. "Short Cuts"

Original Airdate: September 4, 1996   NR/AS: 5.9/9
Writer: Lisa Melamed
Director: Ellen S. Pressman
Guest Cast: Paula Devicq (Kirsten Bennett), Michael Goorjian
(Justin Thompson), Harold Pruett (Cooper), Bruce French
(Dr. Kass), Alan Wilder (Mr. Shiffer)

On his first day of college, Bailey meets Cooper, a student bent on
sailing through college without sweat or effort. Bailey at first refuses
Cooper's offer to help him cheat on his computer proficiency test, but
after failing the test on his own, Bailey accepts Cooper's underhanded
assistance.

As they plan for college, Julia, Justin, and Sarah enter a scholarship
essay contest. When Julia learns that Justin wrote his essay about her
miscarriage, she demands he withdraw it from the competition, but he
refuses. They try to figure out a way to be friends despite their past history together.

Kirsten loses her job at the university when a colleague discovers
that she plagiarized a large section of her thesis. Charlie is disbelieving,

but Kirsten admits it is true. She had been depressed after the wedding was called off, and can't even remember typing the pages. Charlie thinks the school will understand if she explains the situation, but Kirsten refuses to make excuses for herself.

Notes: A rare continuity glitch occurs in this episode. In Justin's essay, he recalls how he felt when Julia told him she was pregnant—on the telephone. But in the episode ("Valentine's Day," 2/14/96) in which it occurred, Julia had climbed in his bedroom window at night to tell him in person.

Writer and co-executive producer Lisa Melamed previously wrote for the Nickelodeon kids series *Hey Dude* and the CBS comedy *Brooklyn Bridge*. She worked with Amy Lippman and Chris Keyser on *Sisters*, where she was an executive story editor. At a Museum of Television & Radio seminar, she said that she and the other writers frequently incorporate events and dialogue from their own lives into their scripts. Melamed said, "You steal from your life, you steal from your friends' lives, you tell your family, 'All bets are off. If you say something funny, it's going in the show. If you do something interesting, you're going to see it in a month on television.'" In this episode, Claudia tries to understand how Kirsten could have plagiarized her thesis. She remembers a time when she heard Julia playing a song over and over through the wall so many times that eventually Claudia thought she wrote it. Melamed says that is actually something that happened during her childhood between her and her sister.

Familiar Faces: Harold Pruett played the recurring role of Parker Lewis' nemesis, Brad, in the 1992-93 season of the FOX sitcom *Parker Lewis Can't Lose.*

47.   "Deal With It"

Original Airdate: September 11, 1996   NR/AS: 6.5/11
Writer: Susannah Grant
Director: Dennie Gordon
Guest Cast: Paula Devicq (Kirsten Bennett), Alexondra Lee (Callie Martel), Harold Pruett (Cooper), Jim O'Heir (Plumber #1), Peter Siragusa (Plumber #2), Norman Parker (Dr. Leto), Carlos Lacamara (Manny), John Webber (Tommy), Dan Bucatinsky (Checkout Guy), Paul Witten (Ray), Peter James Smith (Busboy)

As Kirsten sinks deeper and deeper into a depression, Charlie is powerless to help her. ARCHIVE PHOTOS.

Kirsten sinks deeper into depression, and Charlie feels helpless. She refuses to see a psychiatrist and won't allow him to call her parents. As Kirsten spends her days in bed, Charlie wonders if he'll have the strength to be there for her.

Julia is attracted to Bailey's college friend, Cooper, but Bailey disapproves. He doesn't want his family encroaching on his new life at college. Cooper and Julia continue to date despite Bailey's disapproval.

Sarah is already uncomfortable when Bailey moves in with a young couple, but when the other guy moves out and Bailey is left living alone with the woman, Callie, Sarah is seething with jealousy. But Bailey assures her that he could never be attracted to another woman as long as he has Sarah.

As her siblings are off dealing with their own crises, Claudia is left alone to handle the family's plumbing problems.

Familiar Faces: Carlos Lacamara played Paco Ortiz on *Nurses* (NBC, 1991-94).

48. "Mixed Signals"

Original Airdate: September 18, 1996   NR/AS: 6.7/10
Writers: Amy Lippman and Christopher Keyser
Director: Ken Topolsky
Guest Cast: Paula Devicq (Kirsten Bennett), Alexondra Lee (Callie Martel), Harold Pruett (Cooper), Marla Sokoloff (Jody Lynch), Larry Poindexter (Professor Tom Digman), Stacey Katzin (Secretary), Tony Sirkin (Gary)

Cooper pressures Julia to have sex, but she isn't ready. When he makes it clear he doesn't want to date her unless they sleep together, she says yes, then no again. Bailey ends his friendship with Cooper when he learns he pressured Julia.

Callie asks Bailey to pose as her boyfriend to fend off an overzealous suitor, who happens to be Bailey's professor. Bailey defends Callie when she claims the professor is stalking her, but then he learns that Callie's overwrought imagination has invented the whole thing.

Charlie doesn't understand why Claudia and Jody have been inseparable until Claudia reveals that Jody is afraid to go home because her mother's boyfriend has been abusing her. Claudia pleads with Charlie to keep Jody's secret, but Charlie informs Jody's mother.

Kirsten's new anti-depressant medication makes her obsessively clean the house and organize things. Just as Charlie thinks Kirsten has improved, she tells him she wants to go off her medication. Claudia, angry with Charlie's interference in Jody's situation, calls Kirsten's parents and tells them about her illness.

Highlights: With Bailey living on campus, Julia moves into the attic, and Claudia finally gets her own room. She dismantles her beloved tent, while playing appropriately somber violin music to mark the occasion.

Familiar Faces: Larry Poindexter also played Kirsten's paralegal boyfriend in the first season episode, "Good Sports" (9/26/94). Fans of *Lois & Clark: The New Adventures of Superman* will recognize him from a two-episode stint in March 1996. He played the duplicitous Dr. Deter, whom Lois consults to cure her amnesia.

49. "Going Home"

Original Airdate: September 25, 1996   NR/AS: 6.7/11
Writers: Amy Lippman and Christopher Keyser

Director: Daniel Attias
Guest Cast: Paula Devicq (Kirsten Bennett), Alexondra Lee (Cal-
lie Martel), Kathleen Noone (Ellie Bennett), Nicholas Pryor
(Gene Bennett), Richard McGonagle (Emmett), Alyson Croft (Zoe),
Nick Tate (Professor), Joe Anthony (Phone Guy), Ali Elk (Girl)

Kirsten's parents arrive and want to take their daughter back to
Chicago for treatment, but Charlie objects. When they threaten to get a
court order, Charlie realizes that he has no legal grounds to fight them
because he and Kirsten are not married. Kirsten doesn't comprehend
when she is asked to decide between her parents and Charlie. When he
sees how the fighting is hurting her, Charlie lets Kirsten's parents take
her away. Julia cuts short a visit to Dartmouth when she hears about
Kirsten, and she and the others gather at the house to be there for Charlie as he says good-bye to Kirsten.

Notes: This episode features some of the series' most heartrending
scenes, as Charlie is helpless to prevent Kirsten's parents from taking her
away. At an Academy of Television Arts & Sciences panel discussion,
Chris Keyser, noting the series' propensity towards melodrama, joked
that cues for actors to cry are so widely used in the *Party of Five* scripts,
that the writers have programmed such commands into their word pro-
cessing programs. He said, "On computers, the writers have macros.
Like Alt-B is Bailey, Alt-J is Julia, and Alt-H is 'He holds her as she cries.'"

50. *"Personal Demons"*

Original Airdate: October 30, 1996　　　　NR/AS: 7.0/11
Writer: Mark B. Perry
Director: Michael Engler
Guest Cast: Alexondra Lee (Callie Martel), Tamara Taylor (Grace
Wilcox), Michael Goorjian (Justin Thompson), Taylor Negron
(Dr. Blalock), Kenneth Mars (Earl), Lisa Rieffel (Robin), Daniel
Hagen (Mr. Trimble), Mary Gillis (Costume Shop Lady), Steven M.
Gagnon (Police Officer), Marc Danon (Callie's Date), Sebastian
de Vicente (Rob)

Kirsten's departure and her family's refusal to let him speak to her
leave Charlie in a foul mood. He refuses a request for leftovers from a
homeless organization, and turns away a down-on-his-luck handyman
who comes looking for odd jobs. The handyman reveals that he knew

Charlie's father, and Charlie's mood is softened by hearing stories of the old days.

Bailey doesn't share Sarah's enthusiasm for a high school Halloween dance. She dreams of their going as Sleeping Beauty and Prince Charming, but Bailey is no Prince Charming—after one too many beers he sleeps with roommate Callie.

Claudia concludes that the family's string of bad luck is due to a curse. She hires an exorcist who concludes, "There is a vortex of negative forces here." When they learn that someone has opened up credit card accounts in their father's name, Claudia and Charlie assume it was the exorcist, who had access to their papers in the basement. But the culprit turns out to be the handyman, Earl.

Julia is jealous when Justin begins dating a classmate, Robin. She tries to come between them, but feels guilty when they break up. Though she wasn't the cause of their break-up after all, Julia persuades Robin to give Justin another chance.

Highlights: Scott Wolf's resemblance to Tom Cruise is again the subject of an in-joke (see "Who Cares?," 2/15/95) in this episode. While picking out outfits in the costume shop, Bailey tries on a pair of glasses and says, "Tom Cruise in *Mission: Impossible.*"

Familiar Faces: Comedian Taylor Negron played Gwillem the program manager in the 1995-96 season of NBC's *Hope & Gloria.* Lisa Rieffel played Ann Jillian's daughter on her sitcom *Ann Jillian* (NBC, 1989-90), and has had regular roles on *The Trials of Rosie O'Neill* (CBS, 1990-92) and *Empty Nest* (NBC, 1993).

51.   "Not So Fast"

Original Airdate: November 6, 1996   NR/AS: 7.2/11
Writer: Karen Krenis
Director: Ken Topolsky
Regular Cast Changes: Alexondra Lee was added to the opening
credit sequence
Guest Cast: Mitchell Anderson (Ross Werkman), James Sloyan
(Avery Baltus), Neil Roberts (Gary Prescott), Lenny Wolpe
(Strause), June Claman (Judge), Matthew Bartilson (Todd), Bill
Lee Brown (Security Guard), Adam A. Labaud, Jr., Kevin Moss,
Bryant Woodert (Singing Trio)

Feeling guilty about his infidelity, Bailey decides to break up with

Sarah. Before he can tell her, he contracts chicken pox. While Callie is unsympathetic ("I don't do sick," she tells him), Sarah takes care of Bailey. Bailey tries to push her away, but when he sees how much she loves him, he has second thoughts.

Julia meets Gary Prescott, a novelist she admires, and asks for his critique of her writing. He calls her work unfocused and immature. Her confidence shaken, Julia blows her interview at Stanford. She begins to question her talent and career goals.

Claudia meets her mother's colleague, musician Avery Baltus. Avery thinks that Claudia can surpass her mother's talent and wants to help advance her musical career. Charlie and Ross fear that Avery is pushing Claudia too hard, and when Avery gets her accepted into a conservatory, Charlie won't let her go. Though Charlie explains he wants her to lead a more balanced life, Claudia says she'll never forgive him.

Notes: Acknowledging that *Party of Five* features more tragic than light-hearted moments, Scott Wolf jokes that when the actors ask for direction on a scene, they are frequently told, "Tears would not be inappropriate."

52. "Gimme Shelter"

Original Airdate: November 13, 1996   NR/AS: 7.1/11
Writer: Susannah Grant
Director: Steven Robman
Guest Cast: Tamara Taylor (Grace Wilcox), Ben Browder (Sam Brody), Breckin Meyer (Alec Brody), Dan Lauria (Coach Russ Petrocelli), Dean Robinson (Jim Seely), Wendle Josepher (Lori), Danil Torrpe (Coach Dawes), Eddie Mui (Eddie), Dennis Tragesser (Jimmy Gilbert), Catherine Dyer (Waitress), Phyllis Ehrlich (Homeless Woman)

The winner of Salingers' slogan contest brings a group of homeless people to dine at the restaurant as part of his prize. Charlie ejects the homeless when the other patrons begin to leave. Charlie's actions make newspaper headlines as Grace Wilcox launches a boycott of Salingers. They eventually reach a truce and Charlie agrees to serve the homeless one meal a week in between shifts.

With four days to finish her college applications, Julia is bothered by the presence of construction workers who were hired to repair the roof. One of the roofers, Alec, flirts with Julia, but it's his older brother, Sam, who catches Julia's attention.

Bailey doesn't make the hockey team, but the wrestling coach recruits him sight unseen—a sign of desperation, thinks Bailey. The persuasive coach convinces a reluctant Bailey to give wrestling a chance.

Familiar Faces: Dan Lauria is best-known for his role as Jack Arnold, the patriarch on *The Wonder Years* (1989-93). *Party of Five* co-executive producer Ken Topolsky was a supervising producer on *The Wonder Years.*

Ben Browder began a ten-episode stint as Sam, Julia's roofer boyfriend. Browder previously starred in the very short-lived 1992 CBS series *Boys of Twilight* and had small roles in the feature films *Memphis Belle* (1990) and *A Kiss Before Dying* (1991).

53. "Close To You"

Original Airdate: November 20, 1996   NR/AS: 6.9/11
Writer: Catherine Butterfield
Director: Vicki Jackson Lemay
Guest Cast: Tamara Taylor (Grace Wilcox), Ben Browder (Sam Brody), Ben Savage (Stuart), Colleen Quinn (Police Woman), Clifford David (Mr. Olmstead), David Quane (Guy), Jackie Mari Roberts (Marcia)

As she dispenses "advice to the lovelorn" for her junior high school newspaper column, Claudia discovers she has a knack for detecting romantic strife in her own family. Charlie enjoys spending time with Grace, but when she tries to kiss him, he tells her he's not available—he's waiting for Kirsten.

Julia's crush on Sam leads her to interfere in a dispute between Charlie and Sam, and to use her own money to pay Sam to come back to work when Charlie fires him. Though he enjoys spending time with her, Sam is stunned when Julia kisses him. After Bailey rescues Callie from a date rape attempt, she grows dependent on him. Sarah tries to befriend Callie, but Callie only wants to lean on Bailey. Despite her insights into her siblings' affairs, Claudia remains oblivious to her classmate Stuart's obvious attraction to her.

Familiar Faces: Ben Savage stars as Cory Matthews on the ABC sitcom *Boy Meets World* (1993-).

54. "I Do"

Original Airdate: November 27, 1996   NR/AS: 5.4/9
Writers: Lisa Melamed and P. K. Simonds

Director: Ellen S. Pressman
Guest Cast: Tom Mason (Joe Mangus), Tamara Taylor (Grace Wilcox), Ben Browder (Sam Brody), Anita Barone (Franny), Zoaunne Leroy (Justice of the Peace), Vincent Duvall (Lewis), Don Jeffcoat (Paul), Danette Christine (Singer)

Joe comes to town with big news: he's getting married! Everyone is happy, except for Charlie, who would have been celebrating his first anniversary with Kirsten had he gone through with the wedding. Grace goes to the wedding with Charlie as a favor, but afterwards tells him it's too difficult being his friend because she has feelings for him and he is still hung up on Kirsten.

Joe's relationship with his much younger bride convinces Julia that age shouldn't matter in a relationship. Still in her bridesmaid's dress, she visits Sam at his construction site. Sam, who has been avoiding Julia since they kissed, admits he is attracted to her.

Sarah fixes Callie up with her cousin Paul in order to get her away from Bailey, but Callie insists they double date. Later, Sarah wants to make love to Bailey, but he is unable to perform. Back at the apartment, Bailey drowns his guilt in alcohol and repeats his past mistake with Callie.

Notes: Alexondra Lee spoke of her difficulty filming the rollerblading scene in an interview with *Soap Opera Digest.* "I had no idea how to rollerblade. Scott was like a professional. He plays rollerblade hockey, so he was really good. I had to get lessons, and I was still awful. At one point I was supposed to say to Scott, 'Let's race,' and we had to go really fast; it was just ridiculous."

55. *"Desperate Measures"*

Original Airdate: December 11, 1996   NR/AS: 7.4/12
Writer: Mark B. Perry
Director: Michael Engler
Guest Cast: Paula Devicq (Kirsten Bennett), Ben Browder (Sam Brody), Kathleen Noone (Ellie Bennett), Dan Lauria (Coach Russ Petrocelli), Rose Portillo (Dr. Aguilar), Lenora May (Nurse)

Charlie goes to Chicago to see Kirsten, who appears to have made a complete recovery. Kirsten asks Charlie to drive her back to San Francisco with him, but en route, she begins to suffer a breakdown. She tells him that the wedding triggered her depression and that she can't be with him without bringing it back. Charlie takes Kirsten back to her parents' house and returns to San Francisco alone.

Left in charge in Charlie's absence, Julia takes her responsibilities too lightly. Swept up with her new romance with Sam, Julia ignores Claudia's complaints that she is ill. Then Claudia winds up in the hospital with appendicitis and Julia is forced to reexamine her priorities.

Bailey finally tells Sarah that he slept with Callie. Sarah is devastated, but she can't break up with Bailey because she still loves him.

Notes: Scripting this episode provided Mark B. Perry with his greatest writing challenge, he revealed at the Academy of Television Arts & Sciences "Inside *Party of Five*" event. "That was very difficult—to really delve into the degree of her mental illness and how Charlie was responsible for it. It was painful to write, and it was actually painful to see, because the actors did such a marvelous job."

56. "Christmas"

Original Airdate: December 18, 1996   NR/AS: 7.3/12
Writer: Susannah Grant
Director: Dennie Gordon
Guest Cast: Carroll O'Connor (Jake Gordon), Tamara Taylor
(Grace Wilcox), Dan Lauria (Coach Russ Petrocelli), Ben Savage
(Stuart), Jonathan Hadary (Pete), Ken Magee (Xander)

Grandpa Jake arrives unexpectedly, wanting to spend Christmas with the Salingers. But the Salingers aren't feeling very merry. Charlie ships off Kirsten's belongings to Chicago and tries to move on with his life, but finds that it is empty. With both Sarah and Callie away for the holidays, Bailey stays home alone, ignoring his family's phone calls. Jake buys a tree and insists they celebrate Christmas, but then he departs hastily on Christmas morning while everyone is still asleep. Charlie catches him sneaking out, and Jake reveals that he has cancer and doesn't want to stick around long enough to be a burden to the kids.

Christmas dinner turns out to be bigger than anyone expected, as Bailey arrives with his coach in tow, Claudia invites her classmate Stuart, and Grace shows up with a gift for Charlie.

57. "Life's Too Short"

Original Airdate: January 8, 1997   NR/AS: 7.2/11
Writer: Lisa Melamed

Story: Amy Lippman and Christopher Keyser
Director: Eric Jewett
Guest Cast: Tamara Taylor (Grace Wilcox), Ben Browder (Sam
Brody), Michael Goorjian (Justin Thompson), Bryn Erin (Libby
Dwyer), Jessica Tuck (Lori), Matthew Ross (Aaron), Stan Cahill
(T. J.), Joan McMurtrey (Mrs. Dwyer), Cayce Callaway (Miss
Baird), Saadia Persad (Gail), Ben Rawnsley (Postal Clerk),
Matthew Sutherland (Steve), Darren Campbell (Guy), Ron Ostrow
(Minister)

Julia and Justin feel guilty after their friend Libby commits suicide
and they realize that neither of them had returned her recent phone
calls. Julia reads Libby's journal and discovers that the pressure of getting accepted into Harvard led to her actions.

At his high school reunion, Charlie tries to relive his glory days with
his buddies, T. J. and Aaron, and reminisces with his high school sweetheart, Lori. When he discovers that his Lori and Aaron slept together in
high school, Charlie realizes that his glory days weren't as perfect as he
thought.

No matter what Bailey does, it's never good enough for Sarah, who
can't get over his cheating. Tired of fighting, and hoping to regain her
self-respect, Sarah breaks up with Bailey.

Notes: There are two blunders in the post office scene. First, Julia's
applications cost $1.25 each to mail. At current postal rates, nothing
would cost $1.25 to mail within the U.S. The rate goes from $1.24 for a
four-ounce package to $1.47 for five ounces. When Julia puts the
envelopes in the mail box, there is no postage affixed, even though she
paid the clerk.

58. *"Significant Others"*

Original Airdate: January 15, 1997   NR/AS: 7.2/11
Writer: P. K. Simonds
Director: Ken Topolsky
Guest Cast: Tamara Taylor (Grace Wilcox), Dan Lauria (Coach Russ
Petrocelli), Ben Browder (Sam Brody), Michael Whaley (Michael),
Corrine Bohrer (Karen), Zach Ward (Teddy), Billy Morrissette
(Henry), Jackie Mari Roberts (Marcia), Michelle Azar (Abby),
Dennis Tragesser (Jimmy), Eddie Mui (Eddie), Audrey Wasilewski
(Waitress), Duane Matthews (Bar Patron)

Charlie is happy being "just friends" with Grace, until she accepts a date with a man from the mayor's office. Grace's new relationship arouses jealousy in Charlie, who asks her to stop seeing him.

Julia is surprised to learn that Sam was once engaged. He says it's ancient history, but when his fiancée announces she is getting married, he is obviously jealous. He admits to Julia that he still has feelings for Karen and that he isn't in love with Julia. Julia asks him to give it time.

Bailey throws himself into wrestling, pleading with his coach to allow him to compete in the All-Stars. Claudia cheers him on at the qualifiers and wants to celebrate afterwards, but Bailey goes out drinking instead.

59. "I Declare"

Original Airdate: January 22, 1997   NR/AS: 7.0/11
Writer: Chris Levinson
Director: Michael Engler
Guest Cast: Tamara Taylor (Grace Wilcox), Ben Browder (Sam Brody), Mitchell Anderson (Ross Werkman), Lela Ivey (Mrs. Huffman), Raphael Sbarge (Paul Archer), John Pleshette (Professor Conklin), Fred Sanders (Mr. Burns), Virginia Capers (Grace's Nana), Jose Felipe Padron (Frank), J. D. Daniels (Aaron), Michael Malota (Dempsey), Megan Bouchard (Brooks)

Bailey's drinking jeopardizes his position on the wrestling team. He needs a B+ on his paper in order to stay off academic probation and remain on the team. He tries to quit partying and crack down on the books, but Callie's disruptive presence and his "one-beer-per-page" reward system results in an incomprehensible paper that Bailey, when sober, cannot turn in. He drops the class and takes an incomplete so that the grade won't affect his position on the team.

Claudia learns that Ross is dating Mr. Archer, a teacher at her school, and lets her classmates in on the secret. Claudia's indiscretion upsets Ross and exposes a flaw in his relationship: Ross isn't comfortable dating someone who isn't open about his sexuality.

Charlie and Grace want to take their emerging romance slowly, but they have difficulty fighting their attraction for one another. Julia gets an early acceptance letter from Stanford, but she announces that she is not going to college. Charlie is furious with her decision and blames it on Sam's influence.

Bailey's alcoholism story line dominated the third season and helped the series achieve its highest ratings ever. ARCHIVE PHOTOS.

60. "Misery Loves Company"

Original Airdate: January 29, 1997   NR/AS: 7.3/11
Writer: Mark B. Perry
Director: Rodman Flender
Guest Cast: Scott Grimes (Will McCorkle), Tamara Taylor (Grace Wilcox), Ben Browder (Sam Brody), Lela Ivey (Mrs. Huffman), Walter D. Morris (Coffee Guy), Elliot Woods (Fireman)

Will shows up for a surprise visit from college and is surprised to discover how much—and how frequently—Bailey drinks. He goes to Sarah and suggests that together they get Bailey help. However, Sarah is trying to get over her break-up with Bailey and doesn't want to get involved. Bailey insists he doesn't have a problem, it's just normal college partying.

Grace comes to live with the Salingers after her apartment is destroyed in a fire. Charlie is at first uneasy having Grace in the bed he shared with Kirsten, but then he urges Grace to make the move a permanent one. After Charlie and Julia come to blows over her decision to forgo college, Julia moves in with Sam. Julia's encroachment on Sam's "quiet little life" is made worse when her family problems follow her. Concerned that her family is falling apart, Claudia turns to Bailey, who tells her that the family is no longer his problem.

Highlights: Will sees underage Bailey's fake I.D. and says, "No way you could pass for 27!" In real life, baby-faced Scott Wolf was 28 when this episode was filmed.

The drunk scene between Will, Bailey, and Callie borders on the burlesque, but provides some genuinely amusing moments. Even funnier is the surprise Will and Bailey receive when they wake up in bed together.

61.   "MYOB"

Original Airdate: February 5, 1997   NR/AS: 8.7/13
Writer: Daniel Attias
Director: Lisa Melamed
Guest Cast: Tamara Taylor (Grace Wilcox), Ben Browder (Sam Brody), Sharon Mahoney (Elaine), David Batiste (Eddie), Daren Carlson (Lead Singer)

Julia is disbelieving when Sarah tells her that Bailey has a drinking problem, but then Julia begins witnessing some of Bailey's unusual behavior. Sam gives Bailey a job on a construction site, and some liquor turns up missing, with Bailey the obvious culprit. Julia and Sarah try to talk to Bailey about his drinking, but he pushes them away.

Julia didn't find Sam's (Ben Browder) racial jokes to be funny. EVERETT COLLECTION

Grace feels that she sold out her principles when she moved into the Salingers' middle class, white neighborhood. Claudia volunteers at the Harvest Program in an effort to become friends with Grace, but instead the experience drives a wedge between Claudia and Grace.

Notes: The *Party of Five* writing staff took a unique approach to dealing with racism by initially ignoring the issue. At the beginning of Charlie and Grace's courtship, their racial differences were not mentioned. When the writers did introduce race as an issue, they took an unusual slant. Rather than having Charlie or his family members oppose his relationship with a black woman, the writers had Grace question her decision to become involved with a white man, which, to her, equated with selling out. Amy Lippman says, "We try to look at different sides of an issue. Rather than dealing head-on with racism, we wanted to see it in a way which isn't often portrayed on television."

62. *"Point of No Return"*

Original Airdate: February 12, 1997   NR/AS: 7.7/12
Writer: Susannah Grant
Director: Michael Engler
Guest Cast: Tamara Taylor (Grace Wilcox), Ben Browder (Sam Brody), James Sloyan (Avery Baltus), Clifton Davis (Martin Wilcox), Joan Pringle (Rose Wilcox), Matthew Carey (Marcus), Steven M. Porter (Coco the Clown), Eric Bruce Scott (Record Store Clerk), Karen James (Baker), Phil Barney (Louie), Ian Hernandez (Crying Boy)

Julia ends her relationship with Sam after he makes some racial jokes that she doesn't find funny. Claudia tries to strike up a friendship with fellow musician Avery's 14-year-old son, Marcus, but the recalcitrant lad isn't interested in being friends.

Owen's third birthday is approaching and the Salingers divvy up the party-planning chores. Bailey is charged with hiring a clown, but he spends the clown money on liquor. He shows up at the party in a clown suit, intoxicated, and ruins the festivities with his drunken outbursts.

Despite Bailey's behavior, Charlie refuses to believe his brother has a problem, chalking it up to normal college drinking. Julia, Sarah, and Grace help Charlie to see the truth—that Bailey is an alcoholic.

Notes: In another TV life, Grace's parents were siblings. Clifton

Davis and Joan Pringle played brother and sister on the sitcom *That's My Mama* (ABC, 1975).

63. "Intervention"

Original Airdate: February 19, 1997   NR/AS: 8.9/14
Writers: Amy Lippman and Christopher Keyser
Director: Steven Robman
Guest Cast: Tom Mason (Joe Mangus), Tamara Taylor (Grace Wilcox), Mark Robman (Man at Salingers)

The family plans an intervention to confront Bailey about his drinking. To lure him to the house, Claudia calls him in tears, saying that Owen fell down the stairs and isn't breathing. Bailey races to the house and is astonished to discover that it was just a cruel trick; Owen is fine and all his family, plus Grace and Sarah, have assembled to talk to him about his drinking.

Bailey denies that he has a problem and responds to their accusations by lashing out at them with cruel remarks about their own mistakes. As Bailey is about to leave, Joe arrives and reveals a shocking secret: their father, Nick, was an alcoholic. Bailey thinks Joe's revelation is just another lie, but Joe's stories ring true with events Charlie recalls from his early childhood, before Nick stopped drinking.

In light of this discovery, Bailey admits that he is an alcoholic. But he refuses to seek treatment, saying that drinking is part of who he is, and now he knows it's not his fault, it's his father's. Claudia gives Bailey an ultimatum—either stop drinking or get out of the house and never come back. The family watches in anguished silence as Bailey walks out.

Highlights: In one of several heartrending scenes, Bailey discusses the legacy he received from his father. In a previous episode ("Poor Substitutes," 1/17/96), Sarah had wondered what traits she inherited from her birth mother and asked Bailey how he and his siblings are like his parents. After learning that his father was an alcoholic, he tells Sarah that he has come up with the answer: "Claudia plays the violin, and Julia looks like her, and Charlie looks like him. And this is what I got. This is what my father gave me."

Notes: *Party of Five*'s production coordinator Carol Kravetz appears as an extra in this episode. She's the woman who comes into Salingers and learns that the restaurant is closed for the night.

It's in the numbers

Party of Five:
... ranked in TV's Top 10 of 1995 according to *USA Today.*

Neve Campbell:
... was listed as one of 6 Reasons to tune in to television by *Time*
... has one of TV's 20 Great Faces according to *TV Guide*
... is one of the 20 Hottest Stars selected by *Seventeen* magazine
... made *Entertainment Weekly's* "It" List of the 100 Most Creative People in Entertainment
... ranked 22 in *Rolling Stone's* list of 101 Reasons to Watch TV

Matthew Fox:
... made *People* magazine's 1996 listing of the 50 Most Beautiful People in the World

Jeremy London:
... was chosen as one of the 50 Most Beautiful People in the World by *People* in 1996

Scott Wolf:
... possesses one of TV's 20 Great Faces as chosen by *TV Guide*
... ranked as one of the hottest stars under the age of 30 in *Entertainment Weekly's* 30 Under 30 special issue
... was named as one of the 50 Most Beautiful People in the World by *People* in 1995

"Intervention," the climax in Bailey's season-long struggle with alcohol addiction, received more press coverage than any prior episode of *Party of Five*. Among the sterling reviews the episode received was *USA Today's* four-star (out of four) review, which assessed, "It doesn't overstate this episode's impact to compare it with the strongest story lines of *NYPD Blue*, *ER*, and *Homicide: Life on the Street*. In fact, it's a pleasure to rave about dramatic conflict happening elsewhere than a hospital or a police interrogation room. *Party of Five* hits us where we live: at home."

At a 1997 industry event, Jennifer Love Hewitt called "Intervention" her favorite *Party of Five* episode to date, and revealed that her admiration of costar Lacey Chabert's acting abilities reached new levels in this episode. "Lacey became my role model," she said. "She just *rocks*."

64. "Hitting Bottom"

Original Airdate: February 26, 1997   NR/AS: 9.6/15
Writer: P. K. Simonds
Director: Dennie Gordon
Guest Cast: Jeremy London (Griffin Holbrook), Dan Lauria (Coach Russ Petrocelli), James Sloyan (Avery Baltus), Robert Costanzo (Arnie Horn), Cyd Strittmatter (Nursery School Teacher), Diana Maria Riva (Nurse)

The family worries about Bailey, whom they haven't seen since the ill-fated intervention. They panic when Bailey picks Owen up from nursery school, keeps him out all night, and returns home drunk. Seeing that Bailey has hit bottom, Sarah follows after him. Trying to persuade him not to drive drunk, she gets into his jeep and he takes off, getting them into an accident. Sarah suffers a concussion and several contusions, but Bailey escapes unscathed.

Griffin is back in town again, and Julia turns to him for comfort over her family situation. He reveals that he can no longer work in the merchant marines because of a knee injury he sustained on board his ship. When she learns that the accident wasn't his fault, Julia encourages Griffin to sue for damages. Certain that this time things will work out for her and Griffin, Julia makes love to him.

The discovery that her father was an alcoholic leads Claudia to question her memories of her parents' happy marriage. She probes for information. Resistant at first, Avery eventually tells her about some of Nick's drunken binges.

When Sarah wakes up in her hospital room, she sees Bailey standing in the shadows. He cries as he asks for her help.

Notes: In preparation for his alcoholism stint, Scott Wolf turned to his mother, Susan, a substance abuse counselor, for advice. He told *USA Today*, "Addiction is a difficult thing to understand from the outside," and added that feedback from his mother's clients convinced him that *Party of Five* presented an accurate depiction of the disease.

65. "Leap of Faith"

Original Airdate: March 5, 1997   NR/AS: 8.4/13
Writer: Lisa Melamed
Director: Susannah Grant
Guest Cast: Jeremy London (Griffin Holbrook), John M. Jackson
(Major Holbrook), John Rubinstein (Walter Alcott), Jackie Mari
Roberts (Marcia), Randy Becker (Grace's Colleague), Troy Evans
(Arthur), Phillip Hinch (Craig), Carolyn Hennesy (Alice), Alex
Craig Mann (Dean), Steve O'Connor (Phone Guy)

Bailey cuts up his fake I.D. and announces he has quit drinking. He attends an Alcoholic Anonymous meeting and is stunned to encounter Walter Alcott, the drunk driver who killed his parents. Bailey decides he can do without A.A. and tells his dubious siblings that he has his own 12-step plan: "Steps 1-12, don't drink." Sarah agrees to help him through the tough times.

At the urging of her colleagues, Grace decides to run for city council and sets up her campaign headquarters at the Salinger house. Griffin receives a $100,000 settlement from the ship. His father thinks Griffin should use the money to go into business with his old man. Griffin is excited about the prospect until he learns that his father doesn't want his input in the business, just his money.

Highlights: Julia remarks to Sarah, who stood by Bailey after he cheated on her and nearly killed her in an automobile accident, "You have an amazing capacity for forgiveness, Sarah, I gotta say." Jennifer Love Hewitt revealed during a panel discussion at the Academy of Television Arts & Sciences in North Hollywood, "In real life, I probably wouldn't have forgiven Bailey like Sarah did."

Familiar Faces: John Rubinstein reprises his role from "Thanksgiving" (11/14/94).

Notes: This episode marked the directorial debut of Susannah Grant, one of the show's producers and writers.

66. "Promises, Promises"

Original Airdate: March 19, 1997   NR/AS: 8.2/13
Writer: Mark B. Perry
Director: Lou Antonio
Guest Cast: Jeremy London (Griffin Holbrook), Tamara Taylor
(Grace Wilcox), Jackie Mari Roberts (Marcia), Christopher Gartin
(Drew Bishop), William Newman (Julia's Teacher), Kevin Maloney
(Photographer)

Julia neglects her schoolwork to be with Griffin, who is bothered by Julia's sudden disinterest in school. Grace's political campaign takes over the Salinger house, with phones, faxes, and Xerox machines cluttering up every available space. Charlie is unresponsive to Claudia's claim that Grace doesn't care about her or Owen—she only spends time with the kids when it is good for her public image.

Bailey is jealous when Sarah dates Drew, an intern from her doctor's office. Sarah puts Bailey first when he needs her, but insists she is only interested in being his friend. Callie tries to rekindle her relationship with Bailey, who points out that she was the only person who wasn't there for him when he needed help. Everything about Callie and the apartment reminds Bailey of drinking, so he moves back home with his family.

67. "A Little Faith"

Original Airdate: March 26, 1997   NR/AS: 7.8/13
Writers: Chris Levinson, Amy Lippman, Christopher Keyser
Director: Ken Topolsky
Guest Cast: Tom Mason (Joe Mangus), Tamara Taylor (Grace
Wilcox), Jeremy London (Griffin Holbrook), Mitchell Anderson
(Ross Werkman), Anita Barone (Franny), John Doe (Carter),
Shannon O'Hurley (Newswoman), Michael Paul Chan (Conductor),
Lonna Montrose (Room Service Waitress)
Regular Cast Changes: Alexandra Lee is dropped from the opening
credit sequence

A pregnancy scare gets Grace and Charlie discussing their future together. Charlie is dismayed to learn that Grace doesn't ever want to have children. Griffin and Julia's vacation plans are sidelined when Griffin's motorcycle breaks down. Griffin thinks fate is calling when he has a chance to buy the motorcycle shop, but Julia doesn't want him to be tied down to a business. She had hoped they would use his settlement money to travel together.

Ross is called for jury duty and can't accompany Claudia to L.A., where she is scheduled to perform with the Los Angeles Chamber Orchestra. Charlie is hesitant to allow Bailey to act as Claudia's chaperone, but Bailey pleads for the opportunity to prove himself to his family. In Los Angeles, without Sarah to lean on, Bailey succumbs to his desire to drink, emptying out the hotel's mini-bar while Claudia is at a rehearsal.

Joe and Franny, who are living in L.A., try to prevent Claudia from seeing Bailey drunk, but she guesses what happened and lashes out at her brother. Joe urges Bailey to seek spiritual guidance and points out that he not only possesses what made his father drink, but also what made his father stop. When they return to San Francisco, Bailey attends an A.A. meeting.

68. "You Win Some, You Lose Some"

Original Airdate: April 2, 1997   NR/AS: 9.1/15
Writers: Lisa Melamed and P.K. Simonds
Story: Amy Lippman and Christopher Keyser
Director: Michael Engler
Guest Cast: Tamara Taylor (Grace Wilcox), Jeremy London (Griffin Holbrook), Michael Goorjian (Justin Thompson), Dan Lauria (Coach Russ Petrocelli), Jackie Mari Roberts (Marcia), Joan Pringle (Rose Wilcox), Alyson Reed (Mrs. Reeves), Art Metrano (Justice of the Peace), Kelly Hawthorne (Liz)

Bailey thinks that he has a chance to reconcile with Sarah after they kiss, but she tells him that they have been through too much to ever go back to the way things were. She wants to remain in his life, but only as a friend.

Troubled by Grace's lack of maternal instincts, Charlie breaks up with her. He could accept her decision not to have kids of her own if only she wanted the children he already "has". Though he loves her,

Charlie has to put the kids first, because "that's what parents do."

Julia is eager to see the world, but with Griffin tied to his bike shop, she considers accompanying Justin on a tour of Europe. Griffin fears that he'll lose Julia if she goes, so he proposes and the two are hastily married by a justice of the peace. Her family is stunned when they hear the news. Though he feels she has made a big mistake, Charlie agrees to be supportive. Before she leaves home to move in with Griffin, the family presents her with a wedding gift—their mother's wedding ring.

Notes: *Party of Five* producer and unit production manager Paul Marks appears in campaign flyers and on the TV newscast as Grace's opponent, Wallerstein.

As promotional spots for the third season finale of *Party of Five* stated that one of the Salingers would get married, viewers speculated which couple would be altar-bound, Bailey and Sarah, Julia and Griffin, or Charlie and Grace. Of recovering alcoholic Bailey, suddenly directionless Julia, or mature Charlie, Charlie would have seemed the logical choice. Amy Lippman says she received a lot of criticism for the decision to allow young lovers Griffin and Julia to wed and was surprised by the negative reaction. She told *USA Today*, "I didn't know it was going to be a big deal." Lippman also stated that she agrees the characters acted hastily and hinted that the marriage would prove problematic when the series returns for a fourth season.

One thing that distinguishes *Party of Five* from the majority of continuing dramas (and even many comedies) is that the series' writers do not end their seasons with cliffhangers. Christopher Keyser says, "We've always tried to avoid cliffhangers and the idea that the end of the season was 'we're going to show you something that says "oh I have to come back next year to find out what happens," but more "we're going to show you something so that you feel like you've watched a season and they've gone someplace, and you're interested in how they've grown."''

This episode is particularly poignant in illustrating Charlie's emotional growth. For the first time, Charlie put the kids ahead of his own needs or desires, without feeling resentful or cheated. Whereas in "The Wedding" (12/13/95), he doesn't consider how losing Kirsten will impact the children, and in "Brother's Keeper" (2/22/95), he sacrifices his big career break for the kids, but feels embittered about the lost opportunity, in this episode, he learns what it truly means to be a parent.

Trivia Quiz

Test your *Party of Five* I.Q. with this trivia quiz, which will separate the casual viewer from the diehard *Party of Five* fanatic. There are 100 questions of varying difficulty. Each correct answer is worth one point. Answers can be found on page 236–38.

Bailey

1. What is the name of the imaginary friend Bailey makes up to impress Kirsten?
2. What was Bailey's SAT total score?
3. What is the name of Bailey's high school football team?
4. Which college did Bailey plan to attend in Boston?
5. How can Claudia tell when Bailey is lying?

Charlie

6. For which two events does Charlie shave his beard?
7. What would Charlie's salary have been had he accepted the job in Seattle?
8. On the eve of his near-wedding, how many women does Charlie estimate he has slept with in his life thus far?
9. In what year did Charlie graduate from high school?
10. Where did Charlie attend college?

Julia

11. Who was the first person Julia called after her parents were killed?
12. In what category does Julia find her name written on the boy's bathroom wall?
13. What is Julia's middle name?
14. What is the name of the publishing firm where Julia briefly works?
15. What is the name of Julia's award-winning short story, which gets her into hot water when it is published?

Claudia

16. What school play does Claudia want to try out for in the pilot episode?
17. What is the name of the junior high school Claudia attends?
18. What does Claudia purchase to help her fit in at junior high?
19. What is the name of Claudia's advice column in the school newspaper?
20. Of drinking, smoking, stealing, gambling, and swearing, which vice has Claudia not yet succumbed to on the show?

Justin

21. Name one of Justin's extracurricular school activities in the show's first season.
22. Where is Justin's birthmark and what does it resemble?
23. Name Justin's siblings.
24. What is Julia and Justin's song?
25. What is Justin's father's occupation?

Sarah

26. What is Sarah's birthstone?
27. What is the name of the band with which Sarah performs?
28. What is Sarah's grandmother's first name?
29. How does Sarah acquire a cat in the second season?
30. What is the cat's name?

Will

31. Where do Will and Sarah go on their first date?
32. How does Will win Gina back after dumping her in "Strange Bedfellows"?
33. What items are on Will's list of things to pack for college?
34. What is Will's little sister's name?
35. Who is Will's roommate at college?

Griffin

36. What is the name of the military academy Griffin attends?
37. What does he store at Julia's when he's at military school?
38. What is Griffin's mother's occupation?
39. What is Griffin's middle name?
40. What is Griffin's father's military rank?

Kirsten

41. What is the name of Kirsten's sister?
42. What song does Claudia dedicate to Kirsten on the eve of Kirsten's wedding day?
43. Where do Kirsten's parents live?
44. To what piece of music does Claudia compare the sight of Kirsten in her wedding gown?
45. Whom does Kirsten almost marry (after Charlie jilts her)?

Grace

46. What is the name of the charitable organization for which Grace works?
47. Who is Grace's opponent in the San Francisco city council election?
48. What was Grace's major in college?
49. What's the first movie Grace and Charlie saw together?

Owen

50. Name Owen's four nannies.

Gifts

51. When he has a crush on Kirsten, what does Bailey bring her as a gift from his job?
52. What does Sarah receive from her parents for her 16th birthday?
53. What does Bailey give Sarah for her 16th birthday?
54. What does Bailey present to Sarah for her 17th birthday?
55. What important present does Bailey bestow on Claudia for her 12th birthday that the rest of the family had forgotten?
56. What present does Claudia and Julia give Bailey for his first day of college?
57. What does Bailey get from Sarah for his first day of college?
58. Name the two transportation-related gifts Griffin gives to Julia.

Money

59. How much do the Salingers receive from their parents' estate every four months?
60. How much does Charlie lose in a bad real estate investment?
61. How much does Julia spend on her modeling photographs?
62. Julia's short story wins a cash prize of what amount?
63. How much cash does Griffin steal from Salingers Restaurant?
64. How much does Charlie receive for his share of the furniture building business?
65. What is the amount of Griffin's settlement in his lawsuit against the ship's owners?

Miscellaneous

66. What were the full names of the Salinger parents?
67. What unique physical attribute does Artie possess?
68. What musical instrument does Artie play?
69. What is the name of the principal at Grant High School?
70. What was the winning slogan in Salingers' contest?
71. Where did Joe meet his bride, Franny?
72. What is the name of the moose head in the Salingers' attic?
73. What is the title of family friend Greer's cookbook-in-progress?
74. What college did Mrs. Salinger attend and what was her major there?
75. What is Ross' mother's name?
76. What musical instrument did Avery play?

77. What was Avery's nickname for Diana?
78. What street in San Francisco is Salingers Restaurant located on?
79. How many steps lead to the Salingers' front door?
80. What is the address of the Salinger house?
81. What name does Jake use when posing as Bailey's benefactor?
82. What does Justin's girlfriend Robin nickname her breasts?
83. What is the magnitude of the earthquake that rocks San Francisco in "Aftershocks"?
84. What is Jill's address?
85. What movie stars of yesteryear do Jill and Bailey try to emulate?
86. What is the name of Callie's 17-year-old, half-blind, asthmatic cat with a heart condition?
87. What game do Bailey, Callie, and Sarah play when Bailey has the chicken pox?
88. What phony extracurricular club do Justin and Julia try to establish to beef up their transcripts for college?

Allergies

Match the *Party of Five* character with what makes them itch and scratch.

89. Charlie	A.	strawberries
90. Julia	B.	jicama
91. Sam	C.	wool
92. Grace	D.	walnuts
93. Jill	E.	shrimp
94. Kirsten	F.	Thurber

Party Animals

Match the cast member with their real life pets.

95. Matthew Fox	A.	A cat named Don Juan De Marco
96. Neve Campbell	B.	An iguana named Stevie
97. Jennifer Love Hewitt	C.	A turtle named Yertle
98. Lacey Chabert	D.	A Shih Tzu named Buster
99. Tamara Taylor	E.	A Chihuahua named Big Poppa
100. Andrew & Steven Cavarno	F.	A dog named Abu

Answers

1. Lloyd W. Loomis.
2. 900.
3. The Possums.
4. Hampshire State.
5. His dimples pulse.
6. His wedding and his Seattle job interview.
7. $65,000.
8. 30.
9. 1987.
10. He dropped out of the University of California at Berkeley.
11. Justin.
12. Girls We Most Want to Cheat Off Of.
13. Gordon (after her mother's middle name).
14. Parker Patterson Press.
15. The Children's Room.
16. *The Crucible.*
17. Walt Whitman Jr. High School.
18. An Incredi-Bra.
19. I, Claudia.
20. Gambling.
21. Film society or yearbook staff.
22. On his stomach. It resembles a race car, according to Julia.
23. Sister Jeannie and baby brother, Ben.
24. "As I Lay Me Down" by Sophie B. Hawkins.
25. Attorney.
26. Garnet.
27. The Nielsen Family (named after the Nielsen ratings).
28. Sarah.
29. Her biological mother, Robin, leaves it in her care when she leaves on tour.
30. Amanda.
31. To the ballet ("Romeo and Juliet").
32. He serenades her with "Baby Come Back" with his guitar on her lawn.
33. His lava lamp, Lacrosse stick, and Bob Marley poster.
34. Penny.
35. Tucker.

36. The Allan Wood Academy in Louisiana.
37. His motorcycle.
38. Nurse.
39. Chase.
40. Major.
41. Meg.
42. "If You Wanna Be Happy (Get an Ugly Girl to Marry You)".
43. Chicago.
44. The andante from Mendelssohn's fourth symphony.
45. Michael.
46. The Harvest Program.
47. Wallerstein.
48. She dropped out of law school.
49. *The Wild Bunch.*
50. Mrs. Kelleher, Kirsten, Mona (the drunk), and Bill.
51. Sneaker cleaner.
52. A new red convertible.
53. A star named after her.
54. A fake I.D.
55. A charm for her bracelet.
56. A Jumanji lunchbox.
57. A thesaurus with all the words for boyfriend underlined.
58. A motorcycle helmet and a car.
59. $15,000.
60. $12,000.
61. $800.
62. $1,000.
63. $1,200.
64. $15,000.
65. $100,000.
66. Nicholas Charles and Diana Gordon Salinger.
67. He can wiggle his ears one at a time.
68. The cymbals.
69. Principal Stickley.
70. "Salingers: 'Cause You Gotta Eat".
71. On an airplane.
72. Stanley.
73. *Something Out of Nothing: What to Cook When the Cupboard Is Bare.*
74. She majored in visual arts at Stanford.

75. Mavis.
76. The cello.
77. Digs (from her initials, D.G.S.).
78. Filbert.
79. 52.
80. 3324 Broadway (the actual house used in exterior shots is located on Broadway in San Francisco, but not at 3324).
81. Garrett Williams.
82. Thelma and Louise.
83. 5.1.
84. 667 Presidio.
85. James Dean and Natalie Wood.
86. Peggy.
87. Moral Dilemma.
88. Students for the Ethical Treatment of Students. (Give yourself a half-point for the first suggested title, Future Adults of America.)
89. B.
90. E.
91. D.
92. A.
93. C.
94. F.
95. B.
96. D.
97. A.
98. F.
99. E.
100.C.

Scoring:

Each correct answer is worth one point. If you scored between:

81 - 100	Congratulations, you're an honorary Salinger! Pull up a chair at the booth and join the party.
61 - 80	Way to go! You're on your way to the party, be careful not to make any wrong turns.
41 - 60	Hey party pooper, you'd better work on your Salinger skills.
0 - 40	The party's over. You're in the dog house with Thurber.

Appendices

Matthew, Paula, Scott, Neve, and Lacey with the 1996 Golden Globe Award for
Best Drama Series. Archive Photos.

Appendix A: Awards, Honors, and Nominations

Party of Five has been widely recognized for the outstanding quality of its acting, writing, and production. So it's not surprising that the series has accumulated some impressive awards. Here is a chronological listing of the honors bestowed upon the series:

1995 S.O.S. Winner, *TV Guide*
Party of Five garnered the most votes in *TV Guide*'s fourth annual "Save Our Shows" poll in April 1995. Approximately 28,000 people cast their votes in support of the series. The other shows targeted in the S.O.S. poll—*My So-Called Life*, *Earth 2*, and *Under Suspicion*—were all canceled.

1995 Humanitas Prize
On July 6, 1995, the Pacific Palisades-based Human Family Educational and Cultural Institute awarded a Humanitas Prize to Christopher Keyser and Amy Lippman for their script, "Thanksgiving" (11/14/94). The Humanitas Prize honors film and television scripts that enrich the public. Keyser and Lippman received a cash prize of $15,000.

1996 Golden Globe Award
Party of Five was named Best Television Drama Series at the 53rd annual Golden Globes Awards on January 21, 1996. Up against formidable competition from *NYPD Blue*, *ER*, *Chicago Hope*, and *Murder One*, *Party of Five*'s win took everyone by surprise, including the cast. Scott Wolf later said, "We felt that to be recognized as one of the better shows on television was something we deserved, but to win and stand out among that competition was something that really kind of blew us away." The Golden Globes, awarded by the Hollywood Foreign Press Association, honor outstanding achievement in television and film.

1996 Humanitas Prize Nomination
Christopher Keyser and Amy Lippman were nominated for a Humanitas Prize for their script, "Before and After" (2/21/96), which dealt with Julia's pregnancy.

241

1996 Emmy Nomination - Outstanding Sound Editing

Jeremy Gordon, Charlie Shepard, Amy Morrison, Harry Cheney, and Rich Tavtigian were nominated for an Emmy award for their sound editing on the *Party of Five* episode, "The Wedding." An episode of *The X-Files* won the award.

1996 Viewers Voice Awards

The television advocacy group Viewers Voice named *Party of Five* its "Favorite Drama Series" and Scott Wolf its "Favorite Actor in a Drama Series" at the fifth annual Viewers Voice convention in Studio City, California, on September 28, 1996.

1996 Environmental Media Awards

The *Party of Five* episode "Before and After" (2/21/96) received the Turner Prize from the Environmental Media Association on October 14, 1996. The Turner Prize, which includes a $10,000 cash award, is given each year in recognition of the television show that best deals with the issue of population growth.

1996 William S. Paley Television Festival

The Museum of Television & Radio honored *Party of Five* on October 15, 1996, during its 13th annual television festival in Los Angeles. The Paley Festival celebrates classic and contemporary television at its best. After a screening of the episode "Thanksgiving," several members of the cast and production team participated in a panel discussion and Q&A session.

1996 Nancy Susan Reynolds Award

The *Party of Five* writing staff received a Nancy Susan Reynolds Special Writers Award for the series' portrayals of family planning, sexuality, and reproductive health. The awards were presented on October 23, 1996, in West Hollywood. Nancy Susan Reynolds (1936-1985) was a prominent philanthropist and co-founder of the Z. Smith Reynolds Foundation.

1996 GLAAD Media Award Nominee

Party of Five was nominated as Outstanding Television Series by the Gay & Lesbian Alliance Against Defamation. The series was cited for its positive portrayal of Mitchell Anderson's character, Ross—the first gay man on television to adopt a child.

1997 Golden Globe Nomination

Nominated for Best Television Drama Series, *Party of Five* lost to *The X-Files*. Also nominated were *Chicago Hope*, *NYPD Blue*, and *ER*.

1997 Writers Guild Award Nomination

Mark B. Perry's *Party of Five* script "Falsies" (10/4/95) was nominated for a Writers Guild Award for outstanding achievement in television writing. Also nominated were episodes of *Law & Order*, *Murder One*, *NYPD Blue*, and *The X-Files*. The winner, announced March 16, 1997, was an episode of *NYPD Blue* entitled "Girl Talk".

1997 Gracie Award

The Foundation of American Women in Radio & Television honored *Party of Five* on April 24, 1997, with a Gracie Award. The Gracies recognize achievement in radio and TV programming that advances women and women's issues.

1997 Hollywood Reporter YoungStar Award - Lacey Chabert

Lacey Chabert won the YoungStar Award for Best Performance by a Young Actress in a Drama TV Series for her performance on *Party of Five*. The awards, given by the *Hollywood Reporter*, were presented on May 4, 1997, in Hollywood.

1997 *Seventeen* Magazine Readers' Poll

For *Seventeen's* ninth annual poll, 17,000 readers participated. The results were printed in the July 1997 issue of the magazine. *Party of Five* was named "TV Show of the Year," while Scott Wolf and Neve Campbell were chosen "TV Actor of the Year" and "TV Actress of the Year," respectively.

Appendix B: Party of Five Online

Party of Five had only been on the air a short time when its fans began venturing into cyberspace, networking with other fans to discuss the show, setting up Internet Web sites devoted to the series, or joining electronic mailing lists to keep up with the latest developments in the Salingers' lives. With more than 50 Web sites already devoted to the series, and new pages turning up all the time, it is clear that "cyber-Fivers" have staked a sizable share of the World Wide Web.

The Official Sites

The Official FOX Network *Party of Five* Site
http://www.foxworld.com/po5indx.htm
The FOX site includes cast biographies, episode descriptions, photos, and games.

The Official Sony *Party of Five* Site
http://www.spe.sony.com/Pictures/tv/party/party.html
Sony's official site contains cast biographies, photos, audio and video clips, and a virtual reality tour of the Salinger house.

The Best Fan Sites

TK Baltimore's *Party of Five* Site
http://www.cat.nyu.edu/tkbalt/salingers/
One of the trailblazers, this site was founded in March 1995 and is updated frequently. It
   includes a detailed episode guide, article transcripts, a collection of quotes, previews
   of upcoming episodes, fan fiction, and more. TK started the site to promote the
   show and help keep it on the air and says, "The site kept growing and growing, and
   it turned out to be a pretty comprehensive source of information about the show."

Closer to Free
http://rhf.bradley.edu/ ~ violet/party.html

At Dana Grossman's site, web surfers can listen to the theme song, read episode descriptions, and speak out about the latest plot developments. The site also includes an international page, which lists the countries currently airing *Party of Five*.

Everything *Party of Five*
http://digiserve.com/kmisle/epof.html
The maintainer of Everything *Party of Five* created this site in January 1996 as a means of generating more recognition for the series: "My hope was that with the pictures and information I provided, other fans on the net would start their own *Party of Five* pages, so the show would become more popular, and the powers-that-be at FOX would take notice." The site includes thorough cast biographies, late-breaking news, and photos.

The Salingers
http://www.geocities.com/Hollywood/8061/party.html
A cool design and frequent updating make Kimberly Charette's one of the better fan sites. It includes episode summaries and reviews, cast biographies, and a weekly poll.

The Most Unusual Sites
One can only hope that these sites are not intended to be taken seriously.

Fans Against the Maltreatment of Claudia and Owen Salinger
http://www.geocities.com/Hollywood/Set/5833/lacey.html
"Somewhere in San Francisco, there is a Salinger child crying in the darkness on their violin teacher's doorstep." So proclaims web-master Katie B., who includes addresses where fans should write to express their outrage at the abuse of the littlest Salingers.

Party of Five Drinking Game
http://www.personal.psu.edu/users/h/e/heb112/party.html
The rules to a truly irresponsible drinking game by Heather and her party friends are posted here.

Party of Five Wicked Plot Summaries
http://www.geocities.com/Hollywood/Hills/7214/pof.html
Spex Kowalski rates episodes using the "Ralph-o-Meter," which ranges from "settled stomach" to "emergency room," with colorful rungs like "toilet bound" and "heaving begins" in between. Spex's slogan is, "Everybody one, everybody two, everybody spew."

Other Fan Pages
The Bailey and Sarah Online Fan Club
http://www.stuweeks.u-net.com/bsc/bsfc.htm
Created May 4, 1997, by diehard fans Lynn and Lisa, this page is devoted to a letter writing campaign to convince *Party of Five* producers to reunite Sarah and Bailey.

Bailey's *Party of Five* Home Page
http://www.geocities.com/Hollywood/Hills/3181/Po5.html
This site provides publicity information and photos from the show.

Bill's *Party of Five* Page
http://brill.acomp.usf.edu/~wboulwar/party.html
Bill's site includes show quotations, episode summaries, photos and a video clip.

Black Scorpio's *Party of Five*
http://www.geocities.com/~blackscorpio/pof.htm
Some of the more unique features of Vancouver-based fan Melanie's site are a voting
    booth and live chat room.

Brian Liang's *Party of Five* Page
http://www.mvhs.srvusd.k12.ca.us/~bliang/party.html
Brian's site features cool quotes, sound clips, character profiles, episode summaries,
    and a transcript of "The Fable of Jersey and Geraldine" (Justin's short story from
    "Happily Ever After," 3/20/96).

Byron Go's Page
http://www.csua.berkeley.edu/~byron/PartyOf5/Pof5.html
Launched in late 1994, Byron's page was the first fan site dedicated to *Party of Five*. He
    says, "Back then, few people had heard of the Web, and I was learning HTML for
    work. I've been a big fan of the show since the pilot, so I designed the site as a test
    case." Updated infrequently, the site contains rudimentary show information, pho-
    tos, and cast biographies.

David's *Party of Five* Page
http://www.ozemail.com.au/~ryork/pof/pof.htm
Australian fan David Jenkins established this site in August 1996. The site features
    audio and video clips, an episode guide, cast biographies, photos, and article tran-
    scripts from Australian magazines.

Dianne Smith's Unofficial *Party of Five* Page
http://www.geocities.com/Broadway/7377/pof.html
This site includes information about the show and stars, especially Dianne's favorite
    cast member, Jeremy London.

Eric Blair's Sporadic *Party of Five* Summaries
http://www.his.com/~pavela/po5.html
Eric admits his episode summaries are sporadic ("I have a life, okay?"). The sum-
    maries that are there are quite extensive and amusing.

Erina Nerome's *Party of Five* Page
http://www.geocities.com/TelevisionCity/1405/
Erina's page contains character profiles, show information, and viewer polls.

The First English *Party of Five* Page
http://www.stuweeks.u-net.com/epo5.htm

Stu Weeks's site, launched in March 1997, primarily caters to British fans, but all
nationalities will find the information interesting.

Freddy's *Party of Five* Homepage
http://www.trenton.edu/ ~ friedri2/party.html
Established in February 1996, Freddy's page includes an episode guide, cast biographies, a tribute to "Thanksgiving," and a timeline of events in the show's history.

Heather's *Party of Five* Links Page
http://www.coil.com/ ~ heathera/po5.htm
Heather Arsenault's page is mainly a collection of links to other *Party* sites, but there
are also tidbits of information about the series.

Jamie's *Party of Five* Page
http://www.geocities.com/Hollywood/Set/3087/Pof.htm
Jamie Quick's site has news about the show and many links.

Jen's *Party of Five* Episode Summary Page
http://www.geocities.com/TelevisionCity/4223/
Detailed summaries of several episodes are available on Jen's site.

Julie's *Party of Five*
http://www.txdirect.net/users/julie/party.html
Julie Gumm's site contains lengthy descriptions, cast biographies, and transcripts of
articles about the series.

Liz's *Party of Five*
http://members.aol.com/Lizlou746/partyoffive.html
Liz pays tribute to *Party of Five* and other shows she admires on her site.

Maggie's *Party of Five* Page
http://members.aol.com/MagStar1/party.html
A basic page featuring cast photographs and tidbits about the show.

Max's *Party of Five* Page
http://www.geocities.com/TelevisionCity/4812/
Max Steinman calls his site, created in March 1997, the ultimate *Party of Five* page. It
includes cast biographies, article transcripts, and viewer polls.

Morten's *Party of Five* Page
http://home.sol.no/almeland/party.htm
This page, from a fan in Norway, includes basic information about the show.

The *Party of Five* FTP Site
ftp://ftp.wwa.com/pub/dattier/salingers/
This File Transfer Protocol site includes several downloadable files, including episode
guides, fact sheets, chat transcripts, and music logs.

The *Party of Five* Hidden Gallery
http://www.scrippscol.edu/~home/jjorrits/www/pof5.html
A photo-intensive site with pictures of the cast on and off the show, character profiles, and a history of the series.

The *Party of Five* HomePage
http://www.geocities.com/Hollywood/Hills/5772/
If you read Portuguese, you'll enjoy Guilherme Marquez da Fonseca's site.

The *Party of Five* Page
http://www.geocities.com/Hollywood/Hills/6737/pindah.htm
Launched in December 1996, Lynn's Australian-based site contains cast information, photographs, and lots of links. You can also send a virtual *Party of Five* postcard to your online buddies.

The *Party of Five* Page
http://www.student.uwa.edu.au/student/bj/party.html
Australian fan Brendan Selby's page includes basic information and links.

The *Party of Five* Shrine
http://www.ici.net/cust_pages/jwu012/po5s.htm
Party of Five worshippers will find photos and lots of links at this shrine.

Razman's *Party of Five* Page
http://www.toptown.com/DORMS/hina/po5.html
A list of frequently asked questions and answers, photos, and episode summaries for the third season are included on this site.

Robb's *Party of Five* Page
http://www.tiac.net/users/robbp/partyoffive.html
Among the more unique features on Robb Potter's page are photographs of the real Salinger house, a listing of awards, and article transcripts. Robb says he created his site in March 1995 out of a love of the series and a desire to provide information to other fans.

Russ's *Party of Five* Page
http://home.cc.manitoba.ca/~umloewe3/po5/po5.html
One of the leaner offerings, Russ's page mainly consists of links to other *Party of Five* sites.

Stefani's Unofficial *Party of Five* Home Page
http://www.geocities.com/Hollywood/Lot/1095/POF.html
One of the most recent additions to *Party of Five*'s cyber-library.

Sites for Individual Cast Members
Green Day / Neve Campbell Site
http://www.geocities.com/Hollywood/7026/indexn.htm
Contains photographs and information about Neve's career.

The Jennifer Love Hewitt Page by Teemu
http://bonnie.tky.hut.fi/love/love.html
Finnish fan Teemu Hanninen fell in love with Love after seeing *Byrds of Paradise.*
This site has quicktime videos, photos, and information.

Jeremy London Home Page
http://www2.pitt.edu/~rowst3/Jeremy.html
Rosemary Wally's page dedicated to Jeremy includes photos, information, and movie
clips.

The Lacey Chabert Site
http://qp.com/lacey/
Created in March 1997, this site is dedicated to chronicling Lacey Chabert's career. It
features audio and video clips, credits, news, and information on Lacey's upcoming projects.

Love Access: The Online Magazine About Jennifer Love Hewitt
http://home.sol.no/hestvedt/
Kjetil Hestvedt's site features a slick design and plenty of information, which is updated
frequently. The online magazine includes the latest news on Love's career and regular columns like "Fan of the Month," "Love Sightings," and a trading post.

The Love Hewitt Shrine
http://www.geocities.com/Hollywood/5560/
Created in March 1997 by fan Erik M. Kongsgaard, this site includes biographical
information, a photo gallery and trivia about Love, from her favorite food to her
worst habits.

Neve Campbell: Canadian Princess
http://www.geocities.com/Hollywood/Hills/4253/neve.html
This site includes photos, a filmography, chat transcripts, and other facts about Neve.

The Neve Campbell Obsession Page
http://home.sprynet.com/sprynet/sshanker/
Despite the name of his page, Yohan Shanker says he prefers to call himself a diehard
fan, not an obsessed one. His site contains a biography of Neve, and several photos, including stills from *Scream*, *The Craft*, *Catwalk*, and *Party of Five*.

The *Party of Five* / Jennifer Love Hewitt / Neve Campbell Page
http://www.geocities.com/Hollywood/Hills/9912/
Photos and biographical information on Jennifer Love Hewitt and Neve Campbell.

A Scott Wolf Fan Page
http://www.scott-wolf.com/
Matthew Wagner's site includes Scott's biography, photos, quotes, pictures and article
reprints.

Tribute to Love
http://po5gal.simplenet.com/love.html

The site, devoted to Jennifer Love Hewitt, includes a photo gallery, biography, and
addresses to write to Love.

Other online resources

The *Party of Five* electronic mailing list was started in November 1994 and is moderated by David W. Tamkin. This list had 1,500 subscribers as of June 1997. Subscribers to the list post messages about the series, the cast, and closely related subjects. Spoilers (information about future plot developments that would "spoil" the episode for others) are not allowed. To subscribe, send an email to: salingers-REQUEST@wwa.com

Party of Five bulletin boards

No matter which of the online services you use, you can find fans online who share your interest in *Party of Five*. On CompuServe, the TV Zone section includes a forum for discussing the series. CompuServe has hosted live chats with several *Party* personnel, including Amy Lippman, Scott Wolf, and Matthew Fox.

The America Online *Party of Five* bulletin board has grown from a small but dedicated group of about twenty people in September 1994 to a hugely popular repository of comments and opinions. Several people involved in the production of the show regularly visit the board. Daniel Scott Burnford, one of the founding members and the unofficial group secretary, says, "*Party of Five* touched me from the very start. I don't think I ever missed an episode; nor ended the hour without a tear in my eye. The TV Viewers bulletin board on AOL has also been an experience beyond words. Almost from the start, a group of complete strangers—of various ages and locations around the country—found the board and began to communicate with each other. We posted our thoughts on the characters and episodes; developed a weekly online chat about the series (often joined by the wonderful *Party of Five* cast and crew); and before long, friendships developed."

The *Party of Five* Usenet Newsgroup
alt.tv.party-of-five
Newsgroups are global bulletin boards where people exchange ideas on thousands of topics, from the mainstream to the fringe. They are similar to the message boards found on commercial online services like America Online and Prodigy, but since they are distributed through the Internet, they can be accessed by people using almost any Internet provider or commercial online service. Visitors to the *Party of Five* newsgroup discuss almost anything related to the show.

Note: Web addresses change frequently and new web-pages are constantly being created. The URLs listed here were accurate as of July 1997.

Appendix C: Addresses

To write to any of the stars of *Party of Five*, utilize the following address:
(Star's Name)
c/o *Party of Five*
Columbia Pictures Television
10202 West Washington Boulevard
Culver City, CA 90232

To show your support of *Party of Five*, write to the network:
FOX-TV
P.O. Box 900
Beverly Hills, CA 90213

Jennifer Love Hewitt has an official fan club, which is run by her mother and other family members. For dues of $19.95, members receive an autographed 8"x10" glossy photo, a photo postcard, discounts on merchandise, and newsletters featuring facts about Love and updates on her career activities.
Jennifer Love Hewitt Fan Club
859 Hollywood Way, Suite 523
Burbank, CA 91505

Neve Campbell's mother and cousin operate her official fan club. For $8 membership fee, members receive newsletters keeping them up-to-date on her career activities.
Neve Campbell's Fan Club
Performance Unlimited
Suite 102, 3-2401 Cliffe Street
Courtenay, B.C. V9N 2L5, CANADA

Viewers Voice is a non-profit organization which supports television programming. It has been a vocal supporter of *Party of Five* since its debut. To find out more about this organization, and what you can do to help keep your favorite TV shows on the air, write to:
Viewers Voice, Inc.
P.O. Box 27758
West Allis, WI 53227

Appendix D: Party of Five Merchandise

Album

In November 1996, Reprise Records released the soundtrack album, *Music from Party of Five*. The soundtrack features the theme song, the BoDeans' "Closer to Free," as well as cuts from Big Bad Voodoo Daddy, BT with Tori Amos, Chaka Khan with Bruce Hornsby, Holly Palmer, Bruce Jackson, Laurie Sargent, Nanci Griffith, Rickie Lee Jones, Howard Jones, Rusted Root, Shawn Colvin, Stevie Nicks, and Syd Straw.

New York Daily News reviewer David Bianculli wrote of the album, "[the] songs and performers are relatively quirky, complex and original—just like *Party of Five* itself, which makes this such a fine extension of the TV series. If you like the show enough to trust its musical judgment, you won't be disappointed." The soundtrack is available at most record stores.

Books

Pocket Books produced a series of juvenile books based on Claudia's character. Released in 1997, *Welcome to My World, Too Cool for School, A Boy Friend Is Not a "Boyfriend,"* and *The Best Things in Life Are Free, Right?* are priced at $3.99 each and are available at most bookstores.

Calendars

Landmark Calendars (51 Digital Drive, Novato, CA 94949) produced a 1997 *Party of Five* wall calendar, featuring publicity stills mainly taken from the first season. To order a catalog, call 1-800-365-YEAR.

T-Shirts, Mugs, Hats, and More!

Sony has licensed *Party of Five* T-shirts, sweatshirts, hats, coffee mugs and other items. The following mail order companies carry *Party of Five* merchandise:

Art-Vision Apparel
1565 Cliff Road, Suite 3-289
St. Paul, MN 55122
Fax: (612) 890-7918
E-mail: orders@art-vision.com
Web site: http://www.art-vision.com

Entertainment Weekly Studio Store
Dept. EW-60
P.O. Box 60044
Tampa, FL 33660
Phone: 1-800-EWEEKLY

Movie Madness Merchandise
117 6th Street
Oregon City, OR 97045

Phone: (503) 650-0419
Fax: (503) 722-3867
E-mail: movie@calweb.com
Web site: http://www.moviemadness.com

Power Star Collectibles
35 S. White Horse Pike
Suite 411
Audubon, NJ 08106
Phone: (800) 413-2269; (609) 547-0094
Fax: (609) 547-0294
E-mail: bkushner@ix.netcom.com
Web site:
http://www.pages.prodigy.com/tvmerch/info.htm

Bibliography

In addition to several visits to the set of *Party of Five* and conversations over the years with people involved in the production of the series, the author consulted a number of articles, transcripts, and other sources in the preparation of this book. The following is a comprehensive listing. Where the subject of the article is not evident in its title, that information is included in brackets following the listing, e.g. Garver, Susan. "A Down-to-Earth TV Heartthrob." *Television Today*, Spring 1995, p. 30. [Matthew Fox]

Publications

Adalian, Josef. "Finale Sets a Record for 'Party.'" *New York Post*, April 5, 1997, p. 48.
___. "'Five' Cheers for a TV Legend." *New York Post*, December 12, 1995, p. 81. [Carroll O'Connor]
___. "Fox to Fans: The 'Party's' On!" *New York Post*, March 8, 1997, p. 48.
___. "'Party' Animals Await Word on Fate of 'Five.'" *New York Post*, March, 1995, p. 69.
___. "'Party' Wants Respect in Second Season." *New York Post*, September 27, 1995, p. 70.
Amber, Jeannine. Review of *Party of Five*. *Village Voice*, January 21, 1997, p. 50.
Anderson, Mitchell. "Out in Hollywood: The Party is Just Beginning." GLAAD, May/June 1996.
Archerd, Army. "Just for Variety." *Variety*, December 11, 1995. [Carroll O'Connor]
"At Home With the Stars: Jennifer Love Hewitt." *People*, April 21, 1997, p. 100.
Bash, Alan. "Fox Will Let *Party of Five* Continue." *USA Today*, March 10, 1997, p. 3D.
___. "Hit and Miss: How the Prognosticators Fared." *USA Today*, December 23, 1994.
___. "Inside TV." *USA Today*, April 19, 1995.
___. "Scott Wolf, Hoping to Bring New Life to Fox's 'Party.'" *USA Today*, November 2, 1994.
Beachy, Susan Campbell, and Craig Modderno. "Listen Up: Neve Campbell." *TV Guide Online*, December 5, 1996.
Beck, Marilyn. "*Party of Five* Star Wants to Take Five." *The Outlook* (syndicated column), March 16, 1996, p. E2. [Scott Wolf]

Beller, Miles. Review of *Party of Five*. *Hollywood Reporter*, September 12, 1994, p. 16.

Berger, Lori. "Scott Wolf: Life of the Party." *Sassy*, November 1996.

Bergman, Anne. "Emmy Nominee in Good Company at Sunday's Show." *Los Angeles Times*, September 7, 1994, p. F1. [Michael Goorjian]

"The Best Television of 1995." *Time*, December 20, 1995.

Bianculli, David. "'Party' Begins Its Season With a Bang." *New York Daily News*, August 21, 1996, p. 70.

___. "*Party of Five* Comes Up a Bit Short." *New York Daily News*, September. 12, 1994, p. 64.

___. "Season Over, 'Party' Just Starting." *New York Daily News*, April 2, 1997, p. 70.

___. "TV's Tuning In." *New York Daily News*, November 13, 1996. [*Party of Five* Soundtrack review]

Black, Kent. "Jeremy & Jason London." *Us*, February 1997, pp. 84-88.

Bounds, Wendy and Erle Norton. "Is Party Over for Acclaimed FOX TV Series?" *Wall Street Journal*, March 15, 1995, p. B1.

Bowles, Jennifer. "'Planning *Party of Five*." *Los Angeles Times*, March 9, 1997.

Brasel, Dale and Heather Scott. "The Freshmen." *Detour*, March 1995. [Scott Wolf, Jeremy London]

Braxton, Greg. "Fox Says Patience is Helping Shows Catch More Viewers." *Los Angeles Times*, January 18, 1996, p. F2.

Brooks, Tim and Earle Marsh. *The Complete Directory to Prime Time Network and Cable TV Shows, 1946-Present*. New York: Ballantine Books, 1995.

Brous, Elizabeth. "Lacey's New Look." *Seventeen*, April 1997, pp. 42-43.

Bryson, Jodi. "Alexandra Lee: Luckiest Girl Alive?" *Sassy*, November 1996.

Butterfield, Alan. "*Party of Five* Stars in Trial Marriage." *National Enquirer*, December 3, 1996, p. 33. [Scott Wolf and Paula Devicq]

Byrds of Paradise Press Kit, Steven Bochco Productions, 1994.

Bystedt, Karen Hardy. *Before They Were Stars: In Their Own Words*. Santa Monica, CA: General Publishing Group, 1996, p. 154-157. [Neve Campbell]

Cagle, Jess. "Hour of the Wolf." *Entertainment Weekly*, February 16, 1996, pp. 26-29. [Scott Wolf]

Carter, Alan. "Baby, You Can Drive My Car." *Soap Opera Digest*, Fall 1996. [Michael Goorjian]

___. "Tom Mason Gets Canceled Again." *New York Daily News*, December 26, 1995, p. 79.

Carter, Bill. "Media: After a positive article on a Fox show, *TV Guide* learns the other networks are watching." *New York Times*, December 11, 1995, p. D7.

"Celebrity Dish." *TV Guide*, February 24, 1996, p. 44. [Jennifer Love Hewitt]

Cerone, Daniel Howard. "Campbell's Coup." *TV Guide*, February 8, 1997, pp. 22-28.

___. "Dark Star." *TV Guide*, February 1, 1997, pp. 31-33. [Megan Ward]

The Craft Press Kit, Columbia Pictures, 1996.

Dargis, Manohla. "Neve Campbell: With a star turn in *Scream*, life's more than a *Party of Five*." *Us*, February 1997, pp. 70-71.

Davies, Jonathan. "Creative Force." *Hollywood Reporter*, May 13, 1997, p. S-48. [Christopher Keyser and Amy Lippman]

Dawson, Jeff. "Scott Wolf: Uncanny Resemblance." *Empire*, June 1996, p. 55.

"Death in the Family." *People*, April 10, 1995. [Carroll O'Connor]

Dell, Pamela. "The London Report: Talent Times Two." *Teen*, January 1992, p. 42. [Jeremy and Jason London]

De Moraes, Lisa. "*Party of Five* Gets Early Renewal." *Hollywood Reporter*, March 1, 1996, p. 8.

Double Dragon Press Kit, Gramercy Pictures, 1994.

Dovlin, Rod. "Alexandra Lee: Party of One." *Axcess*, February 1997, p. 42.

Duffy, Mike. "Wolf Sinks Teeth Into Drinking Storyline." *New York Daily News*, January 30, 1997.

Eldredge, Richard L. "Meet the Star: Lacey Chabert, Star of *Party of Five*." *Atlanta Journal and Constitution*, April 8, 1996, p. B3.

Endrst, James. "Here's Hoping the 'Party' Goes On." *Los Angeles Times*, March 5, 1995, TV Times, p. 9.

Epstein, Jeffrey. "Life's a Scream." *Soap Opera Magazine*, February 11, 1997, p. 41. [Neve Campbell]

Erland, Michell, et al. "Kidsday 'Talking With' Lacey Chabert." *Newsday*, March 8, 1995, p. B21.

Esterly, Glenn. "Party Girl." *TV Guide* (Canada), June 17, 1995, pp. 15-19.

The Evening Star Press Kit, Paramount Pictures, 1996.

"The 50 Most Beautiful People in the World, 1995." *People*, May 8, 1995. [Scott Wolf]

"The 50 Most Beautiful People in the World, 1996." *People*, May 6, 1996. [Matthew Fox, Jeremy & Jason London]

Frankel, Valerie and Ellen Tien. *Prime-Time Style*. New York: Perigree Books, 1996.

French, Lawrence. "Neve Campbell, No Scream Queen." *Femme Fatale*, March 1997, pp. 12-15.

Fretts, Bruce. "Altared Formula." *Entertainment Weekly*, December 15, 1995, pp. 56-57. [Review of *Party of Five*]

Garver, Susan. "A Down-to-Earth TV Heartthrob." *Television Today*, Spring 1995, p. 30. [Matthew Fox]

Goldberg, Gabriel J. P. "Neve Campbell: Party of One." *Genre*, May 1996.

Goldman, Steven. "Full Scream Ahead." *Interview*, January 1997, p. 61. [Neve Campbell]

Goodman, Mark and Tina Johnson. "Twins Peaking." *People*, October 11, 1993, pp. 71-72. [Jeremy and Jason London]

Graham, Jefferson. "'Party' Girl Lacey Chabert Is a Pro at 14." *USA Today*, November 20, 1996, p. 3D.

___. "Peter Roth to Take Over Fox Programming." *USA Today*, September 9, 1996, p. 3D.

Gray, Ellen. "*Party of Five*: Fantasy, Family, Value." *Boston Globe*, August 21, 1996.

Greppi, Michele. "Hard Work is No 'Party' for Teen Star." *New York Post*, October 24, 1994, p. 73. [Scott Wolf]

___. "'Party' Politics Intriguing in 'Five's' Season Finale." *New York Post*, April 2, 1997.

Guttman, Monika. "The Fight for TV Favorites." *USA Weekend*, January 20-22, 1995, p. 8.

"He's Got the Look." *TV Guide*, November 28, 1992. [Jeremy London]

Hochman, David. "White Squall." *Us*, February 1996, pp. 72-74.

"Hollywood's Hot Young Stars!" *People*, November 18, 1996, p. 86. [Scott Wolf is profiled as one of 30 hot stars under 30.]

Hope, Darrell L. "Neve Campbell: Bewitching Hollywood Her Way." *Venice*, May 1996, p. 10.

Hueso, Noela. "Ones to Watch." *Hollywood Reporter*, November 19, 1996, p. S-46. [Jennifer Love Hewitt]

Huff, Richard. "Fox Warns: 'Party'-Poopers Are Going to Hang 'Five.'" *New York Daily News*, November 8, 1994, p. 74.

___. "Hey Fans, 'Party' On For Another Season." *New York Daily News*, March 10, 1997.

"I'd Rather Walk." *Soap Opera Digest*, April 8, 1997. [Alexondra Lee]

Imperati, Rebecca. "Festival Brings Writer Home." *Poughkeepsie Journal*, May 28, 1997, p. 1D. [Ken Topolsky]

"The 'It' List: The 100 Most Creative People in Entertainment." *Entertainment Weekly*, June 27, 1997, p. 74-75. [Neve Campbell]

Jarvis, Jeff. Review of *Party of Five*. *TV Guide*, October 15, 1994, p. 10.

Jewel, Dan and Anne-Marie Otey. "Reigning Canadian: At 22, *Party of Five* Star Neve Campbell Graduates to the Big Time." *People*, May 27, 1996, pp. 79-80.

Jobling, Kate. "Neve Campbell." *Dolly*, July 1996.

Johnson, Allan. "Hard to Believe: With Little Fanfare, Fox Prepares to Pull Plug on 'Party' (April Fool)." *Chicago Tribune*, April 1, 1997.

Kappes, Serena. "Totally Music!" *Tiger Beat*, February 1997, p. 82. [Jennifer Love Hewitt]

Karger, Dave. "Neve Gonna Get It." *Entertainment Weekly*, June 21, 1996, p. 24. [Neve Campbell]

Karlen, Neal. "A Family of Struggling Orphans." *New York Times*, August 4, 1996, Section 12, p. 5.

Kerr, Nancy. "Love Child: Party Girl Next Door Jennifer Love Hewitt Manages to Stay Grounded While Growing Up on TV." *Soap Opera Digest*, circa Summer 1996.

Kitman, Marvin. "*Party of Five*." *Newsday*, December 19, 1994, p. B25.

___. "They're Home Alone." *Newsday*, September 1994.

Kleid, Beth. "Survival of the Salingers." *Los Angeles Times*, July 30, 1995, TV Times section, p. 4.

Lambert, Pam and Monica Rizzo. "Party Girl: Bubby teen queen Jennifer Love Hewitt grabs the spotlight." *People*, September 23, 1996, p. 121-122.

Lang, Steven and Anna David. "Sexy Sixth: Tamara Taylor Adds Color to *Party of Five*." *People*, February 3, 1997, p. 107-108.

"Leader of the Pack." *TV Guide*, September 14, 1996. [Matthew Fox]

Leahy, Michael, "Carroll O'Connor's Concern." *TV Guide*, March 12, 1988, p. 8-12.

"Life of the Party: *Party of Five* hunk Matthew Fox would rather just go fishin'." *People*, September 28, 1995, pp. 87-88.

"Love & Brandy." *16 Magazine*, March 1997, p. 34. [Jennifer Love Hewitt]

"Love Rules." *Teen Party*, October 1996. [Jennifer Love Hewitt]

Loynd, Ray. Review of *Party of Five*. *Variety*, September 5, 1994.

"Lucky Lacey." *Tiger Beat*, February 1997, p. 79.

Madans, Nick, Ali Taheri, Tamara Bostram, and Jan Maly. "Real Love." *Real*, Summer 1996, pp. 24-30. [Jennifer Love Hewitt]

Majewski, Lori. "Lone Wolf." *YM (Young & Modern)*, February 1996, pp. 60-62. [Scott Wolf]

___. "Work It, Love." *YM (Young & Modern)*, Special Summer Fitness Issue, 1997, pp. 84-87. [Jennifer Love Hewitt]

Martinez, Jose, Penelope Patsuris, and Ileane Rudolph. "Viewers Vote to Party On and Continue Exploring Earth 2." *TV Guide*, April 22, 1995, p. 51.

Marx, Andy. "If One London Isn't Right, Try the Other." *Los Angeles Times*, October 5, 1991, p. F2. [Jeremy and Jason London]

"Meet the Party Girls." *Tiger Beat*, August 1995, pp. 86-87. [Neve Campbell and Lacey Chabert]

Mendoza, N.F. "As Charlie's Wedding Day Nears, Actor Matthew Fox Tries to Explain His Jitters." *Los Angeles Times*, December 10, 1995, TV Times section, p. 10.

___."Fox's 'Class of '96' Star Megan Ward Proves She's a Quick Study." *Los Angeles Times*, April 25, 1993, p. 74.

___. "It's Charlie's Choice." *Newsday*, December 13, 1995, p. B53.

___. "The 'Sparkle' that Holds Fox's *Party of Five* Together is Called Lacey." *Los Angeles Times*, October 23, 1994, TV Times section, p. 76.

Michaelson, Judith. "Two Series, One Idea: Kids Home Alone." *Los Angeles Times*, October 6, 1994, p. F1.

Min, Janice, Monica Rizzo and Paula Yoo. "Party Time." *People*, March 3, 1997, pp. 78-87.

Mink, Eric. "It's 9 O'Clock: Does Fox Know Where Its Orphans Are?" *New York Daily News*, March 15, 1995, p. 62.

___. "'Party's' Over for Once-Promising Drama." *New York Daily News*, September 27, 1995, p. 70.

"Mitchell Anderson: TV's hottest gay commodity is living his life under the glare of the media spotlight." *The Advocate*, September 17, 1996.

Moore, Roger. "It's Her Party: Neve Campbell Breaks Out of a Naive Stereotype." *Long Beach Press-Telegram*, January 1, 1997, p. S1.

Morales, Juan. "Neve Campbell." *Detour*, November 1996.

Morice, Laura. "Hot Zone: Megan Ward." *Us*, October 1996, p. 47.

Murphy, Mary. "Here's Lacey." *TV Guide*, August 31, 1996, pp. 32-33.

Neve Campbell Fan Club Newsletter, Performance Unlimited, Issues 1 and 2, 1996.

O'Connor, John J. "Trying to Make a House Into a Home." *New York Times*, October 17, 1994.

___. "Show Sags, So It Gets a Wedding for Ratings." *New York Times*, December 13, 1995, p. C22.

Owen, Rob. *Gen X TV: The Brady Bunch to Melrose Place*. Syracuse, New York: Syracuse University Press, 1997.

Painter, Jamie. "Michael Goorjian and Senta Moses." *Back Stage West*, November 7, 1996, p. 8.

"Party Girl." *TV Guide*, February 18, 1995. [Megan Ward]

"*Party of Five*! Meet the Crew Who Wouldn't Quit." *Superstars*, September 1997, p. 64-72.

Party of Five Review. *People*, December 9, 1996, p. 19.

"*Party of Five*r Love Hewitt Takes on Movies, TV and Music." *Teen Beat*, July 1996.

"Party's Other Babe." *Dolly*, August 1996. [Matthew Fox]

Perkins, Ken Parish. "Quietly, *Party of Five* Plays On." *Fort Worth Star-Telegram*, December 18, 1996.

Podhoretz, John. "It's a Great 'Party.'" *New York Post*, September 12, 1994, p. 69.

___. "Join the 'Party.'" *New York Post*, July 15, 1994, p. 102.

___. "Message to Fox: Let This 'Party' Continue." *New York Post*, October 10, 1994, p. 70.

Polly, John. "Mitchell Anderson: The Happiest Man in Showbiz." *Genre*, June 1997, pp. 44-49.

Provenzano, Tom. "Screen Scene." *Drama-Logue*, May 4, 1995, p. 3. [Michael Goorjian]

Rabinowitz, Dorothy. Review of *Party of Five*. *Wall Street Journal*, December 29, 1994, p. A8.

Rochlin, Margy. "Matthew Fox." *Us*, February 1996, pp. 54-57.

Rosenberg, Howard. "'Party' Shows Class; 'Blue Skies' Cloudy." *Los Angeles Times*, September 12, 1994.

Roush, Matt. "Dynamics of Family Life Fuel Quality Drama." *USA Today*, August 21, 1996, p. 2D.

___. "A Family You Should Get to Know." *USA Today*, November 2, 1994.

___. "A House Divided on *Party of Five*." *USA Today*, February 19, 1997, p. 3D.

___. "Intense 'Party' Drew Its Power From Authenticity, Wolf Says." *USA Today*, June 4, 1997, p. 3D.

___. "Let the Good Times Roll: *Party of Five* expects to entertain a bigger crowd." *USA Today*, August 21, 1996, p. 1D.

___. "Little Laughs on CBS; Lots of Sobs for 'Party.'" *USA Today*, November 14, 1994, p. 3D.

___. "'Party' Time After a Season of Trials." *USA Today*, April 2, 1997.

___. "A 'Party' to Crash." *USA Today*, December 13, 1995.

___. "A 'Party' to Cry For: Get Out the Hankies for the Heartfelt Season Finale." *USA Today*, March 27, 1996, p. 1D.

___. "'Party' Worth Celebrating." *USA Today*, September 27, 1995.

___. "Poignant 'Party' Pours on the Emotion." *USA Today*, September 25, 1996, p. 3D.

___. "The Push to Get *People* to the 'Party.'" *USA Today*, June 7, 1995, p. 3D.

___. "Sadly, This 'Party' is Probably Over." *USA Today*, March 15, 1995, p. 3D.

___. "Surprise 'Party': Julia Gets Hitched." *USA Today*, April 3, 1997, p. 3D.

Rubiner, Michael. "The Writers." *Us*, April 1996. [*Party of Five, Seinfeld*, and *X-Files* writers]

Rudolph, Amanda. "The Secret Life of 'The Party.'" *Los Angeles*, August 1996, p. 26.

Russo, Tom. "Scott Wolf: The boy next door on *Party of Five* loses in love and wins viewers' affections." *Us*, November 1995.

"Save Our Shows: *Party of Five*." *TV Guide*, April 1, 1995, p. 33.

Schindehette, Susan and Tom Cunneff. "Who'll Be the Boss?" *People*, March 28, 1994. [Scott Wolf and Alyssa Milano]

Schleier, Curt. "Second Chance from Fox Lets Actor 'Party' On." *Detroit News*, November 15, 1995. [Matthew Fox]

Schneider, Wolf. "After Midnight." *Movieline*, January/February 1997, p. 14. [Neve Campbell]

"Scott Wolf." *Dolly*, July 1996.

"Scott Wolf." *Us*, May 1995, p. 76.

"Scott Wolf's Bailey Blues!" *16 Magazine*, March 1997, p. 69.

Scream Press Kit, Dimension Films, 1996.

Seibel, Deborah Starr. "Fox & Wolf: 'Party' Animals." *TV Guide*, December 10, 1994, pp. 24-26.

Sgroi, Barbara. "Cosmo Q&A: Scott Wolf." *Cosmopolitan*, May 1997, p. 184.

Shales, Tom. "*Party of Five*: A Family Show In More Ways Than One." *Washington Post*, September 27, 1995, p. B1.

___. "*Party of Five*: The Kids are All Right." *Washington Post*, September 12, 1994, p. D1.

Sharkey, Betsy. "Life of the 'Party.'" *Mediaweek*, March 25, 1996, pp. 27-29.

Shaw, Jessica. "Top 'Five' Hit." *Entertainment Weekly*, March 15, 1996, p. 19. [Theme Song, "Closer to Free"]

"63,000 Readers: Save Our Show!" *USA Weekend*, March 3-5, 1995, p. 8.

Slewinski, Christy. "She Strays from the 'Party' Line." *New York Daily News*, August 28, 1996, p. 75. [Neve Campbell]

Snierson, Dan. "Is the 'Party' Over?" *Entertainment Weekly*, March 10, 1995, pp. 16-17.

___. "Life of the Party." *Entertainment Weekly*, February 14, 1997, pp. 16-27.

___. "'Party' Animals." *Entertainment Weekly*, September 9, 1994, p. 67.

Sommers, Susan. "Star Style: Neve Campbell." *New York Daily News/New York Vue*, November 5, 1995, p. 14.

Spillman, Susan. "Life of the 'Party': Fox's Fab *Party of Five* has all the makings of a hit. Now all it needs is more viewers." *TV Guide*, December 9, 1995.

___. "Claudia's First Kiss." *TV Guide*, December 9, 1995, p. 22.

Sterne, Hilary. "Hot Zone: Tamara Taylor." *Us*, May 1997, p. 37.

Stevenson, William. Review of *Jennifer Love Hewitt* (album), *Entertainment Weekly*, September 6, 1996.

Strauss, Bob. "Scott Wolf Weathers the Storm." *Long Beach Press-Telegram*, February 25, 1996.

Teenage Bonnie & Klepto Clyde Press Kit, Trimark Pictures, 1993.

Thompson, Bob. "L.A. Life a Scream for Neve." *Toronto Sun*, December 1996.

Thompson, Malissa. "Interview With a Wolf." *Seventeen*, December 1994, p. 71. [Scott Wolf]

___. "Jeremy London." *Seventeen*, February 1996, pp. 98-99.

___. "Love's Story." *Seventeen*, February 1997, p. 100-107. [Jennifer Love Hewitt]

___. "Neve Campbell." *Seventeen*, October 1995, p. 89.

___. "'Party On': Matthew Fox finds unexpected fame heading up TV's most unusual family on *Party of Five*." *Soap Opera Digest*, November 21, 1995.

___. "Scott Wolf." *Seventeen*, May 1995, p. 93.

___. "The Strife of the Party." *React*, January 1997, p. 9. [Lacey Chabert]

Tucker, Ken. "Orphan Hootenanny (Review of *Party of Five* and *On Our Own*)." *Entertainment Weekly*, September 9, 1994, pp. 66-67.

Tunison, Michael. "Summer of Love." *Entertainment Today*, August 8, 1996, p. 6. [Jennifer Love Hewitt]

"20 Great Faces." *TV Guide*, May 24, 1997. [Scott Wolf and Neve Campbell are among 20 TV stars selected]

"Two's Company Again for *Party of Five* Hunk & *Melrose Place* Cutie." *National Enquirer*, April 1, 1997, p. 41. [Scott Wolf and Alyssa Milano]

Van Tassel, Joan. Review of *Party of Five*. *Hollywood Reporter*, September 27, 1995, p. 12.

___. Review of *Party of Five*. *Hollywood Reporter*, August 21, 1996, p. 9.

Vered, Annabel. "Young Love." *TV Guide*, December 9, 1995, p. 24.

Wedlan, Candace A. "Gooky Golfing is Just One Part of Her Regimen." *Los Angeles Times*, March 20, 1996, p. E3. [Lacey Chabert]

Weinraub, Bernard. "Red Hot Right Now: Neve Campbell." *Cosmopolitan*, January 1997.

Weinstein, Steve. "Party Boy." *Movieline*, January/February 1996. [Scott Wolf]

Werts, Diane. "A Misty-Eyed View of '*Party of Five*.'" *Newsday*, April 2, 1997.

___. "The 'Party' Isn't Over." *Newsday*, July 13, 1995, p. B69.

___. "The 32-Cent Question: Just What Do Celebrities Do with Letters from Their Fans?" *Newsday*, January 7, 1996, p. 10.

___. "Unsettling '*Party of Five*.'" *Newsday*, March 27, 1996, p. B53.

"When Ratings Sag, It's Contest Time." *Mediaweek*, February 24, 1997, p. 29.

Whitney, Dwight. "Why Archie Survives." *TV Guide*, August 8, 1981, pp. 28-30. [Carroll O'Connor]

Wolf, Jeanne. "A Father's Agony and Anger." *TV Guide*, February 24, 1996, p. 5-6. [Carroll O'Connor]

Television Interviews and Transcripts

"Behind the Scenes of *Party of Five*." *In the Mix* (PBS), May 4, 1996. [Interviews with Lacey Chabert, Neve Campbell, Matthew Fox, Michael Goorjian, Jennifer Love Hewitt, Christopher Keyser, Scott Wolf]

Neve Campbell on *Late Night with Conan O'Brien*, December 20, 1996.

Neve Campbell on *The Late Show with David Letterman*, December 19, 1996.

Neve Campbell on *Rosie O'Donnell*, December 6, 1996.

Matthew Fox on *Rosie O'Donnell*, November 11, 1996.

Matthew Fox on *Viewers Voice*, November 26, 1995.

Jennifer Love Hewitt on *Live with Regis and Kathie Lee*, August 5, 1996.

Jennifer Love Hewitt on *The Tonight Show with Jay Leno*, February 1996.

Jennifer Love Hewitt on *The Tonight Show with Jay Leno*, October 22, 1996.

Chris Keyser on *Viewers Voice*, August 25, 1994.

Alexondra Lee on *Access Hollywood*, January 12, 1997.

Amy Lippman on *Viewers Voice*, July 27, 1995.

Scott Wolf on *Late Night with Conan O'Brien*, January 1995.

Scott Wolf on *Live with Regis and Kathie Lee*, January 3, 1995.

Scott Wolf on *Rosie O'Donnell*, February 20, 1997.

Scott Wolf on *The Tonight Show with Jay Leno*, February 28, 1996.

Scott Wolf on *The Tonight Show with Jay Leno*, November 25, 1996.

Events and Seminars

Academy of Television Arts & Sciences, Panel Discussion: Inside *Party of Five*, North Hollywood, CA, June 12, 1997. [Participants: Mitchell Anderson, Mark B. Perry, Michael Engler, Jennifer Love Hewitt, Christopher Keyser, Amy Lippman, P. K. Simonds, Ken Topolsky, Scott Wolf]

Museum of Television & Radio, Creating Prime-Time Drama Seminar: *Party of Five*, Los Angeles, CA, October 29, 1996. [Participants: Chris Keyser, Amy Lippman, Lisa Melamed, Ken Topolsky, Scott Wolf]

Museum of Television & Radio, William S. Paley Television Festival: *Party of Five*, Los Angeles, CA, October 15, 1996. [Participants: Mitchell Anderson, Neve Campbell, Lacey Chabert, Paula Devicq, Michael Engler, Susannah Grant, Jennifer Love Hewitt, Christopher Keyser, Amy Lippman, Jeremy London, Paul Marks, Lisa Melamed, Mark B. Perry, P.K. Simonds, Ken Topolsky, Scott Wolf]

Universal Studios *Party of Five* Event, Q&A/Interview Session, February 17, 1996. [Participants: Neve Campbell, Lacey Chabert, Paula Devicq, Matthew Fox, Scott Grimes, Jennifer Love Hewitt, Scott Wolf]

VQT (Viewers for Quality Television) *Party of Five* Panel Discussion, Los Angeles, CA, September 23, 1995. [Participants: Neve Campbell, Lacey Chabert, Paula Devicq, Matthew Fox, Michael Goorjian, Scott Grimes, Jennifer Love Hewitt, Christopher Keyser, Amy Lippman, Scott Wolf]

Viewers Voice Convention 1994, Studio City, California, October 15, 1994. [Speaker: Amy Lippman]

Viewers Voice Convention 1995, Studio City, California, October 14, 1995. [Speaker: Ken Topolsky]

Online chats and forums

Anderson, Mitchell. America Online chat, December 23, 1996.
Campbell, Neve. America Online chat, February 2, 1995.
Campbell, Neve. America Online chat, December 14, 1995.
Campbell, Neve. Prodigy chat, December 19, 1996.
Chabert, Lacey. America Online chat, February 2, 1995.
Chabert, Lacey. America Online chat, December 14, 1995.
Chabert, Lacey. America Online chat, May 13, 1996.
Fox, Matthew. America Online chat, January 11, 1995.
Fox, Matthew. CompuServe conference, October 10, 1994.
Fox, Matthew. CompuServe conference, November 29, 1994.
Fox, Matthew. CompuServe conference, March 1, 1995.
Hewitt, Jennifer Love. America Online chat, August 8, 1996.
Hewitt, Jennifer Love. America Online chat, October 24, 1996.
Hewitt, Jennifer Love. E! Online - The Star Boards (Q&A), April 1997
    (http://www.eonline.com/Gossip/Star/Hewitt/).
Hewitt, Jennifer Love. Prodigy chat, November 11, 1996.
Lee, Alexondra. America Online chat, December 27, 1996.
Lippman, Amy. CompuServe conference, March 10, 1995.
Party of Five Cast and Crew [Scott Wolf, Matthew Fox, Neve Campbell, Lacey Chabert,
    Paula Devicq, Ken Topolsky, Amy Lippman, and Chris Keyser], America Online
    chat, December 6, 1994.
Party of Five Cybercast. Hosted by *People* Online, November 12, 1996.
Taylor, Tamara. America Online chat, February 26, 1997.
Topolsky, Ken. America Online chat, February 2, 1995.
Topolsky, Ken. America Online chat, January 25, 1996.
Ward, Megan. America Online chat, October 23, 1996.
Wolf, Scott. America Online chat, January 11, 1995.
Wolf, Scott. CompuServe conference, March 14, 1995.

Index

Numbers in *italics* refer to pages with photographs.

About the Author

PHOTO BY M. VICTORIA BATIATO.

Brenda Scott Royce, a freelance entertainment writer and motion picture reviewer, has written for *Movie Marketplace, Classic TV, Autograph Collector, Television Chronicles, Television Today,* and other film and television periodicals. She is the author of *Hogan's Heroes: A Complete Reference.* She lives in Los Angeles, California.

BOOKS

Also available from
RENAISSANCE BOOKS

Hercules & Xena: The Unofficial Companion
by James Van Hise
Over 50 photos with 8-page color insert
296 pages • Index
ISBN: 1-58063-001-4 • $15.95

Coming soon from RENAISSANCE BOOKS:

Alien Nation: The Unofficial Companion
by Ed Gross
Over 30 b&w photos
256 pages • Index
ISBN: 1-58063-002-2 • $14.95

The Ultimate Marilyn
The most complete guide ever to the life
and legend of the amazing and
beloved Marilyn Monroe
by Ernest W. Cunningham
Over 40 b&w photos
256 pages • Index
ISBN: 1-58063-003-0 • $16.95

Pufnstuf & Other Stuff
The weird and wonderful world of
Sid & Marty Krofft
by David Martindale
Over 40 photos with 8-page color insert
288 pages • Index
ISBN: 1-58063-007-3 • $16.95

RENAISSANCE BOOKS ARE DISTRIBUTED BY ST. MARTIN'S PRESS
FOR ORDERS, PLEASE CALL (800) 488-5233